Class Warfare

Class Warfare

Class, Race, and College Admissions in Top-Tier Secondary Schools

LOIS WEIS, KRISTIN CIPOLLONE, AND HEATHER JENKINS

THE UNIVERSITY OF CHICAGO PRESS   CHICAGO AND LONDON

LOIS WEIS is the SUNY Distinguished Professor of Sociology of Education at the University at Buffalo, SUNY. She is the author of many books and most recently the editor of *The Way Class Works*. KRISTIN CIPOLLONE is a lecturer at Buffalo State College, SUNY, and a postdoctoral associate in the Graduate School of Education at the University at Buffalo, SUNY. HEATHER JENKINS is director of academic programs and High School Prep at Buffalo Prep.

The University of Chicago Press, Chicago 60637
The University of Chicago Press, Ltd., London
© 2014 by The University of Chicago
All rights reserved. Published 2014.
Printed in the United States of America
23 22 21 20 19 18 17 16 15 14   1 2 3 4 5

ISBN-13: 978-0-226-13489-5 (cloth)
ISBN-13: 978-0-226-13492-5 (paper)
ISBN-13: 978-0-226-13508-3 (e-book)
DOI: 10.7208/chicago/9780226135083.001.0001

Library of Congress Cataloging-in-Publication Data

Weis, Lois, author.
    Class warfare : class, race, and college admissions in top-tier secondary schools / Lois Weis, Kristin Cipollone, and Heather Jenkins.
        pages ; cm
    Includes bibliographical references and index.
    ISBN 978-0-226-13489-5 (cloth : alk. paper)—ISBN 978-0-226-13492-5 (pbk. : alk. paper)—ISBN 978-0-226-13508-3 (e-book) 1. Education, Secondary—Social aspects—United States. 2. Upper class—Education—United States. 3. Universities and colleges—Admission—Social aspects—United States. 4. Social classes—United States.
I. Cipollone, Kristin, author.   II. Jenkins, Heather, 1972– author.   III. Title.
    LC205.W45 2014
    373.973—dc23

                                                                                    2013040597

♾ This paper meets the requirements of ANSI/NISO Z39.48–1992 (Permanence of Paper).

Contents

Acknowledgments

Numerous people contributed to the ultimate shape of this book. To begin with, we express our profound thanks to the administrators, counselors, faculty, students, and parents at our respective high schools. Without their cooperation and investment in this project, we never could have engaged this research. Although they must remain nameless for reasons of anonymity, these individuals have our deep thanks and genuine respect. Our special thanks go to Elizabeth Branch Dyson, who was relentless both in her support of the project and her insistence that it be an important contribution. She never let us deliver less than our best intellectual work, and we are very grateful for her continued support and involvement. Elizabeth, you are the best.

Colleagues in the United States and elsewhere contributed to the development of this volume in important ways. In particular we thank Michelle Fine, Lois's longtime friend and coauthor, who gave us incredibly helpful feedback on a draft of the manuscript. Michelle's feedback rendered this a far better book than would have ever been the case. Our special thanks to Greg Dimitriadis and Julia Colyar for their purposeful prodding and insightful critiques. Thanks to Philip Altbach, Jean Anyon, Michael Apple, Cathie Cornbleth, Miki David, Greg Dimitriadis, Margaret Eisenhart, Jeremy Finn, Jane Kenway, Jaekyung Lee, Hank Levin, Wendy Luttrell, Cameron McCarthy, Raechele Pope, Sheila Slaughter, and Scott Thomas, all of whom, in one way or another, played a key role in our thinking over the years, and as we crafted this volume. Postdoctoral associate Amy Stich contributed ongoing and important intellectual insight with regard to the project. She also continues to be a part of so many of our research teams and an important asset to all of our work.

In addition, we are grateful for the careful reading of two anonymous external reviewers who offered particularly insightful comments at the draft manuscript stage. The involvement of the anonymous reviewers added a critically important set of changes to our analysis, and we are tremendously thankful for their help. Nancy Campos, Qiongqiong Chen, Chungseo Kang, Khristian King, Miao Li, Keqiao Liu, Ana Luisa Munoz, and Teya Yu, PhD students at the University at Buffalo, offered intellectual insight and technical help with this and related research, and we deeply appreciate their efforts. Lisa Wehrle, Ryo Yamaguchi, and Kelly Finefrock-Creed were incredibly helpful with regard to copyediting, marketing, and all details of production, and we respect and appreciate their enormous skill and evidenced commitment to this project.

We also thank the Spencer Foundation, whose long-term support to Lois enabled some of the work of this volume, and the Baldy Center for Law and Social Policy at the University at Buffalo, which also offered key grant support along the way. We are deeply grateful for the continuing support of these entities. All errors in interpretation, of course, rest with us.

Our final thanks are reserved for our families, without whom we could never have accomplished this work. Lois's husband, Tereffe Asrat, is the bedrock of her life. Tereffe's generalized intellectual take on the world and searing analytical mind with regard to social and economic issues is woven into this volume in more ways than Lois can count. His eyes in so many ways have become her eyes, and she cherishes every moment of their life together. Sara and Jessica Asrat, Lois's daughters, offered intellectual and personal support all along the way. Although always a part of Lois's intellectual endeavors, as young women, they read and reread portions of the book, offering key insight with respect to data, interpretation, and the overall argument, as well as practical help with aspects of technical analysis. Many of the references to issues of law, intersectionality, and the historical underpinnings of race and racism in the United States represent their intellectual contributions.

Kristin would like to thank her parents, Pier and Gloria Cipollone, for their continuous love and support, and for always encouraging her to pursue her intellectual interests. Writing a book, like many other things in life, is a difficult task, and Kristin's parents taught her the value of perseverance no matter the challenge involved. Kristin would also like to thank her husband, Adam Pratt, for his emotional support, love, and patience. Forever Kristin's biggest cheerleader, he was there at every step to urge her on. No matter how many times he heard Kristin discuss this project, he always listened eagerly and offered critical feedback to push her thinking forward. Adam, thank you. I love you.

Heather wishes to thank her daughters, Victoria and Gabriella Augello, and parents, Gary and Cheryl Blaser. Without their patience and support, Heather would have been hard-pressed to complete her contribution to this volume. Victoria and Gabriella selflessly understood the tremendous amount of time that Heather had to devote to this endeavor, and her parents filled in with and for the girls in countless ways. Lastly, every student that Heather has worked with over the past 12 years must be recognized as the inspiration for much of her work.

We end this volume with tremendous respect for those who comprise the subject of this volume. America stands at a crossroads with respect to location in the global economy and the ways in which secondary and postsecondary educational institutions work to position the next generation for privilege and/or the lack thereof. Although this volume focuses largely on positioning for future privilege, our findings have deep implications for the poor and working class as they position for their own futures. Our thoughts are with all of these students as they move toward their own futures in the twenty-first century.

Lois Weis
Kristin Cipollone
Heather Jenkins

CHAPTER ONE

Class, Race, and College Admissions in a Changing US Context

From their former status as peripheral institutions, the colleges and universities [took] on great social importance as the training ground for entrance into the upper middle and upper classes. — (Wechsler 1977, as cited in Stevens 2007, p. 246)

The system that elite colleges and universities developed to evaluate the best and the brightest is now the template for what counts as ideal child rearing in America. . . . Each year's entering class is the product of an elaborate organizational machinery whose upper tiers have been quite consciously designed to send elite colleges just what they are looking for. — (Stevens 2007, p. 247)

You know, there was an article in *Time* magazine, maybe like a year ago when we were starting this (the college admissions process), and talking about the things that kids do to up the ante to get into college, and I remember reading it and going "Oh my gosh, we're bad parents, we haven't done any of that." — (Sandy Jacinovic, Parent, Cannondale High School, 2010)

Stories about the lengths to which parents of middle- and upper-middle-class children are willing to go in light of the increasingly competitive college admissions process flourish in the popular press. For example, one *New York Times* article highlights the rising trend among parents to enroll children, as young as two, in Kumon classes to give them a leg up in competitive kindergarten admissions (Zernike 2011), presumably with an eye toward admission to highly selective colleges and universities.[1] In the documentary film *Race to Nowhere* (2009), a young child reflects on the dizzying array of homework and scheduled activities that undergird his life. Lamenting the loss of free time, he notes that everything is now about "preparing for college."

While more students than ever attend college, admissions, particularly at the most selective colleges and universities, has become increasingly competitive, wherein the most highly valued postsecondary destinations in the United States report markedly increased numbers of applications and commensurate lower acceptance rates. Ranking schemata, such as the *US News & World Report College Rankings*, further fan the flames of competition, serving to exacerbate anxiety among privileged students and families. The fear, it seems, is that failure to gain entry into a "good" college limits long-term economic and social opportunity, a fear that is, by and large, substantiated in the scholarly literature.

Recent studies by Bowen, Chingos, and McPherson (2009) and Stephan, Rosenbaum, and Person (2009) suggest that *where* one goes to school matters, particularly in regard to persistence and graduation rates. This finding was earlier noted by Astin and Oseguera (2002), who suggest that more selective colleges and universities tend to have higher graduation outcomes.[2] So too, as Carnevale (2012) argues, more selective institutions offer better access to jobs and more prestigious graduate and professional programs. In this markedly more competitive context for college and university admissions, parents' "fear of falling" (Ehrenreich 1990) is not completely unfounded.[3]

As Mitchell Stevens suggests, "The system that elite colleges and universities developed to evaluate the best and the brightest is now the template for what counts as ideal child rearing in America" (2007, p. 247). He further argues:

> For the affluent upper middle class, the transition from high school to college is a seamless web of interdependencies: between guidance counselors and admissions officers; between youthful athletic talent and athletic league standings; between high property taxes, large tuition checks, and excellent academics; between aesthetic expectations and architecturally spectacular schools. . . . Colleges rely on affluent families to produce and deliver most of their raw materials, while families in turn rely on colleges to certify those our society calls its most accomplished. The interdependence of privileged families and elite colleges is precisely why the ceremony of selective admissions is so important. It defines college entrance as an almost sacred moment of evaluation, in which supposedly universal standards of merit are applied to each and every applicant regardless of social station. For the most privileged kids in each year's applicant pool, the real question is not if they will be admitted to an elite college, but which ones will offer them spots. Even so, the frenzy of the admissions process serves to bless favored candidates with marks of honor that, however deceptively, seem neutral to class. (pp. 247–48)

Peering underneath such a "sacred moment," *Class Warfare: Class, Race, and College Admissions in Top-Tier Secondary Schools* conceptually and methodologically inverts Stevens's path-breaking study, offering a worm's eye view of the day-to-day and week-by-week *struggles* over class positioning as engaged by differentially located class and race actors in public and private privileged secondary schools in early twenty-first-century United States.[4] As we will argue, rather than a "seamless web of interdependencies," the college admissions process, approached from this point of view, represents the culmination of specifically located and intentionally waged parent and student "class work" that is now linked to an envisioned battleground over forms of privilege represented by admission to particular kinds of postsecondary destinations. Such "class work" is differentially engaged by sector of secondary school, student position in the opportunity structure of the school, and degree of parent/student closeness to the habitus embedded within particularly located privileged institutions.[5] While postsecondary destinations seemingly "bless favored candidates of honor" via admission to specific colleges and universities, thereby *certifying* those "our society calls its most accomplished," we reveal new and complex forms of "class warfare" that lurk just beneath the surface of this "sacred" moment of college admissions.

Taking the perspectives and practices of secondary schools, parents, and students as its central starting point, *Class Warfare* details the extent to which and the ways in which parents, school counselors, teachers, and students at three iconic, privileged, secondary schools in the United States work to "lock in" the next generation's privileged class status via the postsecondary applications and admissions process. In a historic moment marked by deep economic uncertainly and accompanying class anxieties, we argue that a particularly located segment of largely, but not entirely, White and affluent parents and students in relatively privileged secondary schools individually and collectively mobilize all available and embodied cultural, social, and economic capital to carve out and instantiate what we refer to as a "new" upper middle class via entrance to particular postsecondary destinations.[6] Specifically, they seek access to a broadened pallet (beyond the Ivies) of almost entirely *private* institutions that are deemed "Most Competitive" and "Highly Competitive+" in the now ubiquitous postsecondary ranking systems.[7] Underneath the ostensibly "seamless web" of college admissions to highly selective institutions, students and parents at this particular strata of secondary schools now consciously exploit any and all opportunities to position their children for advantage, thereby effectively constricting access to highly and most selective colleges and universities for the rest of the middle class and, by obvious and clear extension, the working class and poor.

Following in the footsteps of Angela Valuenzela (1999), Wendy Luttrell (1997), Douglas Foley (2010a, 2010b), Stacey Lee (2005), Lois Weis (1990, 2004), Michelle Fine (1991), Paul Willis (1977), and others who track and theorize class processes through intense multifaceted ethnographic investigation, we theoretically and empirically *drill down* into the production of a distinctly located upper middle class—one that is increasingly working, we argue, to differentiate itself from the broader middle class within which it is embedded. Employing what Weis and Fine (2012) call "critical bifocality"—a bifocal design that documents at once the linkages and capillaries of structural arrangements and the discursive and lived-out practices by which individuals make sense of their circumstances (Weis and Fine 2012, 2013)—*Class Warfare* connects the story of students, parents, and school personnel to broad social and economic arrangements through specific focus on the secondary to postsecondary "linking process" (Perna et al. 2008; Hill 2008). In so doing, we engage a triplet of theoretical and analytic moves—(1) deep ethnographic work within schools and families in three purposively selected secondary school sites, (2) serious relational analyses between and among relevant race/ethnic and class groups in markedly altered global context, and (3) broad structural connections to social and economic arrangements.

Although seemingly straightforward, the postsecondary application process in the United States has become a dizzying array of complex tasks and activities, with the short- and long-term stakes rendered ever higher by the larger national and global context within which this range of now "normalized" actions and activities are voraciously engaged by students, parents, counselors, and teachers in privileged secondary schools.

Class Warfare takes up this theoretically located "class" project via multiyear ethnographic research with three distinct groups of students in three upper-middle-class secondary schools—defined here as schools serving a largely professional and managerial parental population (Apple 2010; Kivel 2004)—as follows: (1) a representative sample of largely, but not entirely, White students who fall, by virtue of class rank, in the top 10% of their secondary school graduating class in a highly affluent suburban public high school;[8] (2) a representative sample of largely, but not entirely, highly affluent White students and the children of "flexible immigrants" of color who fall, by virtue of class rank, in the top 20% of their graduating class at an NAIS (National Association of Independent Schools) private coeducational day school;[9] and (3) a representative sample of low-income self-identified Black students[10] in two NAIS day schools (one coeducational, one single-sex female)[11] who attended poorly resourced, inner-city public elementary and middle schools and are almost entirely placed at the bottom of the opportunity structure of their respective secondary schools.[12]

Data are drawn from the above three ethnographic studies of relatively elite coeducational secondary schools (elite is defined as high ranking with regard to the educational sector of the nation) located in tier-2, "nonglobal" cities (e.g., Charlotte) in the northeastern United States. Unlike schools in tier-1 cities (e.g., New York City), wherein schools draw from a far wealthier clientele, tier-2 cities are marked by notably less concentration of capital and wealth. Data were collected over one and one-half years during the 2009–10 academic school year, and each researcher was embedded within her respective site for this entire year with some limited engagement before and/or after this year.[13] At the public high school, 37 participants were interviewed and participated in three focus group sessions. Study participants include students (9 purposively selected students in the top 10% of the class), parents (11), school counselors (8), counseling support staff (2), eleventh- and twelfth-grade core subject teachers (5), and administrators (2). All participants were interviewed between one and three times. Additionally, 200 hours were spent in the field observing classes, counselor sessions, college-related presentations, course advisement, parent information meetings, SAT test administration, and many other less-formal occurrences (e.g., spending time in the College Center while students researched schools). Relevant school documents were also collected and analyzed.

Data collection at the private schools was conducted similarly, although two distinct samples were drawn. One sample targeted students in the top 20% of their graduating class, while the other sought out low-income Black students (as defined earlier in note 12) and drew participants from two schools. At the coeducational Matthews Academy, one sample consisted of 38 individuals, including students (13 purposively selected students in the top 20% of the class), Head of the Upper School, Head of College Counseling (one of two counselors in the school), parents (18), and teachers of core junior and senior year subjects (5). All participants were interviewed between one and three times. Additionally, a total of 100 hours were spent in the field observing classes, college-related presentations, parent information meetings, and other less formal interactions (e.g., time spent in the senior lounge as students engaged the college process). As with the public school, relevant school documents were collected and analyzed.[14]

The second sample drew students both from Matthews Academy and Bradford Academy.[15] This sample consisted of students (9 purposively selected students; 5 from Matthews, 4 from Bradford), parents (4), and college counselors (2). Approximately 100 hours of fieldwork were engaged across the two schools in addition to between one and three interviews per participant, with several informal follow-up interviews. Although all parents of this population of students, like parents of the other two student samples, were approached with respect to granting an interview, few availed themselves of this opportunity, a point that will be more fully addressed in the epilogue. As is the case in the other two ethnographic investigations, numerous hours were spent in the field observing classes, college-related presentations, and so forth. In addition, relevant school documents were collected and analyzed.

This purposively selected tri-school student sample enables deep ethnographic focus on actions and activities engaged by differentially located parents, students, counselors, teachers, and other school personnel across class and race/ethnicity in both iconic private and public privileged secondary institutions. While each group independently reveals a great deal about schooling, family practices, and the college process, putting these groups in sharp relief, as we do here, starkly portrays the ways in which "class works" and is put to work by varying groups in schools.[16]

We argue that our tri-school research largely reveals the targeted "class work" of a now highly insecure broad-based middle class that engages in a very specific form of "class warfare," one in which a segment of the middle class individually and collectively mobilizes and enacts its own located and embodied cultural, social, and economic capital in order to preserve itself in uncertain economic times while simultaneously attempting to instantiate a distinctly professional and managerial upper middle class through access to particular kinds of postsecondary destinations. We further argue that although school sector (in this case, privileged private versus privileged public) sets up and facilitates experiences and outcomes with regard to college admissions, both student engagement with the dominant habitus of the school and student location in the structure of opportunities facilitate and/or constrain the college admissions process and subsequent postsecondary entrance patterns. All three phenomena—sector of institution, family/student closeness to the habitus of the institution, and student position in the opportunity structure of the school—work to "produce" varying college admissions outcomes and linked individual and collective position in the US class structure of the twenty-first century. The particular role of race/ethnicity and class in such productions will be explicitly taken up in this volume.

Class Warfare extends the scholarly work on education and the production of social class (Cookson and Persell 1985; Demerath 2009; Fine 1991; Foley 2010a, 2010b; Gaztambide-Fernández 2009; Howard 2007; Khan 2011; Lareau 1987, 2003; Nolan and Anyon 2004; Reay et al. 2011; Varenne and McDermott 1998; Weis 1990, 2004; Willis 1977; among others) centering on the anticipated demise of the middle class in the United States. Affirming the notion that class position must now be "won" at both the individual and collective levels, rather than constituting simply the "manner to which one is born" (with the exception perhaps, of the upper class, which can be understood as constituting the top 1% of the population), we track and theorize the intensified preparation for and application to particular kinds of postsecondary destinations now taking place in affluent and elite secondary schools in the United States. Although, as noted earlier, the media have taken note of such "application frenzy" around postsecondary destinations, little scholarly work tracks and theorizes this frenzy as a *distinctly located class process*, one that represents intensified "class work" at one and the same time as class "winners" and "losers" become ever more apparent. In line with Weis and Fine's (2012, 2013) framework of *critical bifocality*, this must be understood as linked to massively altered national and global circumstances, a topic to which we now turn.

Structural Dynamics of Globalization and Attendant Consequences for US Higher Education

Since the 1970s, we have witnessed a massive realignment of the global economy. In the first wave of this realignment, working-class jobs—primarily in manufacturing—were increasingly exported from highly industrialized countries such as the United States, the United Kingdom, and

Japan to poor countries, where multinational companies can hire skilled and unskilled laborers at lower pay and without benefits. In the current second wave, middle-class jobs are also exported, as members of a new and expanded middle class in countries such as India and China are educated as architects, accountants, medical technicians, and doctors and are willing to work for multinational companies and organizations at a fraction of the salary they would earn for the same work at corporate or other organizational headquarters (Reich 2001, 2008; Weis and Dolby 2012). This evolving set of international economic and human resource relations affects the educational experiences, outcomes, aspirations, and apathies of younger generations in a variety of exporting and importing countries. Those who are highly educated, as well as those who are not, now live and work inside a globally driven knowledge economy that markedly alters the fulcrum of educational experiences and outcomes, irrespective of the extent to which students and families are able to articulate this set of drivers.[17]

The intensified transnational movement of peoples further alters the terrain upon which class productions take place.[18] Of particular importance to this volume is the transnational movement of those with "flexible citizenship" (hereafter referred to as "flexible immigrants"; Ong 1999)— those who can transcend nation-state boundaries by virtue of their inherited and/or earned cultural and intellectual capital (e.g., high-powered intellectuals, engineers, and medical professionals who are seduced to work in economically powerful nations), as the children of such "flexible immigrants" are often in privileged educational settings such as those under consideration here (Lee 2005; Li 2005).[19] The point is that the global knowledge economy coupled with the movement of peoples across national borders *fundamentally* alters the context within which social structure both seeps into the consciousness of students and families, as well as altering the "limit situations" within which this all plays.

This combination of shifting structurally linked drivers, where movement—of capital, cultures, technologies, and peoples—*undergirds* the fundamental structures of our lives (Apple 2010), works to produce altered class relations and sensibilities in a wide variety of nations. Specifically with regard to the population under study here, this set of economic and social drivers, coupled with the US economic crash of 2008 (with attendant global consequences), renders the economic future of the next generation in first-wave industrialized nations highly uncertain. It is in this context that privileged families seek to instantiate opportunities for their children at the same time as such within-nation opportunities are objectively increasingly scarce (Brown, Lauder, and Ashton 2011), as the new global knowledge economy alters the availability of particular kinds of jobs. This is arguably accompanied by the intensified privileging of particular kinds of educational credentials as the availability of such credentials becomes more widely distributed across the globe (Altbach, Riesberg, and Rumbley 2009).

In this context, research related to "maximally" and "effectively maintained inequality" becomes critically important. As Arum, Gamoran, and Shavit (2007, p. 1) argue, "the key question about educational expansion is whether it reduces inequality by providing more opportunities for persons from disadvantaged strata, or magnifies inequality by expanding opportunities disproportionately for those who are already privileged."

Numerous studies conclude that educational expansion does not, in and of itself, serve to reduce class-linked inequalities in education (Raftery and Hout 1993; Shavit, Arum, and Gamoran 2007; among others). This is the case at both the secondary and tertiary levels in a wide variety of nations, whether linked to academic achievement (Campbell, Hombo, and Mazzeo 2000; Reardon 2011), academic attainment (Hout, Raftery, and Bell 1993), or postsecondary entrance patterns (Bailey and Dynarski 2011; Bowen, Chingos, and McPherson 2009; Thomas and Bell 2008). The theory of "maximally maintained inequality" (MMI) sheds light on these findings:

> Inequality between any two social strata in the odds of attaining a given level of education persists until the advantaged class reaches the point of saturation. Saturation is defined as the point at which nearly all sons and daughters of advantaged origins attain the educational level under consideration. Until that point, the advantaged group is typically better equipped to take advantage of any new and attractive educational opportunities, and class inequalities will persist or even increase as opportunities are expanded. (Raftery and Hout 1993, as cited in Shavit et al. 2007, p. 3)

More recently, scholars like Ayalon and Shavit (2004) and Lucas (2001) argue that "once saturation has been reached with regard to a given level of education, inequalities in the odds of this level's attainment may be replaced by inequalities in the odds of placement in the more selective track" (Shavit et al. 2007, p. 4). Known as "effectively maintained inequality" (EMI), this framework recognizes that educational expansion at any given level is often accompanied by increasing institutional differentiation and/or heightened internal systemic stratification, thereby rendering the *status* of any given institution, within a range of hierarchically possible options, increasingly important. Put another way, the battle over *qualitative* distinction in educational opportunities can be expected to intensify, as more generalized access to any given level of education is achieved.

Although the quantitative data are striking in this regard, and often affirm notions of "effectively maintained inequality" (Shavit et al. 2007), they cannot, by their very nature, illuminate the ways in which qualitative distinctions are struggled over at the point of access to any given institutional location, thereby taking hardened shape and form as individuals and groups drive toward *particular* locations in a space of numerically broadened educational opportunities. Through deep ethnographic work in three purposively selected school sites, we argue that the intensified battle over college admissions, and particularly admissions to "Most Competitive" and "Highly Competitive+" private colleges, constitutes an increasingly critical space where future class position is struggled over, engaged, produced, and lived out.

Class Productions in New Time and Space

Based on recent work in the United Kingdom, Diane Reay, Gill Crozier, and David James (2011) suggest:

> Despite the advent of the "age of anxiety," the emergence of the "super rich," and economic upheavals (Apple 2010), it appears that the white middle-classes continue to thrive, their social position strengthened and consolidated. However, there are also growing signs of unease, the exacerbation of anxiety, and a lack of ontological security, "the sense of continuity and order in events, including those not directly within the perceptual environment of the individual" (Giddens 1991, p. 243). (pp. 1–2)

Although not detailing the drivers of new context as we do above, the authors go on to state that, "these insecurities are particularly evident in their children's education" (Reay et al. 2011, p. 2), where it is arguably the case that such insecurities surface in anxieties related to where their children go to school; what they learn in school in contrast to what other people's children learn in different schools; and, in the US context, how specific secondary schools, and experiences within these secondary schools, position their children for the now global knowledge economy in which access to highly valued postsecondary destinations is conceptualized as increasingly paramount. This all sits, it can be argued, inside

> a growing sense of insecurity that was once the purview of the working class but now permeates almost the whole of society. If this is the case, it can be further argued that just as the integrity and value of the working class was undermined over the last decades of the twentieth century (Skeggs 2004), the beginning of the twenty first century may herald the unraveling of white middle-class identity. (Reay et al. 2011, p. 4)

Such anticipated unraveling must be understood in light of our earlier discussion regarding the drivers of new global realities as well as increasing competition for admission to particularly located postsecondary destinations. Such competition over postsecondary admissions, however, must itself be contextualized inside marked changes in the US postsecondary sector.

The *Marketplace* of College Admissions

Espenshade and Radford (2009) state "college admissions angst has probably never been greater, mainly because more students are now competing for relatively few spots at the nation's most prestigious colleges and universities" (p. 15). While colleges and universities overall are now more open in their admissions than they were in the past—that is, they have democratized to a certain extent (e.g., women can now attend Princeton and the vast majority of Harvard's entering class no longer transitions from independent private schools)—and while more students than ever before are applying to college (Espenshade and Radford 2009), the system is increasingly marked by noticeable and reworked forms of stratification, particularly in terms of family income (Bowen, Chingos, and McPherson 2009; Shavit, Arum, and Gamoran 2007). Karen (2002) argues that due to this increase in college applicants and attendees, one must attend more prestigious schools to reap the advantage that a college education presumably provides, a position that affirms notions of EMI as discussed above.

Yet space at these prestigious schools is limited, and applications to these schools are skyrocketing (Soares 2007). Hoxby (1997) points to the fact that students increasingly apply to colleges outside their home states, indicating that the college application process has become much more national (and, more recently, international) in scope, particularly for top students. While students compete for access to particular institutions, institutions also compete for students, always searching for high-achieving/performing students who can raise the academic profile (and rank) of the school. Such institutional competition does little to increase access for lower-income students, as many institutions have transitioned away from need-based aid to offer more "merit" aid to the students they seek:

> Institutional competition simultaneously increases postsecondary quality and inequality. Happily, the number of selective and highly selective colleges in Barron's Guide to the Most Competitive Colleges has grown by more than 30 percent since the 1990s. Unhappily, the share of students from the bottom income quartile at the 200 selective colleges has stalled at less than 5 percent. (Carnevale 2012, n.p.)

Drawing upon the work of Frank and Cook (1995), Attewell (2001) discusses the ways in which education, both at the secondary and postsecondary levels, functions as a "winner take all" marketplace:

> In these special markets, sellers whose goods are viewed as the best (or are thought of as the top performers) reap far greater reward and capture a disproportionate share of the market than do other sellers whose goods are also of high quality. Sellers immediately below the top may perform almost as well as those at the top, but gain far fewer rewards. (p. 269)

Attewell's work (as well as the work of Frank and Cook upon which he draws) is useful for understanding both the real and perceived stakes attached to college admissions. If institutions at the top of the academic hierarchy reap the greatest rewards, then they should be the institutions that confer the greatest advantage, a relationship that further fuels postsecondary admissions competition. Students and parents desire access to top institutions because they believe that these will provide the most secure pathway to good jobs and hence economic security.

College access—that is *who goes where*—is further complicated by the job market, the economy, and the larger social structure (both nationally and globally). Kerckhoff (1993, 1995) argues that where one is located within the structure of educational opportunities works to enhance or constrain future options. He states that we must "view these structural locations both as hierarchically ranked and as providing varied opportunities for later moves and access to various kinds and levels of attainment" (1995, p. 324). In this context, the particular location in the structure of opportunities of K–12 schools matters in relation to how one is positioned for college, and parents increasingly struggle to position their children via particular kinds of educational experiences. As Brown and Tannock (2009) argue, this has implications for school selection as privileged parents struggle for class position for their children:

> In the fields of primary and secondary education, past commitments to comprehensive schooling have been abandoned as middle- and upper- class families seek to position their children in the most desirable and prestigious schools and programmes, to become one of the select members of the internationally sought after, high-skill elite (Ball 2003; Brown 2000; Tomlinson 2007). This process is now being driven by the global war for talent, which rejects a model of universal meritocracy, in which the talent and educational achievements of all are incrementally rewarded. Alternatively, it promotes a form of "hyper-meritocracy," characterised by "winner-takes-all" markets (Frank and Cook 1995). Those defined as the "best" are disproportionately rewarded as the war for talent devalues everything other than "top" performance (Brown and Hesketh 2004; Frank 1999). (p. 384)

College admissions, then, becomes a key site in the fight for economic and social advantage, a fight that not all students and families are equally positioned to play and win.

In the United States, for example, working-class and poor students are entering colleges and universities in greater number than ever before (Ellwood and Kane 2000), reflective of what Altbach, Reisberg, and Rumbley (2009) label a worldwide "academic revolution." Although research on the linkage between family background and type and selectivity of postsecondary institution attended is certainly not new (Karabel 1972), evidence suggests that the class-related gap in type of institution attended is *widening* in the United States under conditions of massification, a finding that is largely, but not entirely, replicated in the global arena (Shavit et al. 2007). Tragically, of course, although it is historically disenfranchised people of color in the United States who struggled most fervently for access to a broadened range of educational opportunities, it is this group that, with notable exceptions, disproportionately bears the brunt of deepening inequalities.

Thomas and Bell (2008) demonstrate that while less-privileged students attend higher education in the United States in greater numbers than ever before, attendance at the most selective such institutions is increasingly comprised of students from more privileged backgrounds. Using Pell Grants as proxy for low-income/poor, Thomas and Bell (2008, p. 281) note that that "it is not just the most selective institutions which are seeing lower numbers of low-income students. Low-income students are less likely to be in four-year institutions in general than they were a decade ago." Looking across years 1992–93 and 2000–2001, "there was a 2.9 percent drop in the enrollment share of Pell Grant recipients at four-year institutions across all states, with 48 of the states seeing a decline in their Pell enrollment shares" (Mortenson 2003, as quoted in Thomas and Bell 2008, p. 281). Conversely, during the same window of time, Pell enrollment at two-year public colleges increased by 1.2% (Mortenson 2003), continuing a longer-term trend beginning in the 1970s (Mortenson 2006). Although the net gain or loss in percentage points may appear small, this represents a very large number of low-income students who are increasingly locked out of higher-prestige institutions at one and the same time as more low-income students are attending college.

More recently Bowen, Chingos, and McPherson (2009) argue that the state "flagship" universities (e.g., University of Wisconsin–Madison, University of Michigan; University of California, Berkeley) have become much more selective over time, and that such selectivity has been accompanied by changes in the social class background of admitted students (Cook and Frank 1993; Hearn 1991; Kingston and Lewis 1990). Even in the less-selective, public four-year institutions detailed by Bowen, Chingos, and McPherson, it is still the case that "more than 40 percent of undergraduates come from families in the top-quartile of the income distribution" (2009, p. 17). This means that an increasingly higher proportion of low-income students attend two-year institutions. Although eventual transition from the two-year to four-year college sector is certainly possible, research by Clark (1960), Weis (1985), Brint and Karabel (1989), and Dougherty and Kienzl (2006) suggest difficulties associated with such movement. In the final analysis, the transition from the two-year to the four-year sector is not as robust as originally anticipated and/or desired.

In fact, factors specifically linked to colleges and universities increasingly press toward the production of social class inequalities and arrangements. Recent changes in financial aid policies and processes that reduce grants to low-income students in favor of loans make it more and more difficult for poor, working-class, and lower-middle-income students to attend and persist in postsecondary institutions (Avery and Kane 2004; Heller 2001; Hoxby 1997; *Losing Ground* 2002; Roksa 2012; St. John 2003). As family incomes have not kept pace with college costs, students shoulder a larger financial burden, making financial aid that much more critical for this group at the same time as middle- and upper-middle-class students have more sustained access to family funds, thereby attending and completing college in record numbers.

Concurrently, the emergence of a nationally integrated market for elite and highly selective colleges (Bowen et al. 2009; Hoxby 1997) serves to intensify pressure for admittance to this strata of postsecondary institutions, thereby encouraging or forcing greater numbers of privileged students to seek entrance to the somewhat less-selective four-year sector, relative to the elite and highly selective sector, than was the case in prior decades (Ellwood and Kane 2000; Mortenson 2003, 2006; Thomas and Bell 2008). In other words, it is now increasingly difficult for even privileged students to gain entrance to the most highly competitive schools in the country. In response, they seek entrance to the next, somewhat less-competitive sector in the rankings hierarchy. By way of example, if a student cannot gain entrance to Williams College; University of California, Berkeley; or a similarly ranked institution, he or she will logically strive to enter a somewhat lower, but still relatively highly ranked, public or private school. As competition for admission becomes increasingly intense throughout the system, it becomes that much more difficult for less-privileged students to gain entrance to a broadened range of institutions, as they have fewer resources upon which to draw during the college admissions process. This means that lower-middle- and working-class students are increasingly "locked out" of highly selective and selective public colleges and universities, in particular. Sadly, of course, it is these institutions that offered a key mechanism for social mobility for past generations of (largely White) working-class and low-income students (Bowen et al. 2009; Thomas and Bell 2008).

Ironically, many currently designated flagship publics were established by the Morrill Act of 1862 to "promote the liberal and practice education of the industrial classes in the several pursuits and professions in life" (Morrill Act of 1862, sec. 4, as cited in Thomas and Bell 2008, p. 274). This worthy goal is less and less actualized, with specifically located implications for poor and working-class students of color. To put it bluntly, access to a broadened range of postsecondary opportunities is shutting down at exactly the same time as increased numbers of poor and working-class students, and particularly those of color, are poised to enter postsecondary institutions.

In this regard, evidence is quite clear that flagship state institutions are now becoming the purview of the children of the privileged (Bowen et al. 2009; Shavit et al. 2007; Thomas and Bell 2008). As we suggest in this volume, however, a particularly located high-end slice of the broad middle class—those who attend privileged private secondary schools and those who are located at the top of the academic hierarchy at privileged public schools—increasingly attempt to carve and more deeply instantiate "distinction" via entrance to "Most Competitive" and "Highly Competitive+" postsecondary private colleges. Additionally, and as we will detail in chapter 6, low-income Black students who enter privileged private secondary schools also drive toward highly selective private postsecondary destinations. As these groups collectively attempt, whether consciously or not, to carve and maintain "distinction" via access to *particularly* located colleges, they experience varying levels of "success." Nevertheless, the majority of these students both position and are positioned for highly valued postsecondary *private* destinations. This has clear implications for both class structure of the future and public flagships more generally.

McPherson and Schapiro (1998), Gumport (2007), and Slaughter and Rhoades (2004) point to specific economic and organizational changes that encourage colleges and universities to shift from selecting students as a "charitable" function to balancing full-paying students or high-"merit" students with low-income and first-generation college students. This makes it less and less possible for the vast majority of low-income and minority students to attend a wide range of colleges. An important driver here, of course, is intensified state disinvestment in public higher education (Slaughter and Rhoades 2004). This contributes both to a marked increase in tuition bills and less institutionally linked money available for scholarships tagged specifically to students from low-income backgrounds.[20] In this context, the "advantage" with regard to college admissions accorded to low-income Black students who attend elite private secondary schools, both today and in past decades, will be discussed further in chapters 6 and 7.

As noted earlier in this chapter, recent research suggests that persistence and completion rates are linked to particular types of postsecondary institutions, and these are the very postsecondary institutions that the vast majority of lower-middle- and low-income students are increasingly locked out of. Work by Bowen, Chingos, and McPherson (2009) and Stephan, Rosenbaum, and Person (2009) clearly suggests that *where* one goes to college/university predicts persistence and graduation rates above and beyond the entering characteristics of admitted students. For example, Stephan, Rosenbaum, and Person (2009, p. 14) argue "academic preparation is an important mechanism of stratification at college entry, but even comparable students (similar on many characteristics, including preparation) have different degree completion chances at different types of colleges."

Bowen, Chingos, and McPherson (2009) additionally spotlight different persistence and graduation rates as independently linked to type/selectivity of institution, expressing great concern for what they call "undermatching"—students who "choose" not to attend the best college they can get into by virtue of their dossier, thereby fundamentally decreasing their chances of persistence and graduation simply by virtue of where they "elect" to go to college. This presses toward the conclusion that selectivity of institution *in and of itself* matters with regard to postsecondary outcomes, above and beyond the characteristics of entering students.[21]

Beyond higher rates of persistence and graduation, we also know that selective institutions are better resourced than less selective institutions (with private research universities now rising head and shoulders above the state flagship universities; Leslie, Slaughter, Taylor, and Zhang 2012) and confer on their graduates both special entrée to the best graduate and professional programs in the country (Eide, Brewer, and Ehrenberg 1998) and well-documented labor market advantages (Bowen and Bok 1998; Rumberger and Thomas 1993; Thomas 2000; Thomas and Zhang 2005). As with persistence and graduation rates, this relationship holds even when characteristics of entering students are held constant in the analysis.

In spite of these empirically documented overall deepening inequalities in educational achievement and attainment in both the secondary and postsecondary sectors, research simultaneously directs our attention toward marked progress in educational opportunities for previously excluded groups in the population, a finding that has important implications for ethnographic work engaged in this volume (Hurtado, Inkelas, Briggs, and Rhee 1997; Perna 2000; St. John, Musoba, and Simmons 2003). This body of research serves to mark possibility with regard to the linkage between the secondary and postsecondary sector at one and the same time as it raises some concerns.

To begin with, researchers do not always take seriously enough the wide variation in postsecondary matriculation patterns, either at the purely descriptive level (who goes where) or as linked to opportunities afforded by attendance at differentially located secondary schools. In other words, although previously excluded groups in the population may enter the postsecondary sector at greater rates than ever before, the "access to what" question coupled with detailed empirical information about the segmented secondary to postsecondary pipeline needs considerably more attention.

Aside from the historically entrenched and simultaneously loosening of race, and, to a lesser extent, class inequalities evidenced in elite private institutions like Harvard, Yale, and Princeton (Bowen and Bok 1998; Bowen, Kurzwell, and Tobin 2005; Karabel 2005), evidence clearly presses toward the conclusion that massification in the United States has been accompanied by a reorganization in the opportunity structure of higher education, with the upper middle class solidifying its grasp on elite and highly selective public/state institutions in particular. As we argue here, however, such solidification represents the culmination of considerable "class work" on the part of schools, teachers, and students. In particular, a segment of the broad middle class is increasingly driving toward "locking up" its own grasp on particularly located postsecondary destinations—those that, as we see above, both produce the highest graduation rates and provide entrée to the most valued graduate and professional schools in the nation.

As the above makes clear, the intensification of educationally linked inequalities in the postsecondary sector and the importance of postsecondary education in the now increasingly competitive global knowledge economy makes higher education a key site of "class struggle," as families and students attempt to carve out economic and social stability in the face of hardening educational and economic inequalities.

Class Warfare: Class, Race, and College Admissions in Top-Tier Secondary Schools

Drawing upon the three data sets discussed earlier, we organize chapters to take into account both marked empirical similarities and differences in pathways to postsecondary destinations. Most important in terms of substance and method, the three site-based studies were comparably conceived; in other words, all three investigators—Lois, Kristin, and Heather—focused on the secondary to postsecondary transition, with particular emphasis on parent, teacher, counselor, and student actions and activities in relation to the college admissions process. In this sense, we held method constant as we worked across the three school sites with three distinct populations of parents and students. Our interview questions with counselors, parents, teachers, and students across the sites/populations reflect a core set of questions and follow-up questions, and the participant observations center on similar actions and activities within the school space across site. In addition to the core set of interview questions, additional questions were posed with each population as relevant, based on responses to the initial interview protocol.

What is most stunning is that although our method was largely held constant, the topics that surfaced as most important for each group/sector of school differ in key ways, and it is these major themes, or topics, that constitute the core substance of each data-driven chapter. This is simply good ethnographic practice, as data led us to our conclusions rather than our conclusions leading us to cherry-pick particular data segments. Again, in line with good ethnographic practice, data were carefully coded, sorted, and analyzed, a set of practices and procedures that we take up in great detail in the epilogue.

In the case at hand, a preponderance of our data gathered from the top 10% of students and linked parents at the affluent public school reveal targeted focus on *early* positioning work by parents and the later transfer of this positioning work to students. Students take up identities centered upon attendance at highly selective universities and engage a good deal of positioning work—such as making "decisions" about specific course placement in the Advanced Placement or International Baccalaureate (AP/IB) track—extending the early work of parents. Data such as these direct our focus in chapter 3 to this particular form of "class work" in the affluent suburban sector. Similarly, the fact that a preponderance of our data gathered from the top 20% of students and linked parents in the independent coeducational private school reveal intense focus on parental micromanagement of the college admissions process, drives our analysis with respect to this group in chapter 4 (somewhat in contrast to comparably affluent students and parents at the secondary suburban public).

In the case of low-income Black students in the independent private day schools, the preponderance of our data drives toward articulation and analysis of their status as "outsiders-within." The fact that this takes a *particular* race, and linked classed, form in the independent private sector becomes highly salient to our analysis and conclusions with regard to this group in particular. This set of conclusions about the ways in which race and class collectively work in privileged settings stands in marked contrast to our analysis of students and parents of color whose own closeness to the dominant *class* habitus of the school renders them fundamentally *class* insiders rather than raced/classed "outsiders-within." Putting these three ethnographically derived data sets and associated findings in constant conversation with one another enables us to theorize class and race/ethnic productions in relation to the struggle over postsecondary destinations in key and critical ways. Our key point, though, is that the driving themes and analysis *within* each individual ethnographically driven chapter stem from the ethnographic investigations themselves, rather than being imposed by the investigators in any kind of ad hoc or a priori way.

The remainder of this volume unfolds as follows: chapter 2 details the three school sites, employing rich ethnographic data garnered by virtue of the three ethnographies, with specific focus on similarities and differences in course offerings and college counseling. In this chapter, we provide an overview of the school culture and communities, paying particular attention to the academic environments of each, and highlight the structure of the college process at each institution. In many regards, the processes are largely similar across site, with one notable exception; in the private sector, college counselors devote all of their time to college-related planning while in the public sector, counselors are expected to engage in college advising *in addition to* their other responsibilities as school counselors.

Following this rich description of the three sites, chapters 3, 4, and 5 focus attention on salient actions and activities linked to specific schools and targeted student populations. These chapters draw upon and present rich ethnographic interview and participant observation data involving parents, students, administrators, and counselors, as relevant, who comprise the particular Cannondale, Matthews Academy, and Bradford Academy communities under investigation. These chapters reflect and present deep ethnographic work at one and the same time as we analytically draw conclusions based on the data at hand.

In chapters 6 and 7, we more intentionally "plunge beneath the surface of ethnography in a more interpretative mode" (Willis 1977, p. 119). Although ethnographic data certainly are embedded within all chapters in this volume, we work to break from ethnographic form in chapters 6 and

7 to probe, at a more deeply analytical and theoretical level, the short and possible long-term meaning behind data reported in chapters 3, 4, and 5, in particular. Specifically, although chapter 6 is, like prior chapters, comprised of in-depth interview and participant observation data with regard to class and race productions, we go well beyond the actions and words of the participants themselves to theorize, in new ways, class and race productions in the twenty-first-century United States. Working to theorize important aspects of class positioning and class productions, particularly in relation to race and class intersectionality (Crenshaw 1991), we both take account of and simultaneously theorize around what the participants themselves articulate, whether verbally or performatively, through interviews and participant observations. Much of our analytical work around race, class, and "flexible immigrants," for example, falls into this latter category.

At a more specific level with regard to the flow of the chapters, chapter 3 focuses on students and parents in an iconic affluent public suburban secondary school, one that bears marked similarity in socioeconomic status of student population served to that of our NAIS schools in the particular geographic area in which we collected our data. In this chapter, we trace how parents position their children for advantage beginning at an early age, a topic that takes center stage in our rendition of "class work" with respect to this particular group. We additionally trace the ways in which students and parents enact and conceptualize their work in the secondary school as well as the ways in which they go through the distinct process of preparing for college and university entrance. Following the students through the college application and admissions process, specific attention is paid to all college-related activities in school, including the work of the school counselors as related to the top 10% of students.

Chapter 4 picks up the same set of questions among students and parents in a NAIS coeducational day school in a tier-2 (nonglobal) city. As in chapter 3, we follow the students through the college application and admissions process in a highly detailed manner, with specific attention paid to all college-related activities among the top 20% of students in the class.

Chapter 5 addresses the same broad question that frames the work of chapters 3 and 4, with specific focus on low-income self-identified Black students who, by and large, are placed at the bottom of the school opportunity structure given their prior education in poorly resourced, predominantly Black and Latino inner-city public middle schools at a time of deepened disinvestment in the public sector generally (Anyon 2014; Lipman 2011). The primary focus of this chapter is students, teachers, and counselors at two NAIS day schools, one single-sex girls and one coeducational.

Chapter 6, as noted above, moves into new and more deeply theoretical terrain, specifically attending to the extent to which democratizing impulses around race/ethnicity in the privileged private secondary sector embody deep contradictions, both perpetuating and demanding the continued articulation of a particular kind of "racial other" that serves both to partially maintain Whiteness as privilege and simultaneously to distance low-income self-identified Black students from their historic social and political base. We then focus on what students, both White and of color, are learning about race and class as they go through elite private schools and transition to the postsecondary sector, as we subsequently interrogate the particular location of privileged Black families in this sector of schools, whether multigenerational US born or "flexible immigrants" of color. We close chapter 6 with a detailed account of college matriculation patterns at the three schools and with the three relevant populations under consideration.

In chapter 7, we take up three interrelated theoretical and empirical points, as follows: (1) class formation in the twenty-first-century United States, with specific focus on the power and complexities of race/ethnicity/ national origin as linked to class, in what will arguably become a "new upper middle class" of the twenty-first century, one that is specifically linked to intensified struggle over particular kinds of postsecondary destinations; (2) the extent to which women's surge into highly valued postsecondary destinations within this class fraction portends altered roles and responsibilities for men and women of the new upper middle class; and (3) the ways and extent to which this ties to the workings of the postsecondary sector of the future, particularly as linked to segmented pathways in a sector that itself is riddled by deepening stratification, linked inequalities, and division. Here we circle back to Kerckhoff's (1995, 2001) charge of the mid-1990s and early 2000s, with specific focus on the extent to which student location at each stage in the structure of educational opportunities limits their possible locations at the next stage. We pay particular attention to the possible implications of this statement for both class structure and the workings of the postsecondary sector more broadly.

In our epilogue, "Details and Reflections on Theory and Methods," we offer detailed information with regard to the ethnographies and our own ethnographic practice. In addition, we reflect on the power of ethnography to reveal the complex interconnections of individual lives with the shaping powers of class, race, and gender. In so doing, we ponder Willis's trenchant statement of 2004, that "class needs ethnography to show its long reach into the fine details of human destiny and . . . ethnography needs 'class' to draw out its full analytic and historical powers and potentials" (Weis 2004, book jacket).

We close this chapter with two important disclaimers. To begin with, we do not mean to imply, or employ, any kind of oversimplification or essentializing conception with regard to our analytical "categories in use." This includes "White," "Whiteness," "flexible immigrants," "low-income Black students," among others. For any one of these categories, we are well aware that considerable within-group variation exists. As Leong (2013, p. 2) notes in a recent article in which she introduces a framework of racial capitalism:

> Within the group of those we might call "white," there is considerable variation in the benefits whiteness confers. . . . The intersection of race with other identity categories, such as gender, class and sexual orientation, affects the degree of privilege that any individual white person in fact experiences—and consequently, the value of that person's whiteness.

Leong's important points hold for all groups under consideration in this volume, and although we focus specifically on self-identified "low-income Black students," "White students," and "children of 'flexible immigrants' of color," we are well aware that individual students within any given category experience varying degrees of privilege, inclusion, and exclusion based on a range of factors beyond race and class. Moreover, we are aware of ethnic variations within broad racial categories such as "White" and "Black." Having said this, it is critically important that we continue to acknowledge the deeply rooted shaping power of such categories in historical and current contexts—in this case, a US context marked by historic and current legally and racially apartheid arrangements and associated sensibilities, and the predominant current ideology of "color-blind racism" (Bonilla-Silva 2006). As Weis and Fine (2004, p. xviii) argue:

> While we refuse essentialism, resisting the mantra-like categories of social life—race, ethnicity, class, gender—as coherent, in the body, "real," consistent, or homogeneous, we also take very seriously that these categories become real inside institutional life, yielding dire political and economic consequences. Even

if resisted, they become foundational to social identities. Even as performed, multiple, shifting, and fluid, the technologies of surveillance ensure partial penetration of the politics of social identities (Butler 1000; Foucault 1977; Scott 1990). You can't just hang out in poor and working class communities, a suburban mall, a prison, or an elite suburban golf course and believe that race, ethnicity, and social class are simply inventions. Thus, with theoretical ambivalence and political commitment, we analytically embrace these categories of identity as social, porous, flexible, and yet profoundly political ways of organizing the world. By so doing, we seek to understand how individuals make sense of, resist, embrace, and embody social categories, and, as dramatically, how they situate "others," at times even essentializing and reifying "other" categories, in relation to themselves. This is, we argue, what demands a relational method.

Although cognizant of any and all complexities, then, we nevertheless employ relevant categories of social life to further our analytical understanding of the workings of class, race, and national origin with regard to the production of what we call a new upper middle class via struggle over access to particularly located postsecondary destinations.

Our second disclaimer is as follows: As we move through the ethnographic chapters, empirically and analytically driving toward the conclusion, it may feel at times as if we are uncritically celebrating the intensified "race" to particularly located postsecondary destinations with all commensurate mobilization of capital and privilege. In this sense, readers may suspect that our focus on parents that choose to "play the educational game," as they attempt to garner specific kinds of choices for their children, means that we uncritically reproduce, and even embrace, relatively narrow notions of quality and "success," much as our students and parents do throughout several chapters in this volume.

To be up front with regard to the task at hand, then, we do not intend to draw specific attention to narrowly defined indicators of quality, with an eye toward envisioning alternative conceptions of "quality outcomes," as this is simply not our intended purpose. Although we certainly do not celebrate narrowly conceived conceptions of "quality" outcomes, our goal in this volume is to analytically unpack the production of a new upper middle class as uncovered ethnographically in privileged secondary school sites, one that swirls around access to a broadened pallet of particularly located postsecondary destinations (beyond the Ivies). In this regard, we emphatically state that it is not our intent to uncritically accept, or script, particular kinds of postsecondary matriculation patterns as the only marker of "success." Rather, based on the resultant data and analysis linked to our multisited ethnographic investigations, we conceptualize the postsecondary admissions process as a site of "class warfare," one engaged most vehemently by a particular slice of the broad-based middle class that employs all available capitals to situate the next generation for privilege.

In this regard, it is important to reflect upon the potential costs—both emotional and economic—of struggles over continued class advantage as currently playing out in privileged secondary schools. Students in privileged secondary schools are now under enormous pressure to gain entrance to particular colleges, a form of pressure that prior generations in the United States have not experienced. Although pressure to attend college in the United States has certainly been in evidence among a particular segment of the population for many decades now, and the elite has long struggled to maintain its stranglehold on the Ivies, Americans strongly believed that there were many roads to "success" and that one did not *necessarily* need to attend the most competitive postsecondary destinations in the country to reap future economic rewards. As we see throughout the volume, for particular populations this sentiment is no longer evident, as access to particularly located postsecondary destinations—specifically "Most Competitive" and "Highly Competitive+" private colleges as per Barron's *Profiles of American Colleges*—now dictates the pace of life for privileged students and their families, ultimately constituting the seemingly lone moniker of student and family success.

Having said this, the short- and long-term consequences of this "race" as currently engaged within this privileged class fraction remains to be seen. Family incomes have not kept pace with rising tuition, even among the top 20% of the income distribution, which means that students, and often families, are responsible for a greater portion of college expenses (*Losing Ground* 2002). Although privileged families are largely able and willing to pay college tuition and living expenses for their children at the current moment, soaring tuition at public and particularly private postsecondary institutions suggests that even privileged families may have little remaining flexible income after putting their children through college. This suggests that this population of current students will increasingly have to borrow enormous sums of money to help defray the costs of graduate and professional school, while also being called upon, dependent on the extent to which parental investments and other resources are depleted by virtue of their children's attendance at particularly located colleges, to help their parents in their retirement years.

In addition, given America's sinking position in the global economy (Brown, Lauder, and Ashton 2011) and the uncertain degree to which even elite undergraduate and graduate education will prove to be a "good investment," we can anticipate that even those who have been educated in America's most prestigious postsecondary institutions may find it difficult to repay their loans. If so, this will create a further educational "debt bubble" that goes beyond that forecast for those with far less highly prized educational credentials. To be clear, then, although our explicitly engaged task is not to critique the current "race to the top" of the postsecondary hierarchy or the extent to which "success" is narrowly defined by the class fraction largely under investigation, we are not unaware of the potential short- and long-term consequences of these practices.

Employing "critical bifocality," our goal in this volume is to work across a range of macro and micro levels, keeping the broader social structures in continual play as we simultaneously probe the lived experiences and practices of young people, their families, and secondary school personnel who both attend and are otherwise linked to privileged public and private secondary schools. In so doing, we chart the complexity and nature of "class work" in twenty-first-century America, presenting powerful evidence with regard to the new ways in which upper-middle-class privilege is currently consolidated across race/ethnic and class difference by virtue of access to particularly located postsecondary destinations. Such class consolidation, we argue, is taking place at one and the same time as deepening divisions are in evidence within and between existing class and race/ethnic communities. Our data and analysis drive toward the conclusion that although the twenty-first-century United States will continue to be marked by significant class and racial apartheid, such apartheid will prevail in complex and newly evolving forms, rendering the class structure markedly different from that which defined the experiences and practices, including those related to the secondary to postsecondary transition, of prior generations.

CHAPTER TWO

Schooling in Privileged Spaces

Organizational habitus shows how high schools' organizational cultures are linked to wider socioeconomic status cultures, how social class operates though high schools to shape students' perceptions of appropriate college choices, thereby affecting patterns of educational attainment, and how individuals and schools mutually shape and reshape one another.
— (McDonough 1997, p. 107)

We have "College Information Night," not "Job Information Night,"[1] so you know . . . and we have like 800 kids taking the PSATs next week, they are not taking the ASVAB[2] test. It's all that stuff, and it's [discussion about college] all over the place, which is fine. I think it should be that way, but it hits you in the head everywhere. — (Tom Cherub, lead counselor, Cannondale)

A growing but still small body of literature focuses on the production of privilege in schools, both public and private. Cookson and Persell (1985), for example, offer early work on private school advantage, specifically focusing upon the "select sixteen" boarding schools. More recent work by Proweller (1998), Howard (2007), Khan (2011), and Gaztambide-Fernández (2009) in private secondary (day and boarding) schools, and Varenne and McDermott (1998) and Demerath (2009) in affluent public schools, pinpoints specific family- and school-based mechanisms that confer advantage, including a sustained and intense focus on high-status knowledge; new competitions and tests that require "ever more difficult displays of proficiency" (Varenne and McDermott 1998, p. 111); specific attention to tutoring and preparation for college entrance tests; and editing college essays/applications, all of which serve to confer specific and targeted advantage to those who already possess such advantage.

In a related and important vein, McDonough (1997) documents a range of class/race-related opportunities for college counseling in secondary schools, which are linked to differential postsecondary destinations, paying particular attention to the role of counselors in the college search and application process. Stevens (2007), while directing his attention to the ways in which selective universities (with particular focus on one institution) assemble a class, highlights the ways in which families and schools draw upon college admissions criteria to make childrearing and curricular decisions. He argues that advantaged families use the college admissions process as a method of transmitting social and economic advantage to their offspring, and that schools and colleges are complicit in the reproduction of privilege.

As noted in chapter 1, the popular press has also taken an interest in the college admissions process and related positioning work of families. Steinberg (2002), for example, takes a journalistic look at the admissions process at Wesleyan, a prestigious liberal arts college in the northeastern United States. By acting as an admissions representative for one year, Steinberg offers an upclose examination into a largely secretive process. In particular, he alerts the reader to the importance of the forged relationship between any given high school counselor, the high school itself, and college admissions representatives with regard to facilitating student access to given colleges. This important point was made fifteen years earlier by Cookson and Persell (1985) and confirmed a decade after Steinberg's journalistic account by researchers Hoxby and Avery (2012). A corpus of evidence now strongly suggests that particularly located secondary schools—those whose counselors have established connections to college admissions personnel—tend to fare better in the college admissions process, a fact that belies the instantiation of privilege and its reproduction.

Robbins (2006) also provides a journalistic account of the college admissions process. She locates herself inside an affluent public high school in Bethesda, Maryland, and reveals the extent to which issues of college positioning in middle- and upper-middle-class communities has entered the popular imagination. She follows a group of students who excel in various areas (academics, sports, leadership, popularity, etc.) to demonstrate the current pressure on students who attend high-powered, affluent public schools. Robbins documents the social, academic, and extracurricular lives of these students to illustrate how the frenzy to prepare for college has taken on an intensely competitive nature in affluent settings.

A small number of scholars have focused upon family practices to understand the intersection between social position and education. For example, Lareau (2000, 2003) studies families across race/ethnicity and class, ultimately locating *specific* childrearing strategies that are endemic to one's class position. She argues that working-class and low-income families, irrespective of race, tend to abide by a philosophy of natural growth—an approach to parenting that maintains hard boundaries between children and parents, involves limited interventions in schooling by parents, and allows children a good deal of autonomy to organize their own time. Conversely, middle- and upper-middle-class parents, similarly irrespective of race, engage what Lareau calls "concerted cultivation." Parents who adopt this method are notably hands-on, intervening in their children's schooling, scheduling their free time, and actively working to develop their children's negotiation skills so they may speak to adults as equals. Brantlinger (2003), too, focuses on young children and the positioning work done by parents (mothers) on their behalf. She argues that parental intervention by middle- and upper-middle-class parents advantages their children at the expense of less-advantaged children.

While the work on childrearing patterns and parental intervention vis-à-vis schooling in the United States certainly complements our work, prior research focuses to a greater extent on young children, usually elementary school age. Further, such work is not theorized as *specifically* located inside current economically driven and increasingly complex class/race processes, thereby not intentionally engaging the burgeoning literature on the ways in which "class works" in our rearticulated contemporary moment. In addition, with the exception of McDonough (1997), Horvat and Antonio (1999), Lareau and Weininger (2010), Perna et al. (2008), and Hill (2008), there has been remarkably little attention paid to the specific secondary to postsecondary linkage and the ways in which entrance to increasingly valued postsecondary destinations in a now national marketplace must be theorized as an attempt to "maintain distinction" and mark class boundaries.

Description of Sites

As detailed in chapter 1, data reported in this book were drawn from three research sites: one affluent, public high school; one NAIS independent (private), coeducational day school; and one NAIS single-sex girls' independent (private) day school. All three schools are located within the greater metropolitan areas of nonglobal, tier-2 cities in the northeastern United States, the implications of which will be discussed more fully in chapter 4.[3] Data were largely collected during the 2009–10 school year, when students were in their senior year of high school. Student selection criteria are detailed in chapter 1. Further particulars with regard to sampling procedures are discussed at length in the epilogue. As noted in chapter 1, participant observation data related to college counseling meetings and classes were collected over a one-and-a-half-year period, spanning both junior and senior years, although the majority of data collection was engaged during the students' senior year.

Cannondale High School

Cannondale High[4] is located in the community of Cannondale, a third-ring, affluent suburb of Riverside.[5] Riverside is located in the northeastern United States and is considered to be a large, metropolitan area.[6] Cannondale has consistently been named one of the "Best 100 Places to Live in America" and draws people with its small-town charm and reputation for "good" schools. The community is overwhelmingly White, with fewer than 10% of the population identifying as Black, Asian, and/or Native American. The school largely mirrors these demographics—although, due to an optional integration program that busses in students from Riverside, the student body is slightly more diverse in terms of race and class than the surrounding community. Riverside itself was once home to a number of technology giants and has a distinctively white-collar identity despite its more recent economic decline and high rates of poverty. The city and its suburbs are both economically and racially segmented. The city is within close proximity to a number of well-known, highly selective colleges and universities, well-regarded state colleges, and a smattering of small, private liberal arts institutions.

Cannondale High School is a large, comprehensive public high school that serves between 600 and 700 students per grade level. The school mission statement prioritizes the development of individual students' talents and aspirations while simultaneously emphasizing the importance of interdependence and an appreciation for difference (paraphrased from the school's website). There is no explicit diversity statement or diversity club, yet the school projects values that support individual differences in many regards.

The grounds consist of one large two-story building, built in the style typical of the late 1960s, with an inner courtyard and an expansive array of sports fields. Additions and renovations have been made over time to accommodate a growing student population and its needs. Inside, the school is immaculately clean, brightly lit, and extremely inviting. Photographs of current and former students line the halls, and celebrations of students' accomplishments—be they artwork, trophies, humanitarian work, and so forth—abound. Cannondale prides itself on its family environment (students and family are often addressed as the "Cannondale family") and consequently has organized the school space to exemplify this.

In addition to the family atmosphere CHS wishes to project, the other aspect of the school culture that a visitor would notice immediately is a focus on college. Embedded into the very fabric of the school, the importance of college physically manifests itself everywhere. Teachers and counselors proudly display pennants and degrees from their alma maters; academic departments devote entire bulletin boards to where faculty went to college; the school counseling department arranges numerous displays detailing college information, visits from college representatives, test prep information, interactive maps highlighting where students in the previous class matriculated; and daily announcements share college-related information. As lead counselor Tom Cherub explains, college "hits you over the head" in a place like Cannondale High School.

Classroom space occupies both floors of the building. The building is largely divided into informal wings, and subject-area teachers are clustered together such that all the English rooms are found in one area, science rooms in another, and so on. Classrooms are updated with modern technology. All classrooms are outfitted with audiovisual equipment (student-produced announcements are often made through the TV), smartboards, dry-erase boards, and computers. According to district-level data, fewer than 10% of teachers in the district have less than three years' experience and roughly 15% at least 30 credit hours beyond a masters (including doctorates). No teachers are teaching outside of their certification area.

CANNONDALE ACADEMIC HABITUS.   Cannondale High maintains rigorous academic standards. A wide range of Advanced Placement (AP) (21, in fact), SUCP (Selective University College Prep), and Honors-level courses are offered, both in traditional subject areas (math, English, foreign language, social studies, and science) as well as in art, music, and technology.[7] More than 800 AP exams were administered to the class of 2010 over their high school tenure, and a stunning 90% of students scored a 3 or better on their AP exams (some students took multiple exams).[8] In addition, the school operates the International Baccalaureate (IB) program,[9] offering 13 IB courses. Students can opt for the "full diploma," the "certificate," or just take any IB course of their choosing. The IB program is relatively new to Cannondale, and in the class of 2010, approximately 60 students sat for 160+ exams, and almost one-third of those students who sat the examinations (including 2 in this sample) received the full diploma.

Data for the 2009–10 school year also indicate that CHS students score above the national average on traditional college entrance standardized tests (such as the ACT and SAT), and the senior class had several National Merit Semifinalists and 28 Commended Students. One of the students in the sample (Michael Penn) was a scholarship winner. Once graduated, more than 90% of the total graduating class immediately goes on to attend either two- or four-year institutions, with the majority matriculating at four-year schools (about 70%). Students apply to and attend a number of selective and highly selective institutions such as Cornell, Dartmouth, Colgate, and others, as well as local colleges and universities.

Course selection uses an open enrollment process, although in practice, it takes on the characteristics of a soft tracking system, wherein the same group of students tend to be clustered in a particular track across subjects. In particular, a tight-knit group of students tends to be identified and identify themselves as the "AP/IB track," with attendant consequences for the college admissions process, a topic that will be taken up more fully in chapters 3 and 6. Students are initially placed in courses using a combination of factors: previous course placement history and grades, teacher and counselor recommendations, and student (and parent) requests. Prior course history, grades, and teacher recommendations are the factors with the greatest determining strength. For example, a student who was placed in Honors math in ninth grade and scored well would be recommended for Honors 10 math. In some cases, a teacher may not recommend a student for a given course; yet, if students and parents advocate for placement in that course, the student may be placed in that class nevertheless. If the student does not perform well, he or she will be scheduled into a less accelerated section.

AP and IB courses are also technically open enrollment. Any student is able to take an AP course or an IB course, and the IB full certificate program is open to all students. A large percentage of CHS students opt to take at least one AP class over the course of their high school careers. Counselors often encourage students to challenge themselves by taking at least one AP course, highlighting that doing so will have a favorable effect vis-à-vis the college admissions process and/or preparation for college more generally. Interestingly, participant teachers were less than enthusiastic about this practice, arguing that AP courses had become less rigorous over time because of a greater number of students who now enter the courses from the state (examination) "track." Again, however, a core group of students comprises the majority of these AP and IB classes, and they tend to "travel together" through the AP/IB track in high school with a highly distinctive identity.

Matthews Academy

Founded in the late 1800s as an elite college preparatory school for boys, Matthews Academy later merged with Hamilton Academy to become an elite coeducational private school. The Matthews mission is not explicitly about academics; rather, it speaks to the importance of character and service and preparing students physically, psychologically, and mentally for life's rigors. At the turn of the century, the school added to its mission a set of core values that are mounted in every classroom in the school and found in the student handbook: pursuit of excellence, integrity of character, tradition and change, rigor and balance, and diverse community. Additionally, the school also has an honor code, which addresses respectful interactions between students, and respect of property and diversity. Interestingly, while very little in the school's stated mission and values explicitly addresses college preparatory academics, the culture of the school, as a preparatory institution, fundamentally centers on preparing students for college—academically, socially, and personally.

In addition to these policies and statements, the school has a Statement on Multiculturalism that is listed in its handbook and on its website. This statement confirms that the school values diversity in multiple forms (race, class, gender, religion, sexual orientation) and seeks to address diversity through policies and procedures, curricula, and instruction. More recently, Matthews has convened diversity committees and appointed an informal diversity practitioner to be charged with mentoring low-income students of color, aiding the admissions office with recruitment and matriculation of these students, advising the student diversity committee, and initiating school-wide "awareness raising" events.

Despite the stated scope of the diversity practitioner position, it was a position in name only, as it came with no authority or budget to enact the broadly stated diversity agenda. Since its inception, three Black females have held this position. Recently it has been reduced from a half-time to a quarter-time position, with the diversity practitioner's main efforts now revolving around classroom instruction. While a detailed analysis of the school's stated mission on diversity, and its incongruence with respect to actual institutional practice, is beyond the scope of this study, this brief description provides a glimpse into the context that helps to produce the felt "outsider within" status among low-income Black students, as discussed at length in chapter 5.

Matthews Academy is a sprawling 25-acre campus that includes several brick buildings equipped with state-of-the-art facilities for academics, athletics, and the arts. The McDonald Center for the Performing Arts (MCPA) has an impressive theater that seats 500, as well as classrooms for instruction in instrumental and vocal music. Hamilton Hall, which houses the offices of the Head of School, the Dean of Students, and the Director of Development, along with humanities classrooms, sits behind the MCPA. When walking through the hallways, visitors are often struck by the rows and rows of student-created art adorning the walls—we say struck, as the sophistication of the pieces gives the feel of adult artists. Next to Hamilton Hall is Davidson Hall, which houses several classrooms and the school library, which includes a computer lab and more than 12,000 books. Lastly, the newly founded science and math building, Atkins Hall, is a state-of-the-art facility equipped with a "green" roof, laboratories, classrooms with smartboards and mounted projectors, and several college-style lecture halls. The open layout of the campus, complete with an academic quadrangle, gives the school the look and feel of a small version of a liberal arts college.

In addition to facilities for academics and the arts, Matthews has athletic facilities that are far more extensive than other schools in the area. The school has two gymnasiums, which include squash courts, basketball courts, exercise rooms (with treadmills, weights, and rowing machines), a wrestling room, and spacious locker rooms. The school has five athletic fields, two of which are artificial turf, for soccer, lacrosse, field hockey, and football games and practices. Lastly, Matthews has an impressive ice hockey rink, situated in a building comprised of one large and one small rink, a heated observation room, and a concession stand. The school earns considerable revenue from the rental of this facility, as local hockey teams continually seek use of the rink.

The neighborhoods immediately surrounding Matthews are predominantly White, middle- and upper-middle-class communities. The homes are large and well maintained; along nearby side streets and driveways are parked expensive cars and SUVs. However, a few blocks from Matthews and from these surrounding communities are predominantly Black, working-class, and lower-income neighborhoods. The homes are not as well maintained, and there are fewer cars, most of which are less expensive than in the predominantly White neighborhoods. The public middle and high schools in these Black communities are ones that student and parent participants in this study (particularly those discussed in chapter 5) refer to as being underresourced and lacking academic rigor.

MATTHEWS ACADEMIC HABITUS. Students who gain admission to Matthews spend their years inside a very distinct academic habitus, one built upon a foundation of excellence, tradition, and rigor, a reputation it maintains both locally and nationally. To this end the school employs highly educated faculty chosen for expertise and recognition in their fields; 75% of teachers hold masters degrees, 10% hold PhDs, and 14% are graduates of the school. Students are able to reap the benefits of their teachers' knowledge and expertise in class sizes of approximately 15 students.

Course placement decisions at Matthews are made based on a combination of individual student and organizational factors, depending on the course. Generally, the Freshman Dean and the Academic Department Chairs use a combination of admissions test scores (which includes mathematical reasoning and reading comprehension), IQ scores (when they are available), and students' middle school teacher recommendations to place students into their freshman courses. The Department Chairs spend a significant amount of time looking over students' files and assessing what types of academic content students have been exposed to, in an effort to make fair, appropriate placement decisions. In some instances—mathematics and science, in particular—the school administers a placement test to assist in those decisions.

In response to an opportunity structure that sets limits on the courses available to students over their high school career, the math department developed a new system whereby all students complete geometry by the end of ninth grade, thus allowing *all* students to take a math course beyond precalculus during twelfth grade. The Dean of Students states that the school has always "felt badly about kids being placed in Algebra I" (in grade 9) due to lack of prior exposure and preparation, and wanted to try to equalize students' opportunities, especially considering the important role mathematics, and particularly high-level mathematics, plays in college admissions (Muller, Riegle-Crumb, Schiller, Wilkinson, and Frank 2010; Riegle-Crumb and Grodsky 2010). Students in this section start with some Basic Algebra I and ideally end up completing the requirements for geometry by the end of freshman year. This change requires one of the math teachers to meet with relevant students (eight students total during the 2009–10 academic year) outside of their math class for "lab sessions" to cover all necessary additional content, thereby enabling students to move to Algebra II as tenth graders. The Dean notes that some of these students could still end up being placed in Basic Algebra II (a lower section) rather than Algebra II in grade 10, as they may still be behind those students who entered the school with stronger math preparation. Over the course of their high school career, however, all students, even those who entered the school with notable academic disadvantages, are positioned to access a high-level math course such as AP Probability and Statistics, AP Calculus AB, AP Calculus BC, or Regular Calculus, in their senior year.

Bradford Academy

Founded in the mid-1800s as an independent, private, college preparatory school for girls, Bradford Academy has maintained a reputation for academic excellence and leadership. The Bradford mission is to foster an environment that facilitates active participation, academic rigor, leadership, and a commitment to service. Like Matthews, the stated mission is less about college preparation explicitly and more about preparation for life, which certainly, implicitly, includes four-year college preparation in schools such as Matthews and Bradford. In addition to this mission, the school has both academic and social honor codes. The academic honor code focuses on academic honesty and integrity in regard to all assignments and tests. The social honor code centers on respect for self and others, and lists serious consequences for any student who harasses or bullies another girl because of any part of her identity, and for the use or possession of alcohol or drugs at school or school-sponsored events. Unlike Matthews, Bradford does not have a formal statement with respect to diversity—either separate from or included in its mission—and the school does not employ a diversity practitioner, but does have a student diversity club. The school also evidences some elective courses for seniors on multiculturalism, and the school's mission and philosophy statements signify that they prepare students for "a global community" and "value people from diverse backgrounds."

Entering the foyer of the school a visitor feels as if he or she is entering a large Victorian-style home rather than a secondary school. Bradford has two large staircases that wind from the first to the third floor, and several almost secret hallways and staircases where the students carve out study spaces. On the first floor, one is immediately drawn to the library complete with plush wingback chairs, a baby grand piano, and a wood-burning fireplace. The library is small, but appropriate for the size of the student body. On the opposite end of the hallway is one of the student lounges, which is a rather large room with rectangular wooden tables and chairs; this room sits just to the right of the office of the Head of School.

The chapel is on the second floor; although not used for worship, as the school is not religiously affiliated, this stunning room is used for school-wide meetings and for senior and junior class college events.[10] Stained glass windows line the walls of the chapel, as do six doors on either side that lead to small alcoves where students study and "hang out." Academic classrooms are on the first, second, and third floors of the school. Most are equipped with smartboards and projectors so that faculty (and students) may use their school-issued laptops in the classroom. (As of fall 2009, all incoming students are equipped with their own laptop to use throughout their years at Bradford.) The classrooms, again, feel as if they are rooms in someone's richly appointed home, as most rooms are carpeted with plush, ornate rugs, and are small, as they only need to accommodate about 10 students at a time.

Bradford recently invested nearly $1 million in renovating their athletic facilities. The gym is now divided into two practice courts for basketball, has two new squash courts, and includes a fitness room complete with treadmills, elliptical machines, weights, and yoga mats. As the school does not have its own athletic fields for soccer and field hockey practices and games, the students have access to space on small practice fields at a local college. Likewise, the school's crew team uses the facilities at the East Bank Rowing Club, an exclusive private club, for their practices.

Bradford is located in a predominantly White, affluent neighborhood. The neighborhoods immediately surrounding the school contain some of the largest, most expensive homes within the city, all of which are immaculately maintained. There is also a strip of high-end shops, boutiques, and restaurants on a main city street a few blocks from the school. Traveling a few miles down this street, one crosses over (literally) into the predominantly Latino, lower-income neighborhood. Like Matthews, the communities surrounding Bradford reflect the segregation and social geography

of the city, in that one can move a few miles or a few blocks and find themselves in what seems to be a different world—different stores, different
homes, different people, and visibly different resources.

BRADFORD ACADEMIC HABITUS.   Students who are accepted into Bradford
spend the next four years inside an intimate academic habitus, one designed to foster not only growth academically, but also intellectual confidence. As one of the oldest of the elite private schools in Blair, Bradford
has maintained a reputation for academic excellence and rigor. As such,
Bradford employs faculty highly regarded in their fields; three-quarters of
the faculty hold advanced degrees, some of which are terminal. With class
sizes of approximately 10 to 12 girls, students are able to interact with their
peers and teachers in a unique manner.

Course placement decisions at Bradford have undergone changes
designed to bring greater equity and access regardless of the type and
quality of middle school attended. Like Matthews, in years past students
who were not in an advanced or accelerated math section in eighth grade
(being exposed to Algebra I) were automatically placed in Algebra I as
opposed to geometry for ninth grade (which was the placement organization for the students in this study). Again, like Matthews, beginning in fall
2009, all students are placed in Geometry as freshman; those students who
were not accelerated as eighth graders are placed in a section or sections
where they begin the year with a focus on Algebra, but end the year completing geometry. This requires additional meetings outside of class with
their math teacher. The Dean of Curriculum states that the school found
it "unfair" that some students, due to lack of exposure and opportunity,
were not able to take a math course beyond Precalculus during their time
at Bradford. Thus, this decision is explicitly designed to "level the playing
field" between students coming from different types of middle schools.

Ninth-grade placements in English, science, history, and foreign language are based on entrance exam/placement scores, academic transcripts,
and teacher recommendation forms, which specify the course content cov-
ered in middle school (particularly eighth grade) and the student's level
of proficiency. Thus, for example, a student who took a Spanish I course
in eighth grade that did not meet every day and exposed the student only
minimally to the language may be placed in Spanish I as a ninth grader
at Bradford, based on the recommendations of the Dean of Curriculum
and the Foreign Language Chair. One major difference between Matthews and Bradford is that Bradford does not offer a Basic (the section

below Regular in the opportunity structure at Matthews) section in any course; students are either placed in Regular or Honors sections for all courses.

The Structure of College Counseling

College is clearly an integral part of the organizational habitus at Cannondale, Matthews, and Bradford. As McDonough (1997, p. 107) states:

> Organizational habitus shows how high schools' organizational cultures are linked to wider socioeconomic status cultures, how social class operates though high schools to shape students' perceptions of appropriate college choices, thereby affecting patterns of educational attainment, and how individuals and schools mutually shape and reshape one another.

The organizational habitus of a school shapes not only the appropriate college choices for a given locale (McDonough 1997; Robbins 2006; Souza 2004), but also the appropriate career choices (Kaufman 2005), which is clearly evidenced in focal students' aspirations across the three sites.

As McDonough (1997), Hossler, Schmit, and Vesper (1999) and others (e.g., McDonough 2005; Perna 2005; Williams 2011) argue, school counselors play a germinal role in crafting the college-going culture of a school. As McDonough (1997, p. 89) states, "the counselor is critical in constructing the school's expectations and formal planning for college" in addition to having a "direct impact on students." While expectations and norms regarding college aspirations are shaped by one's larger social environment—including, but not limited to family, friends, community, and social class (Demerath 2009; Hossler et al. 1999; Howard 2007; MacLeod 1995; McDonough 1997; Weis 1990)—the school counselors play a primary role in establishing and maintaining the college advisement services, services that often act—particularly in middle- and upper-middle-class schools such as those discussed in this volume—to reinforce the expectations and aspirations of attendant students and their families (McDonough 1997), or at least those most dominant. Counselors, to a lesser extent, also have a hand in shaping curricular offerings and then directing students in course selection.

As Grodsky and Riegle-Crumb (2010, p. 14) argue, "many students do not really choose [to attend college] at all; they have always *assumed* that they will attend college. For these students, the decision is not whether but *where* to attend" (see also Hoxby 2004; Mullen 2010). Grodsky and Riegle-Crumb describe students with this disposition toward college as possessing a "college-going" habitus (p. 14). The implications of such a disposition at the student level and its relation to academic identity formation are explored in greater detail in the following chapters, yet it is imperative to consider here how a college-going habitus interacts with the way in which Cannondale, Matthews, and Bradford structure college counseling and, hence, their college cultures.

In many ways, it is not the task of these schools to create a college-going habitus for students, per se, as this is already present among families and the larger community. The three schools in this study maintain a college culture focused upon admissions to four-year selective schools—this is even true at a place like Cannondale, that, as a comprehensive high school, sends a smaller proportion of its overall student body to four-year institutions than places like Matthews or Bradford. College counseling, while somewhat different by sector—for example, Matthews and Bradford employ college counselors whose only job is to focus on the college process whereas Cannondale counselors, while highly engaged in the college process, also take on additional responsibilities more typical of school counselors—becomes a process of helping students to pick "where" to go. In other words, counselors assist students in selecting the college that is "right" for them, simultaneously helping them prepare to do this through proper course selection.

In many regards, the *dominant* college cultures are similar across the three schools, and the process for preparing for and enacting the college admissions process are largely the same.[11] Developing student academic and extracurricular portfolios, holding several college-related meetings for students and parents, bringing in college representatives and the like occur at all three institutions, and all *officially* begin the college admissions process at approximately the same time: junior year. Since the processes are nearly identical across the three sites, we briefly and broadly outline the structure of college counseling at our three iconic secondary institutions, noting meaningful differences between sites and sectors when and where they occur.

The college process begins upon students' entry into high school and is one that facilitates students' college options. The schools, through their counselors, provide a multipronged approach to planning and enacting the process, one that seeks to maximize student choice and advantage.

Students receive both group and individual college counseling, and sessions are also organized specifically for parents. Further, there is a very clear process in place for filing applications, complete with well-developed timelines. College advising in the early high school years focuses more on assessing student aspirations and assembling the types of résumés students will need to realize such aspirations. In this regard, course planning takes priority. Counselors meet one on one with students each year to plan the following year's schedule, helping students to select classes that position them well vis-à-vis college admissions. In addition to course scheduling, early college advising activities include prepping for and taking the PSATs in tenth grade and regular grade-level meetings that are held for parents. While these meetings, in theory, are devised to discuss information pertinent to the specific grade, ninth- and tenth-grade-level meetings inevitably devote at least some time to a discussion of college preparation. Counselors attempt to temper parents' zeal with regards to the college process in these early grades, suggesting that if they intend to do any college visits, that these visits be incredibly casual and done separately from the official tours offered by the colleges. Counselors warn parents that students are not fully ready to begin the college search process at this point and may be turned off if it becomes too intense too early.

Direct college advising intensifies junior year. Students are strongly encouraged to prep for and take the PSATs, for two reasons: (1) PSAT scores provide a preview of how students will perform on the SAT (giving students a sense of just how much additional preparation they will need to earn the scores they desire); and (2) if students score well enough, they may qualify for Merit Scholarships. Once scores are received, counselors advise students on the meaning of the scores and what students' next steps should be. At Cannondale, this occurs in small group meetings in English class; at Bradford and Matthews, this occurs individually with the college counselors.

Junior and senior years are filled with college-related meetings for both students and parents. All three sites hold a number of information sessions that outline the basics of the college process, advise parents on how to approach the college search with their children, and what to expect (academically as well as emotionally) as they execute the process over the next two years. Students attend meetings on how to start devising a list of potential colleges, highlighting the questions they should consider while doing this. Numerous college fairs, both onsite and in the community, are held for students and their parents. Additionally, students visit in small groups with an array of college representatives—particularly those from private colleges that have a budget to support such visits and activities— who routinely embrace privileged institutions as appropriate recruitment grounds (Hoxby and Avery 2012). There are also information sessions on locating, completing, and filing financial aid and scholarship forms. Once students make their college decisions, there are various student and parent meetings and events designed to celebrate their decisions and prepare families for the transition. While the minutia of how all this is enacted may vary ever so slightly in the three sites, the overall process is largely the same at Cannondale, Bradford, and Matthews.

Where the processes across sites noticeably diverge is with regard to the work of the counselors themselves, specifically how the counselors' time is allocated in a given day. Counselors at CHS report spending a large portion of their time (upwards of 50%, especially when course advising is included) on college advising, which for a public school is significant given scholarly accounts of demands on and responsibilities of public school counselors (see, e.g., McDonough 1997; Perna et al. 2008). While Cannondale counselors spend greater time engaged in college advisement as compared with other public school counselors, and particularly other school counselors in far less-privileged institutions than Cannondale, this constitutes an important distinction between the school sectors. Unlike Matthews and Bradford, CHS does not employ "college counselors" whose job duties *solely* revolve around planning for college. At CHS, counselors, who juggle student loads between 200 and 250, must conduct college counseling *in addition* to other duties. While the counselors themselves are incredibly experienced (all counselors, with two exceptions, had more than five years' experience) and have the support of two secretaries and two guidance support staff who assist with college searches and processing college applications, they are unable to devote all their attention to college planning in the way that college counselors at both Bradford and Matthews can.

Where we see these differences play out is primarily at the point of one-on-one time students and parents receive from the counselors. At both Matthews and Bradford, both parents and *all* students are expected to at least meet with the college counselor in junior year. The purpose of these meetings is for the college counselors to gain some background information on the students in regard to family, academics, extracurricular activities, aspirations, goals, and so on, and to gauge how much college research each student has already done. Students are expected to have at least one individual meeting with their counselor, as well as one meeting with their counselor and their parents, during the spring of junior year, leaving for summer vacation with a list of potential schools—some offered by the counselors based on their assessment of "fit" for the students and some based on the students' preferences. Students and parents are encouraged to continue researching colleges of interest during the summer and to visit colleges of interest during the summer, taking guided college tours. Per the College Counseling Office, students are advised to spend "at least two hours" at any given school, and often considerably longer. In addition to this personal advice, all students receive a copy of a college applications process handbook (now online), created by the Director of College Counseling, with step-by-step information on researching colleges, seeking letters of recommendation, writing letters of interest, visiting colleges, interviewing (generally conducted by alumni of the college in the city of student residence), essay writing, and numerous other aspects of the college process. Although expected of all students and parents at Matthews and Bradford, not all students and parents follow through with such requirements. This is made particularly clear in chapter 5.

In theory, all Cannondale students also meet with their respective counselors in the early spring of junior year. Counselors meet with juniors individually in February to plan course schedules for senior year. At these meetings, counselors also spend time engaged in college advising. CHS counselors ask similar questions of their students as those asked of Matthews and Bradford students: what are their plans after high school; what are their interests; what are their preferences in terms of size, setting, and location of college; have they registered for the SATs, ACTs, and SAT Subject Tests (specifically required for highly selective colleges); are they enrolled in test prep; and so on. After this meeting, counselors encourage their students to come back and schedule further one-on-one meetings so that they can work together to begin devising a list of prospective schools. Many students (including focal students and other students in the top 10% of the class) avail themselves of these meetings. However, due to the size of their caseloads and other responsibilities, it is nearly impossible for counselors to meet with all students more than once.

The structure of individual college counseling converges across the three sites during senior year. Matthews's process appears to be somewhat more intensive than either Cannondale's or Bradford's, but nevertheless, students receive a combination of individual and small-group college advisement at all three sites. At Matthews, where students receive the most individualized assistance, students take what is called the College Seminar, which is a class taught by the Director and Assistant Director of the College Office. The goal of this seminar, per the Director, is to meet with students in small groups and review some "nuts and bolts" of the college process, such as essay writing, filling out the Common Application,[12] and discussing what students can expect once they get to college. This course meets once every other week during the fall for a full 40-minute class period. In addition, students (and their parents) meet individually with their college counselor, as needed (determined by the student and/or parent), during the application and admissions processes.

At Bradford, while students do not take a class in college planning, they do participate in a college simulation in which they view and evaluate mock college applications complete with transcripts and SAT scores. The Bradford counselor brings in a college admissions officer from a highly selective college or university to run the students and parents through this simulation, which concludes with parents and students in small groups making decisions about whether to admit, reject, or wait-list the three mock applicants. After each group makes and justifies its decisions with specific references to the students' application packages, the admissions officer goes through his or her decisions, clearly articulating the reasons for each one based on what his or her and similarly situated colleges are looking for as they structure an incoming class. Students also sit through a workshop on the "nuts and bolts" of college admissions, which focuses attention on how to complete the Common Application and how to complete applications generally, including the often required and lengthy school-specific supplements (often essays) that almost always accompany the Common Application at highly selective colleges. Beyond these group advisement sessions, students have the opportunity to work with the Bradford counselor one on one should they seek that.

Senior year college advisement at Cannondale looks quite similar to Bradford. Counselors push into classes and hold a "nuts and bolts" session that clearly outlines the process for applying to colleges, how Cannondale processes applications, a walk-through of the Common Application, and general advisement on testing and selecting colleges. Cannondale counselors also conduct "senior interviews" in the fall of senior year to check in with every senior to ensure they have a postgraduation plan in place. Counselors continue to encourage students to schedule appointments and seek them out as much as possible, but, as is the case at both Bradford and Matthews, the onus to do this is largely placed upon the students. As such, some students receive considerably more one-on-one advising than others, as they make it a point to demand the counselor's attention.

As is clearly the case, the structure of college counseling is largely similar across the three sites. College advising begins early and informally and progresses to an intensive process that officially begins junior year. Advising takes on numerous forms—whole-group, small-group, and individual sessions—and information sessions for students and parents are plentiful. The expectation of college attendance is woven into the very fabric and culture of the three sites under investigation, and college advisement is structured with this in mind. Basic information about college is readily available and more in-depth advisement via individual sessions with the counselors is available should students take advantage of it. The most significant difference among the three school sites centers on the role of the counselor. At Cannondale, counselors are responsible for much more than the college applications process, and this is simply not the case for independent privates such as Bradford and Matthews. In contrast to Cannondale, Bradford and Matthews each have a dedicated college counselor whose sole task is facilitating college advisement (Matthews has two counselors dedicated to the college process; Bradford, which is half the size of Matthews, has one). This, coupled with the fact that both Matthews and Bradford have fewer students, means that the opportunity for more in-depth counseling is clearly present, should students take advantage of it. In most cases, students at the top of their classes (and their parents) use the counselors a great deal, as will be shown in chapter 4. Conversely, some students, such as the low-income Black students discussed in chapters 5 and 6, feel somewhat distanced from their schools and the college process, thereby relying far less upon their counselors than one might expect.

Conclusion

In this chapter, we take great care to detail the school sites and their respective modal college processes. Although Cannondale, Matthews, and Bradford differ in numerous important ways, the fundamental centrality of college preparation in their academic cultures is unmistakable. While neither Cannondale, Bradford, nor Matthews explicitly state college process or matriculation goals as unequivocally connected to their mission, ensuring that students are prepared for selective four-year colleges is clearly ingrained in the very fabric of each institution, and implicitly assumed to be part of one's preparation for life. As we argue throughout this volume, the college admissions process, in many ways, has become *the* place where middle- and upper-middle-class families wage the most important battle in the war for class position. As we will see in the following chapters, privileged families, as a result of their own class standing and the extent to which such located class position intersects or interacts with the habitus of the school, invest all available resources into positioning their children for the college applications process. The hope, it seems, is that if students are positioned to enter "good" schools, they will be on the pathway to greater economic security in the long term.

While certainly no guarantee, families and schools nevertheless view the transition from high school to college, and specifically matriculation into highly selective colleges, as a key site for the transmission of privilege in increasingly harsh and contested economic times. As we will argue in this volume, this struggle is primarily and increasingly waged over access to "Most Competitive" and "Highly Competitive+" (as per Barron's *Profiles of American Colleges*) private institutions, with flagship and other public colleges across the competitiveness index taking a distinctly second place in the now intensified race for privilege with respect to the next generation.

We now turn our attention to the individual school sites. Chapter 3 will take an in-depth look at how the families of Cannondale prepare for and enact the college applications process, revealing the particularly located ways that families of affluent public school students lay the groundwork for, and subsequently specifically enact, the college admissions process. As we suggest here, although the *basic formal* practices that surround college admissions in privileged institutions are largely similar, key differences emerge in relation to *how* specifically located class actors within particularly located privileged educational institutions actually engage what appears to be, on the surface at least, almost identical formal processes with regard to college admissions. In chapters 3, 4 and 5, then, we carefully track the *insertion* of the *informal* response to the college admissions process, as forged and subsequently codified as normative practice, within and by particular school sectors and varying classed/raced constituencies.

Class Practices and the College Process in a Suburban, Public High School: Creating Distinction around the Highly Selective College-Going Self

Did I talk about [college]? Yeah, I guess, yeah, I guess we talked about it but I don't think it's been a focus. I think the career thing has been more of a focus, you know, "What are you going to be and college is a way to get to what you want to do with your life." . . . I don't think consciously I said "Okay, now I'm going to talk about college." I'm sure all the way along, it's been in the background. . . . — (Sandra Whitcome, Cannondale parent)

In this chapter,[1] we examine the class (and classed) practices that students and families engage vis-à-vis the college application process, focusing specifically on the ways in which top students in an affluent public suburban high school are encouraged to create and enact identities as "selective college-goers" (colleges with highly selective admissions such as those classified as "Most Competitive" and "Highly Competitive+" [Barron's 2009]). In assuming such identities, students envision themselves as capable of entering the most elite colleges and universities in the nation. We first explore the parental investments made on behalf of children that begin to position them for college and beyond, arguing that parents invest a great deal of work "up front" to position their children for future advantage. We pay particular attention to student identity development processes, demonstrating the way in which attending a four-year (highly selective) college is not only an expectation, but is presented as the only acceptable option for students. We then argue that students incorporate their presumed status as selective college-goers into their identities, creating a frame through which to judge themselves and others. Such identities are steeped in notions of meritocracy and hard work, frameworks that allow students to legitimize their own position and rationalize their aspirations to attend the most selective colleges and universities in the country. In making our case regarding student identity development, we draw upon Ball's (2003) work on class practices to examine how students' identities are adopted and subsequently naturalized.

We then move to discuss the ways in which the school, through its exclusionary practices of tracking, works to reify the boundaries between students in the top 10% (from which participant students are drawn) and the remainder of the student body. Despite the fact that AP and IB courses are ostensibly open to all students, a number of school-based constraints are in place, which work to limit the number of students *not* in the top 10% who actually take these classes.[2] This serves to reinforce the status hierarchy within the school and similtaneously affirms participants' perspectives regarding their personal actions, self-perceptions, aspirations, and broader notions of meritocracy. Such exclusionary practices are inextricably tied to the way in which entitlement filters through students' identities, serving as a feedback loop through which parental and, subsequently, students' ambitions and expectations are affirmed and entrenched. By virtue of the track structure, the school acts to privilege those in the top 10% both by providing them with access to higher status knowledge *and* by underscoring their special status, all of which serve to naturalize what students and parents assume is their rightful place within the academic status hierarchy. Such entitlement leads to high expectations vis-à-vis the college application process and beyond.

The school garners much of its distinction or distinctiveness from the college aspirations and outcomes of the top 10% of the class—the entire college admissions process favors this small yet dominant group, taking on a hegemonic quality in the sense that all competing *nonselective four-year and two-year college-going* identities become marginalized. This, coupled with the fact that top students have been groomed to assume identities as selective college-goers, enables and encourages parents to take a "lead from behind" approach to the college process. Although more than willing to intervene when needed, parents are confident that they can step back (relatively) and let students (with the help of their counselors) drive the college admissions process.

Although practices detailed in this chapter are somewhat similar to those described in chapter 4, they are also notably different, as the site of the public affluent secondary school *itself* works to encourage different emphases with regard to college applications and admissions behavior than what becomes *normative practice* within the independent private sector. In so stating, and as we will argue in chapter 4, the class background of families in the top academic track at the two schools under consideration is largely similar, thereby suggesting that it is the site itself that works to encourage varying behavior around college admissions.

Class Practices and the College Process

Ball (2003, p. 28) explains that "classes, and here specifically the middle class, are to a great extent, constituted through their practices." Similarly, Walkerdine, Lucey, and Melody (2001, p. 27) refer to these as "the social and psychic practices through which ordinary people live, survive and cope." In other words, class categorization has much to do with the particular day-to-day practices and social and cultural experiences one engages (in addition to types of careers one pursues and the attached income and prestige). As Ball, and Walkerdine, Lucey and Melody, among others, argue, much of what it means to be middle class or upper middle class in Cannondale is ineluctably connected to ways of behaving and acting, which, while certainly related to income, are heavily influenced by other families and their practices, and by schools (Ball 2003; Weis 2008). The acts of preparing for and applying to college, then, are practices that are influenced by classed ways of being—affected by habitus—and are shaped by what others in this social class category consider to be appropriate choices and actions.

Choosing Schools: Buying a "Public" Education

Early on, often before children are even born, Cannondale parents begin the process of investing in the education of their (future) children. One key way that parents do this is by buying homes in districts with excellent public schools.[3] However, Cannondale is not a community that just anyone can buy into, a fact not lost on the student participants in this study, as the brief exchange between Nicholas Stowe and Kelly Tran demonstrates:

NICHOLAS: There was something in the Riverside Gazette, and I think that there
is a large percentage of people in Cannondale that have gotten their bachelor's
degree and gone on to get some kind of graduate degree and I think that if you
look at that percentage that yields, well it's their children that go through the
educational system so that's where you get—
KELLY: Well to live here, you kind of have to.
KRISTIN: What do you mean?
KELLY: Well to live here, it's expensive so you have to have a good paying job in
order to even buy a house here or something.

Kelly is correct in her assertion. Less than 20% of the available housing in the community is comprised of rental units, and the median home
price at the time of this research was close to $200,000. Approximately
2% of the population accessed Food Stamps and less than 1% receive
cash assistance (welfare). Additionally, more than 50% of the population
has at least a bachelor's degree, and the median household income hovers
around $75,000, placing Cannondale, as a community, in the fourth-highest
economic quintile in the United States. The majority of the participants
in this study, however, exceed that income level, placing them in the top
economic quintile.[4] Given these descriptive statistics, Cannondale is one
of the most exclusive and affluent communities in the greater Riverside
area.[5] Given its (relative) affluence, it also has a reputation as a district
with strong schools, which is a major selling point for real estate agents,
further entrenching its reputation as a good place for affluent people to
live and send their children to school.

It is not uncommon for parents to purchase homes in particular neighborhoods to gain access to certain public schools. Recent studies by Holmes
(2002), Brantlinger (2003), Andre-Bechely (2005), Lawrence (2009), and
others highlight the ways in which middle- and upper-middle-class parents make very specific housing choices as directly related to school reputations. As Lawrence (2009, p. 209) states, "exercising one's capital for
'residential mobility' or 'selection by mortgage'—that is the practice of
families relocating themselves closer to the 'best' schools to ensure entry via the catchment zone—is not a new phenomenon (Sutcliffe 2000)."
In this respect, Cannondale parents are no different. Of the 9 families
(11 parents) interviewed, all but 2 indicate that the reputation of Cannondale schools played a significant role in their purchase of a home.[6]

Similar to Holmes's (2002) findings, parents relied primarily upon their
social networks of families, friends, colleagues, and acquaintances who are
similarly situated (financially), as well as their knowledge of the area, to

assess the relative reputation of the educational sector. As Allison Gruzina tells it, part of why she and her husband opted to purchase a new home (which they needed for their growing family) was because "people said 'Oh, the schools were good and blah, blah, blah,' stuff like that." In line with Holmes's (2002) findings, parents do not make mention of test scores, college placement, curriculum, or instruction, criteria that much of the relevant scholarly literature relies upon to assess educational quality. Rather, reputation and knowledge of the area—geographically and demographically—constitute the driving force behind parents' residential choices. A number of the parents grew up and/or spent time in the greater Riverside area prior to choosing to settle in Cannondale. For example, the Penns, Roger Stowe, the Swansons, Richard Rogers, Alan Gruzina, and Sandra Whitcombe all grew up in the surrounding area. The Gruzinas, the Jacinovics, and the Tran family all lived in the Riverside metropolitan area prior to having children.

Significantly, Cannondale is also a place where many of the participants felt comfortable.

KRISTIN: And did you, I know you said you're from Oxford (town about ten minutes from Cannondale) so you're from the Riverside area, but why Cannondale?

JAN STOWE: The school district was known to be good. Cannondale and Haverford [are known to be good] and we felt comfortable here.

ROGER STOWE: We could afford Cannondale.

JAN STOWE: I was going to say, Haverford was . . . not going to work.

ROGER STOWE: Well, Cannondale had a little more small-town charm. I mean not that Haverford doesn't. I'm sure you've been through Haverford, strong place and all that but it's a little more expensive.

KRISTIN: There's a different feel to the two, for sure.

JAN STOWE: Right, so Cannondale is great! It's on the canal, [has] nice trails, [it's a] beautiful place. You can't beat it! It's lovely, so that's why we settled on here— townhouse first—until we found a house that was reasonable, and we took it from there.

KRISTIN: So you were happy with the school and seeing that as—

ROGER STOWE: That was a big driving factor, the academics, [the] schools. So you know, you talk about academics. Right there, *even before our kids were born, we were thinking about the opportunity to get the best education* (emphasis added).

The Stowes emphasize two factors that drove their decision to settle in Cannondale: educational opportunity and comfort/affordability. Education, long viewed as an engine of social mobility and/or a mechanism through which parents can ensure that their offspring will have *at least* the same level of economic security as they do, is the first move parents make to transfer advantages to their children.

Comfort is also a factor and certainly has class connotations. Comfort can be interpreted in multiple ways: comfort in knowing that there are other people *like them* socially, economically, perhaps even racially; comfort in the material and physical space that Cannondale affords; and comfort in a Bourdieuian sense—one's habitus and with whom one feels comfortable interacting. To Cannondale residents, Haverford has a reputation as being haughty and more exclusive, whereas participants view Cannondale as more down to earth. As Caroline Swanson states, Cannondale is "less income-focused" and "more like us."

"What the Joneses Are Doing Is Pretty Damn Important."

Aside from deciding where to purchase homes, parents and students are cognizant of what similarly situated people in their geographic area are doing. As teacher Robert Parker states matter-of-factly, a lot of what drives the structure of the college process at Cannondale, as well as the "concerted cultivation" families engage in (Lareau 2003), is the result of "parents saying, 'Well over at Haverford [neighboring, affluent town] they do it that way, why don't you do it that way?' So, suburbia is a place, no secret, where what the Joneses are doing is pretty damn important."

"What the Joneses are doing" drives, in contradictory fashion, community identity in Cannondale. In spite of expressed concerns surrounding haughtiness embedded in neighboring suburban areas, Cannondale scripts itself as largely comparable to a wide variety of affluent suburban communities in US cities, including Scarsdale, a very wealthy community just outside of New York City. There is constant comparison and assessment of the extent to which Cannondale "measures up" to other affluent communities, and a subsequent weaving of stories or justification if it is deemed that it does not.

The notions of relative privilege and deprivation become important here. Cannondale, on the one hand, compares itself to the greater Riverside area, a comparison that reinforces feelings of intense affluence and entitlement. Yet Haverford, one of Cannondale's closest neighbors, serves as an immediate counterpoint to this identity, a reminder that as affluent as Cannondale believes itself to be, it is not as privileged as its closest neighbor. This elicits considerable discursive negativity with regard to more economically privileged communities—that is, Haverford is "too snotty" or too focused on income. Such sentiments, however, do not pierce Cannondale's image of itself in economic or class terms, in that residents continue to declare themselves wholly similar to Haverford, just more "down to earth."

Cannondale in fact routinely constructs itself as on par with a range of exceptionally affluent communities. This sense of entitlement has implications for actions, activities, and expectations with regard to the college admissions process, a set of expectations and related practices that is arguably rooted in the now national marketplace for college and university entrance (Hoxby 1997), as discussed in chapter 1. Although college admissions is becoming more competitive, the most selective colleges in the nation are simultaneously now *perceived* to be "within reach" of a far broader group of individuals than was the case historically (see chapter 1 and elsewhere in this volume). As a consequence, communities like Cannondale envision themselves as potentially reaping the benefits of broadening access and opportunities. For students in the top 10% of the class, this translates into a deeply felt sense of entitlement and expectation to attend the most prestigious universities in the country.[7]

ACTIVITIES AND EXPERIENCES.   As Mitchell Stevens (2007) astutely notes, middle- and upper-middle-class childrearing is often done with an eye toward selection criteria at selective colleges and universities. Consequently, Cannondale focal students participate in a range of school and out-of-school activities such as sports, church groups, artistic endeavors, volunteer work, paid jobs, internships, and academic pursuits (e.g., taking astronomy courses at the local planetarium). Résumés are jam-packed with activities, often reaching two and three pages. CHS facilitates and supports this form of childrearing by creating greater opportunities for students to be involved and offering more and more "unique" experiences for students, much of this in response to parental demand. Veteran teacher Robert Parker speaks at length about the ways in which parents stake out activities and experiences as a way to provide advantage for their children, thereby creating *distinction*:

> From the get go, as soon as the kids are in seventh grade, and we accelerate in math, they are very concerned if their child . . . especially if their parents are literate in the game [positioning for college admissions], you know, you can't lump all of the parents together, some of them are not literate. They find out, hey, if

I had found out how this game was played, I would have played it differently. They learn from their first child, especially if they are not heavily networked. Most of our parents are heavily networked here. They are clustered in these little ticky-tacky neighborhoods and they talk to each other. And so, they are positioning the kid in the sense that if there is an opportunity . . . I mean we had one school trip to Ireland 14 years ago and now we have an exchange with Italy, Ireland, Germany, France, a humanitarian trip to India. We are doing a humanitarian trip to Peru, which is a sign of the affluence, but is also a sign that the parents want every opportunity for their kids to say, to reflect on, to grow from, to put on, if you will, the college application. So, my SAT prep class and my ACT prep class, almost half the students take it in the school because there is this perception that the other kids are taking it.

Robert Parker, who is seemingly somewhat disdainful of the Cannondale community and the practices of some of its residents,[8] provides a clear example of the ways in which parents use their class resources—social networks, financial assets—to provide opportunities for the next generation. Those who are "literate," by his estimation, are more strategic (in a non-Bourdieuian sense) as they attempt to use particular opportunities to leverage advantage for their children—alternately, one could speculate that parents who are more "literate" have greater resources and knowledge at their disposal. At the same time, Robert Parker's account makes clear that some parents pursue opportunities for their children because *other parents* are doing the same thing. In this way, action is somewhat divorced from meaning, as it becomes more of an act of emulation—parents are playing the game without, perhaps, fully understanding the rules. Rather than consciously engaging positioning work that is (fully) informed by social location and habitus, a portion of Cannondale parents appear to mimic what other "comparable" class actors are seen and/or imagined to do in other suburban schools.[9]

Students' involvement in activities is multifaceted, and their motivations for participation are complex. Yet, being involved is normalized within this space (top 10% at Cannondale). While there are certainly activities that are engaged only for the sake of applying to college—for example, some volunteer work, accepting nominations to Honor Society—students tend to get involved in things that they enjoy, that they are good at, and/or that their friends are involved in. A few students, like Jacob Jacinovic and Nicholas Stowe, denied (and in Jacob's case, vehemently denied) taking on activities to boost their college résumés, proclaiming that they do only what interests them (both) or what comes naturally (Nicholas).

These examples affirm the assumptions of appropriate middle-class childrearing—children are involved and parents provide them with opportunities to explore interests, academic talents, and travel (see, e.g., Lareau 2003). Parents expend (or activate) capital so as to procure opportunities for their children (Lareau 2000), opportunities that can act to advantage them in the college application process. Ironically, in many cases, parents do not view their actions as prepping their children for college and specifically the college admissions process. Yet, this is exactly what it is, whether considered consciously or not. More often than not, focal parents consider their actions to be simply what "good" parents do. Rather than conceptualizing such "goodness" as materially based, however, they analytically bury the knowledge and/or finances it takes to accomplish such opportunities, simultaneously establishing themselves as "good parents" in counterdistinction to "bad parents" who do not care enough or work hard enough to garner opportunities for their children. As Caroline Swanson states in reference to the broader Riverside community, some parents, "for whatever reason," do not set the "appropriate" expectations or provide the "appropriate" opportunities for their children.

Such shared class understandings work to establish that positioning for college entrance is predominantly linked to childrearing practices rather than available social and economic resources. Like consciously purchasing homes in areas with a reputation for strong schools, parents at Cannondale continue to actualize their social and economic capital "up front" to normalize the expectation of student involvement. Whether engaged by Cannondale parents consciously or not, such involvement helps to position children favorably vis-à-vis the college applications process and beyond.

Watching, Waiting, and Deciding When to Intervene

Lareau (2008) analyzes the ways in which Black middle-class parents use their class-based resources to ensure educational advantage for their children. Drawing from her study of middle- and upper-middle-class[10] and working-class families' childrearing patterns (Lareau 2003), Lareau (2008, p. 128) suggests that self-identified Black parents are "*selective* in their activation of cultural capital," opting to choose their battles rather than constantly intervening on behalf of their children.

Participants from Cannondale express similar sentiments, particularly with regard to high school experiences and the college process. Based upon parent and counselor interview data, participants note that while there are some hyper-involved parents, these "helicopter" parents are, for the most part, few and far between. The conception of the "helicopter parent" must itself be contextualized. Unlike stories in the *New York Times* about the suburbs surrounding New York City in which parents employ a cadre of professionals to manage their children's college process (and at times actually do the work associated with applications), parents in Cannondale are comparatively laid back. Nadine Powell's comments, which are representative of the counselors as a whole, suggest "some parents are over-involved [in the process] but for the most part, parents are pretty actively involved," mostly, she explains "by driving the process." Rather than micromanage the process at all relevant points, however, in discursive contrast to the *New York Times* rendition, CHS parents prompt their children to make their *own* critical decisions. Nadine Powell provides what she considers to be a typical example of parental involvement: "OK, we are going to visit some colleges over Columbus Day weekend. Tell me what campus you want to visit."

In point of fact, Cannondale parent and counselor accounts indicate that direct intervention by parents on behalf of students somewhat drops off in high school, suggesting that parents are much more involved at the elementary and middle school levels, a finding certainly supported by Lareau (2003), Brantlinger (2003), and others. Parents, like Sandra Whitcombe, recount stories of approaching the principal of Brad's elementary school after she felt his second-grade teacher passed him over for the "gifted and talented" program. Requesting that he be *formally* tested for admission rather than simply relying upon the teacher's judgment, the gifted designation was ultimately granted. Placement in the gifted program set in motion an educational trajectory that, as discussed later in this chapter, traveled with him into middle and high school, ultimately positioning him in particular ways vis-à-vis the college admissions process. Angie Penn, in similar fashion, intentionally sought a teaching position in the district—in fact she went back to school to become a teacher explicitly to teach in Cannondale—so that she could "have [her] hands in everything," thereby attempting to ensure her child's future rather than leave it entirely up to the school.

Abby Bronstein, a school counselor who has spent some time working at the middle school level in the district, shares her perspective:

> Well, they have this accelerated and twice exceptional [label] and they label them in elementary school, whether they are advanced or not, and that kind of sticks with them. And the parents are constantly (knocks on table to simulate

knocking on a door) "My kid has been labeled twice exceptional" and it's constantly like "What can I do to get my kid ahead?" And, it's constant, you know, "What can I do?" You see it in the Honor-thing in middle school, it's like math and science are the only places where they are going to be able to get ahead high school-wise, so parents are always wanting to, you know, "I want my kid in Honors, I want my kid in Honors!" There is a lot of that pressure from parents.

Jamie Cucchiara, another school counselor, affirms Abby Bronstein's comments, indicating that parents push for their children to be classified as exceptional and/or gifted early on and placed in Honors-level classes in middle school because they are interested in "what's going to make their kid competitive when they apply to college." Parents intervene, particularly in the younger grades, to ensure academic advantage for their children by way of positioning for access to high-level, gate-keeping courses in high school. By high school, however, where the course tracking system is somewhat more entrenched, direct intervention of this type becomes less frequent. Once students are placed in the most rigorous courses, parents take a step back and let students and the school, engage the positioning work.

COURSE SELECTION.   Course selection and placement is instrumental to the creation of a college dossier that will position one for the college admissions process (Riegle-Crumb and Grodsky 2010). Parents attempt to get their children into accelerated tracks prior to high school so that they can access the Honors and AP coursework that will presumably make them attractive candidates to college admission counselors. In fact, all but two students from the sample of top students were in the "gifted and talented" program, which, of course, is a stepping-stone to the accelerated route in middle school.[11]

Once in high school, while parents certainly appear to be encouraging children to continue in such tracks, students themselves drive the push for AP and other high-level courses, wherein admission to a highly selective four-year college (what Barron's [2009] would define as "Most Competitive" or "Highly Competitive+") becomes an integral part of student identity. Based on prior schooling experiences, parental advocacy in regard to course placement, and parental guidance, students come to take ownership of their own academic careers, making choices that continue the positioning work that was once the domain of parents.

KRISTIN: And Kelly took a number of APs, right?

SUE TRAN: She took a few, yes.

KRISTIN: Is that something that you and your husband encouraged?

SUE TRAN: Well, yeah, we did encourage her, just because of her ability. You know, we'd rather see her struggle a little bit than coast through.

Sue Tran states that she and her husband encouraged Kelly to enroll in advanced coursework, including several AP classes during her junior and senior year. Cannondale, like virtually all high schools in the country, employs a (soft) system of academic tracking, wherein students can theoretically choose to take advanced courses such as APs and IBs, but in practice are often excluded from such courses because they do not have the necessary academic résumé to position them for access to such courses. Due to Kelly's initial designation as "gifted and talented," as accompanied by "logical" subsequent enrollment in high-level courses in middle and high school, Kelly is now in a position to *choose* to take APs and do well in them, clearly not an option open to all students despite the "open" enrollment policy for AP and IB classes. While Kelly is certainly intelligent, we can see how by virtue of her placement in the gifted program in elementary school, she is able to convert such placement into later academic advantage with regard to course selection. While other students may work equally hard or even harder than Kelly, because she had been previously placed in the accelerated track, she has access to higher-level courses and is now deemed to have greater "ability" than most of her peers at CHS (Anyon 1980; Oakes 1985; Rist 1970). In addition to Kelly's intelligence, such ultimate advantage often rests on parental intervention at an early age. This, coupled with the available opportunity structure, such as "gifted and talented" programs in given districts, serves to shape school outcomes, both offering more to certain students while designating them as "more intelligent" and accomplished by the end of high school. This sheds light on the ways in which schools, as middle-class institutions, praise and reward family practices that are in line with their values (Hochschild and Scovronick 2003; Spring 2004).

Other parents also describe course selection in high school as driven by students while monitored by parents. Students meet with counselors and bring home schedules, which parents then sign off on, provided they approve. When asked about her level of involvement, Caroline Swanson, who, along with the Tran family, exhibits a relatively high level of micromanagement (within the given sample) with regard to course selection and the educational process more generally, states:

CAROLINE SWANSON: So, I tried to [be involved], to a certain degree, I would say. Did we choose the things (courses)? No. Did we oversee and just make sure it was going in the right direction? Yeah.

KRISTIN: And "in the right direction" meaning?

CAROLINE SWANSON: With her . . . academic ability, making sure she's on the level that she should be, you know, she took the AP classes that she should have.

Most parents, however, do not articulate this level of involvement. The Penns, for example, typify the sample parent population. Both Frank and Angie Penn note that they do *not* choose courses for Michael and that he takes AP classes because he *wants* to. For example, when Michael heard about the IB program, the Penns attest that he *chose* to enroll. Provided that students choose classes that reflect parental desires and, more important, their perceived "abilities," parents are quite willing to cede course decisions to their children. In fact, Sandy Jacinovic intervenes on Jacob's behalf only because the counselor wants him to take an AP class that Jacob did not want to take (AP English). Jamie Cucchiara, Jacob's counselor, initiates the phone call in which she asks Sandy Jacinovic to encourage Jacob to take AP English, in addition to the AP math and science courses in which he was already enrolled. Rather than demanding that her son take the more challenging course, she states: "You know, I can encourage, but Jacob makes up his mind and Jacob does what Jacob wants to do for himself, which is fine."

Students are clearly aware of the academic edge garnered by enrolling in higher-level classes. Highly cognizant of the fact that they are competing against other students with competitive résumés, focal students generally opt to take the most rigorous schedule available, often choosing to forgo lunch or take a class over the summer to make room in their schedule for more demanding courses junior and senior year. Despite the fact that Kelly's parents, for example, also want her to take AP classes, Kelly owns the decision to enroll, providing a stark assessment of the market value of APs in the college process:

Um, I signed up for a lot of APs and stuff for my classes, which I probably wouldn't have taken if they weren't for, like, college.

Michael is more emphatic about the ways in which academics are related to college positioning. Michael, like Nicholas (another focal student), opts to take the full IB track, a decision he makes because he thinks it will make him more attractive to the highly selective schools he was thinking about as early sophomore year:

> I feel like more and more people, more and more kids are exposed to these higher-level programs like IB or AP, and so more and more people are apply- ing to colleges and more and more people already have these feathers in their cap that would have stood out maybe, I don't know, 10 or 15 years ago. It feels like . . . it's expected that kids who are competitive about school take APs . . . my doctor, so [he told me that] he asked a guidance counselor a question like he said, [and] a lot of parents ask this, it's a common question, but "Is it better to take an AP if you think you are going to get a worse grade or should you take the easier class to get a higher grade?" and the guidance counselor said to him, "The answer is you have to take an AP *and* get a higher grade." So I feel like there's more of that attitude these days, not just a question of do I take grades or hard classes? It's no, you have to have grades *and* hard classes. It's sort of like that. . . .

This tension between taking an easier course load and getting higher grades or taking more difficult courses and potentially sacrificing higher grades is heightened at Cannondale because CHS does not weight grades along the lines of course difficulty. Students in the top 10% of the class, acting on the information they have regarding the college process (from friends, par- ents, counselors, etc.), opt to take the more rigorous course load, with an eye toward positioning competitively for the college application process. That said, the examples reveal the ways in which course selection is con- strained and shaped both by social class and prior schooling experiences. If students had not been tracked into accelerated courses early on, they would not, in all likelihood, have been positioned to "choose" to take AP and IB coursework. In this sense, then, advantage is clearly cumulative. Further, and perhaps more important, such students have been *trained* from early on, both implicitly and explicitly, by their schools, community, and families to make such choices, and, therefore, parents can take a step back, lessening their direct involvement. However, there is a strong sense that if students do not make the "correct" choices, they will not be poised to partake in the highly selective, ultracompetitive college admissions game, with the ultimate goal of entrance to highly selective colleges. In this case, parents may need to step in so as to redirect students toward the "correct" choice.

When College Is the Only Option

Parents in Cannondale are clearly invested in their children's academic futures and engage actions and activities early on that potentially position their children to access the most elite postsecondary institutions in the country. These actions send particular messages to their children about the expected next step after high school. As Ball (2003, p. 65) so eloquently articulates:

> Parents' commitment to providing for their children what Allatt (1993: 153) calls a "landscape of possibilities" has to be set against the deeply inscribed grammars of aspirations which circumscribe choice. For some families certain possibilities are unthinkable. The "transgenerational family scripts" (Cohen and Hey 2000: 5) of some middle-class families "exert prospective and regulative influence on actual life chances and choices" (Cohen and Hey 2000: 5). They are pursuing what Du Bois-Reymond (1998) calls a "normal biography"; although on occasion these can be resisted. Normal biographies are linear, anticipated and predictable, unreflexive transitions, often gender- and class-specific, rooted in well-established life worlds. They are often driven by an absence of decisions.

The "decision" to attend college for participants from Cannondale is in fact a nondecision, a predictable and nonreflexive transition (Mullen 2010). College is the expected "next step" for seniors at CHS, a school that boasts a college attendance rate of more than 90%, although students matriculate at a wide range of institutions in terms of their competitiveness rating (see chapter 6). It is a step that students rarely think about, at least in terms of its possibility.

BRAD: [I probably first started thinking about college] when I figured out what it was. I mean, it's always been kind of a given . . . higher education is what you need to do to get a better job, to be more successful. . . . I think that I just sort of picked it up. I guess that is what society expects of you.

MICHAEL: Yeah, I feel like even as a little kid [I knew I would be going to college]. I feel like there is an expectation to attend college. Especially, I don't know if it's Cannondale as a community or my family, but, like, you know, if I was in a position where I was not going to attend college after high school, that's sort of a sign that you failed in some way. Whether right or wrong . . . you know what I mean by that?

Among respondents, and affluent suburban students generally (Demerath 2009; Grodsky and Reigle-Crumb 2010; Kaufman 2005), Michael Penn and Brad Whitcombe are very typical. For every student in the Cannondale sample, going to college has become an embedded, engrained step in their life trajectory and it is simply taken for granted (Ball 2003). "Would I go to college? Of course, what else does one do?" In fact, when asked the question, "When did you first start thinking about college?" students are visibly confused and perplexed. Many ask for clarification and are unable to pinpoint a specific time because the expectation has always been there (Ball 2003; Grodsky and Reigle-Crumb 2010). As Chloe Rogers demonstrates, college is "part of the air [they] breathed" (Sacks 2007, p. 23).

CHLOE: I always wanted to go [to college] because it's kind of been embedded into my head that "You are going to college," like, that's just what my family does, we go to college, and we always kind of place emphasis on education and really like to proceed and further [ourselves].

Chloe's acknowledgment that aspiring to and attending college is "just what my family does" speaks to the degree to which parents transfer expectations to their children and the extent to which children internalize such expectations, reflective of what Ball (2003, p. 108) refers to as the "normal biography."

NICHOLAS: It was just the natural thing. Both of my parents were fortunate enough to go to college and I think they just—the American dream, you know? That the next generation gets a little, has it better, so they have been working to offer that opportunity and they just expect that [I go to college].

Parents and the larger school community scaffold the transfer of this "normal biography," affirming and facilitating adoption by the students. In this way, students' identities are ineluctably tied to college attendance. Their academic and extracurricular lives are organized with an eye toward college, if not explicitly for college (Stevens 2007). Students interpret college as the mechanism for success and social status, modeling the trajectories they have witnessed among parents, siblings, and other relatives. Such student understandings are reflected in their articulations of the purpose of postsecondary education. For example, Nicholas explains how "the stereotype of college equals good job is key . . . like this idea that society believes that you have to go to college to get a good job has created this sort of *natural tendency* that [college] is just what's next, after high school (emphasis added)." Nicholas's choice of the phrase "natural tendency" is important (as is his understanding of "society"), as it reveals the extent to which college attendance is simply taken for granted (Mullen 2010). This nondecision decision, or what Bourdieu refers to as "intentionality without intention" (Bourdieu 1990, p. 8, as cited by Ball 2003, p. 65) and Nicholas calls a "natural tendency," belies the automatic nature of college attendance for Cannondale participants, students, and families that occupy a particular niche in the middle class.

Nicholas's comments are additionally important as they establish the premise that one goes to college so that one can be successful in the job market, a sentiment with which all students in this study identify. Students *like* Nicholas are constructed as those who get "good jobs" and therefore must go to "good" schools (Ball 2003). In this sense, college attendance is constructed instrumentally: as a means to an end (Weber 1902/2003). As college becomes the instrument for obtaining a "good" job and derives its value from the extent to which it is perceived to deliver in this regard, students increasingly focus upon institutional prestige, under the assumption that more prestigious postsecondary institutions provide stronger pathways to "good" jobs, and ultimately greater economic and social security and standing (Carnevale 2012).

Within this college-going habitus—assuming they will go to college, attend specific types of institutions (four-year, highly selective schools, those defined as "Most Competitive" and "Highly Competitive+" per Barron's [2009]), and assuming college is what *naturally* follows high school—students develop an identity. In this way, students' understandings of college—particularly, its role and purpose—act as a cultural tool with which to shape themselves.

Cultural tools in the form of ideologies provide individuals with a coherent world view, something that, in [Erikson's] view, youth desperately need to fashion an identity. In that way, these ideologies are empowering, providing youth with a compass in a contradictory and complex world. At the same time, [however], these resources are, according to Erikson, constraining, in that individuals are limited in who they can become by the array of choices and ideologies, career, and self-expression. (Penuel and Wertsch 1995, p. 90, as cited in Howard 2007, p. 26)

The fact that resources, while providing opportunities, also act as constraints is particularly useful for making sense of focal student experiences at CHS. Despite the fact that students attend college, ostensibly increasing their opportunities long term, they learn to constrain their decision making with regard to college attendance. Specifically, they limit the types of colleges to which they consider applying and, at least at this point, insofar as they can fashion an identity tied to future careers, the types of majors they deem feasible. While the option not to attend college altogether is certainly present (as is the option to pursue employment that does not require a college education or to join the military), it has never been presented as a "real" choice to this group of students, who subsequently reject this as an alternative (Kaufman 2005). Not going to college is the reality of "other" students; those whom they perceive to be less motivated, less hard working, less deserving, and/or less academically able.

Similarly, attending a two-year college or less prestigious four-year college are also possibilities; however, they are, again, scripted as options for those who are less able and less motivated, and therefore they are not *real* options for students like themselves. Attending a four-year, highly selective college is both an expectation and an identity marker, and increasingly the "norm" for those at the top of the Cannondale class. The reification of highly selective, four-year college attendance to normative status among this particular group of students simultaneously creates a binary opposition for focal students, one that differentiates between those who plan to attend colleges of lesser prestige, including a wide range of two- and relatively less selective four-year schools, versus highly selective (largely, in this case, those marked as "Most Competitive" and "Highly Competitive+" by Barron's [2009]) four-year institutions. This particularly constructed binary between lesser and greater institutional prestige and the accompanying now hard line between what "we" deserve and what "others" deserve with regard to college attendance, renders the condition and linked identity of the noncollege-going population wholly irrelevant. While a hard line has historically been drawn between those who attend college and those who do not, *this group of relatively privileged students are explicitly redrawing this line to reflect entrance into particularly located institutions—predominantly those deemed Most Competitive and Highly Competitive + versus all the others.*

Due to the expectation of college attendance in the school and broader community, in addition to the participants families' academic histories and assumptions regarding college, and in conjunction with larger perceptions about the affluence of Cannondale residents (and the particular class practices specifically related to education and tied to affluence), students are blind to the fact that there are, in fact, some Cannondale students (8% from the class of 2009) who do not attend college directly upon completion of high school. Because not going to college is anathema to student participants, they in fact pay virtually no attention to such students, positioning themselves in contradistinction to the larger group of nonhighly selective college-goers, who comprise the vast majority of students at CHS.

This newly drawn *line of distinction* closely maps onto the track structure at Cannondale High, in which those possessing identities that assume admission to institutions ranked "Most Competitive" and "Highly Competitive+" find themselves insulated in the AP and IB classes. While there are certainly students not in the top 10% in some of these classes, their presence does little to pierce the dominant culture within this track.[12] This is true for mainly two reasons. First, the students in the top 10% tend to move together as a unit throughout the top classes, something they have been doing since entering high school (and often before, for example, in their gifted and talented programs and middle school acceleration). The added presence of a few students from the state examination track is little noticed. Additionally, despite that fact that there is "open enrollment," gaining access to top-level courses is in fact constrained by one's previous course placement history. For example, to be in a position to take AP Calculus senior year, one must have been accelerated in math since the eighth grade or have doubled up on two years of math at some point during high school. Courses in subjects such as English or social studies, which are less sequential than math, tend to provide greater pathways to higher-level courses for nonaccelerated (and non-top 10%) students—and this is in fact where greater AP enrollment of non-top 10% students is found. However, because of the structure of the schedule and the way in which top students tend to move together throughout all the top classes, those students not in the top 10% less frequently end up in classes with the core group of top students. As such, the identity of highly selective, four-year college-goers is maintained, unchallenged by the presence of a few students who fall outside this dominant group.

This identity of highly selective, four-year college-goers is marked as superior in relation to the inferior, less-selective, and nonselective college-goers. This particular "college-going habitus," as linked to the top 10% of students in the school (Grodsky and Reigle-Crumb 2010), reinforces the parental and community expectations that college attendance is the automatic next step after high school. In addition, however, it systematically establishes the parameters for what are and are not acceptable college options, thereby delimiting the colleges and universities students in the top 10% of the class initially consider and to which they subsequently apply (Ball 2003).

NOT JUST ANY COLLEGE.   While families assume early on that the particularly located students under consideration here would attend college, the expectations around this become increasingly specific over time. In today's social and economic climate, an expectation of college attendance is neither novel nor unique. Students of varied class and racial backgrounds often aspire to and in fact attend college (Bloom 2005; Jenkins 2011; Kozol 2005; Macleod 1995; McDonough 1997; Schneider and Stevenson 1999). What is noteworthy here is both the sense of entitlement to attend college and the expectation linked to the caliber of college deemed *worthy* of attending. While students in both Kozol's (2005) and MacLeod's (1995) work may express a desire to attend college, they do not view college as the "logical progression" of schooling as Nicholas refers to it, or "just what you do. You go to high school, then college, and then graduate school," as Jacob asserts. In other words, while many students in the United States now realistically strive to attend college, fewer see such attendance as inevitable. Further, students, as well as parents in the instance under consideration, have a very narrow view (at least initially) as to what constitutes a viable option for acceptable college choice (Ball 2003). In the next section, we discuss *which* colleges students aspire to and how their classed (and privileged) experiences shape these aspirations.

    As demonstrated previously, the expectation to attend college is ever present and something that both parents and students buy into rather unquestioningly. When participants talk about the desire to attend college, however, what is actually meant by *college*? As the school profile data make clear, the majority of students at CHS (more than 90%) go on to attend some type of postsecondary education. Of those who choose to attend college immediately upon high school completion, approximately 70% attend four-year colleges (CHS 2010 School Profile).[13] In this regard, community college is not, and never has been, in contention. Conversations with focal students over the course of the year emphasize that ending up at the local community college, RCC, is a running joke among students, particularly more highly ranked students. Kelly's perception that "the majority of people who go to schools *like that* [emphasis added] go because they can't get into other schools because they [slacked off]" is ubiquitous. Such sentiments are indicative of the nonreflexive privileged position in which participants sit. They see their own hard work through this prism, failing to see how their own advantage propels their worldview and associated options. By extension, of course, they fail to see how those without such advantages might be propelled in the opposite direction. These statements additionally reveal what it means to be a college-goer in this community. RCC is certainly a college, yet to participants, community college is not granted this distinction.[14]

Students are not alone in their perceptions of the viability (or lack thereof, more appropriately) of community college. Sandra Whitcombe is not only responsible for coordinating the college application process of her son Brad, but she is also assisting her niece. The types of schools she regards as appropriate for her niece are not the same as those in contention for Brad. Sandra states, "I was really impressed with RCC, too, not for Brad, but I mean the guy we talked with knew his stuff." While Sandra does not write off community college in the way many students do (i.e., only lazy students go there), she does think that her son's academic ability outdistances what RCC can offer.

Frank Penn expresses similar sentiments. When talking about his son Michael, who is class valedictorian, he states that if Michael had not been "on the right path or wasn't applying to the schools of his caliber, then we might have intervened." Of course, statements like these by Sandra and Frank are not without context. Their children have been identified as academically talented for some time now. Both had been marked as "gifted and talented" since elementary school; they now take the highest-level courses available at the high school and rank in the top 10% of the class. Although problematic, it is often the case that academic success (as measured by high class rank and test grades) is simply equated to merit. Speaking of students who attend an exclusive private school, Howard (2007, p. 35) argues:

> Although students undergo an advantaging education that many children in the United States cannot even imagine, most members of this community—including parents who wield great influence to secure their children's advantages and success in school—believe that academic success depends primarily on ability,

talent, effort, and attitude, rather than on wealth or personal connections. Within this culture, class advantages are rarely acknowledged, but individual merit and effort are frequently and openly celebrated.

Like the students in Howard's (2007) study or those "overachievers" from Robbin's (2006) work, Cannondale participants work hard; however, they are also highly privileged by virtue of their social class standing and the concerted cultivation (Lareau 2003) their parents have provided. In this way, privilege meshes with merit, which furthers the belief in meritocracy and ultimately affirms student identities as highly selective college-goers, while simultaneously shaping their aspirations and deepened feelings of entitlement.

In this sense, students and parents for the most part, seek out schools that offer more than a four-year degree program; they are, in fact, interested in very specific four-year schools. Claire Lombard, one of the two guidance support staff, articulates what she sees as a troubling trend in expectations around what constitutes an acceptable four-year school choice:

> Personally I—it's very interesting for me. I have three daughters and they are all going to [state universities] and you know, we routinely get the comment [from others] that they work *too hard* to go to [state universities], so you know, it's interesting to work in that office [guidance] and hear the comments and you know, well that is just the perception here. . . .

Bottom line is that students, parents, and the community at large are focused on selectivity and prestige. Not only is community college a place where the "lazy" or those who "slack off" find themselves, but state colleges are often similarly seen as places where top students simply do not go. In this sense, perceptions of what constitute viable colleges (largely four-year, "Most Competitive" and "Highly Competitive+" private institutions) filter through students' perceptions of their identity as college-goers. For example, Jacob discusses how his mother "made him" apply to one in-state state university. When the acceptance letter arrives, he does not even open it. Instead, he gives the letter to his mother as he has already been accepted at the University of Rochester, a more prestigious and private institution. To be a college-goer in the way students in this study craft themselves is to apply to and attend *a very narrow band of postsecondary institutions*. In addition to community colleges, then, state schools simply do not count. This sensibility parallels, and is undoubtedly fueled by, classification schemata such as Barron's (2009), where less than 9% of US colleges ranked as "Most Competitive" are public, and only 23% of Highly Competitive+ colleges are public (see chapter 6 for further exploration of this issue).

Such stigma is generally applied to state schools uniformly, with two notable exceptions: "Highly Competitive+" State College (a local school) and top-tier state schools in other states, such as University of California, Berkeley. Despite being a state university, "Highly Competitive +" State College tends to be the one state school that students are not ashamed to put on their lists. The school has a reputation for being incredibly selective and challenging and is a particularly strong institution for those interested in teaching.

Many students complain that their parents direct them to apply to at least one state university, usually done as a point of cost comparison. Jacob's response to his acceptance at a Research I state university is telling and reinforces the earlier point: namely, that community colleges and four-year state institutions are simply not worthy of consideration. For Jacob, his acceptance to the University of Rochester made the Research I state university irrelevant.

Reputation, selectivity, and prestige matter to students in this study. Students feel strongly that they worked hard and want a college environment that they imagine will reward that hard work (via name recognition later in life). Sandy Jacinovic explains her son Jacob's criteria when initially creating his list of potential schools:

> He was smart. He did fill out things that he wanted and one of the things he wanted was a school where their admissions rate was mostly from the top—I think he put the top 25% of the graduating high school classes—because that was one of the things you could do, do you want the top 50%? Do you want someone that takes everyone? And he really wanted a place that just took the top 25% because he really wants to be challenged and wants that kind of education and not . . . I think that was important, that was a good choice. I think that is a good choice, as far as you're coming out of school, to have that challenge.

Kelly's mother, Sue Tran, concurs:

> We knew that she, I mean she wasn't like a genius or anything but for her SAT scores . . . we knew that our [older] daughter got into certain schools so we knew that [Kelly] would get into some schools, probably even better than the schools my [older] daughter had gotten into.

When students and parents speak of college, their points of reference tend to be almost entirely highly selective ("Most Competitive," "Highly Competitive+," and, to a less extent, "Highly Competitive" per Barron's [2009] classification) private colleges and universities. While this fixation on more highly selective institutions applies to all students in the focal group, it is clear that those students who self-select into more rigorous APs and the IB program are more intent on gaining entry to top-tier colleges. Nicholas, who graduates second in his class, explains:

NICHOLAS: I have to say it's sort of scary [but] a person in the IB program, well there are a number of people in our full diploma program who consider the [local "Most Competitive" University] now as a sort of fall back plan now . . . because they have either applied to Brown or Dartmouth or . . . Harvard. And so they consider—well, I guess, "We all will go to [local "Most Competitive" University] almost as a running joke, and that's scary because I consider the [local "Most Competitive" University] to be my top choice and I think their education is phenomenal. But I guess, talking about the hierarchy, it's the Ivies, and I think Stanford would be included as well, and then, at least in IB, [local "Most Competitive" private college] is considered to be . . .

KRISTIN: Of lower prestige?

NICHOLAS: Even though it's a phenomenal school. It's kind of scary to me.

Nicholas's comments about perceptions of the local university, an institution ranked as "Most Competitive" by Barron's (2009), reveal the extent to which the high school plays a marked role in shaping and affirming student identities vis-à-vis college admissions. Being identified as an AP/IB student (not just for one class but as an overall track), a celebrated distinction and one, for all intents and purposes, results in a separation from the remainder of the senior class, has deep ramifications for how students manifest their privileged identities, influencing *which* colleges they both desire to attend and feel entitled to attend. We turn now to the last piece of this identity formation process: school exclusionary practices.

Exclusions from Within: Tracking, Entitlement, and Identity

Affluent parents are competing as never before to give their children an edge, pressing schools to carve out havens of privilege with "gifted and talented" programs, accelerated classes, and other methods of separating students in ways that reward upper-class status. (Sacks 2007, p. 7)

In analyzing how it is that students (and their families) come to understand their privileged identities as highly selective college-goers, it is imperative that we examine the ways in which the school supports and facilitates the creation and maintenance of "distinction." Scholarly work suggests that schools serve the primary function of sorting students (see, e.g., see Anyon 1980; Bowles and Gintis 1976; Oakes 1985; Rist 1970; Spring 2004; Willis 1977). As Hochschild and Scrovronick (2003) remind us, "schools are the arena in which many Americans first fail. Failure there almost certainly guarantees failure from then on." Using the American dream as a framework, they go on to argue that for the majority of Americans, the perception is that "failure results from lack of individual merit and effort" (p. 5).

While schools are often a place where some experience their first taste of failure, for others, school is a place where they encounter great success. Similar to the ways in which failure is perceived, student success in school is largely explained through individual merit, talent, and effort. While this may be the prevailing common sense, research consistently demonstrates the correlation between the social structure and individual and collective position within such structure—race and class inequality, for example— and academic achievement.

Focal students from Cannondale are used to being in the most advanced classes with generally the same students, which acts to shape both how they conceive of themselves as well as how they construct others. As Brantlinger (2003) reminds us, "those who excel have a sense of superiority and entitlement" (Brantlinger 1993, as cited by Brantlinger 2003, p. 20), sentiments that are clearly felt in the lengthy focus group exchange that follows.

KRISTIN: What about the courses you select? Does that have anything to do with— [preparing for college]? . . . Like the courses that you took and why you took them?

BRAD: Yeah, oh yeah!

KRISTIN: Oh yeah? Say more . . .

NICHOLAS: Well, I took IB and part of IB was the college stuff. It has good recognition—growing recognition at colleges, and I think that is a way to *differentiate* [emphasis added] myself from students that may have similar academic qualities, let's say—I don't know if that's the right word. But the electives that I took, it wasn't about college, I mean I took journalism for two years, loved journalism! I didn't have to take the Leadership class because of the IB history requirement. I took it because I wanted to be part of it, so I don't think *all* the decisions I am making about courses was for college, it's not all about college. I think part of it is personal interest.

BRAD: Yeah . . . I am trying to think, you know, I do all the Honors and AP stuff and that might just be for college, but it is also for me to know that I can do it and feel good about myself, too [snickers].

KARINA: And I don't feel good in like state[15] classes because I feel like a lot of time the stuff is common sense.

BRAD: And also, some of those kids . . . I am taking Health, which is like my first like state-level class in a long time, and I am like "Where did all these douche bags come from?"

KELLY: Oh, that's on tape!

BRAD: Alfonso is a mean kid but he's honest! [Brad referring to himself as Alfonso to "hide" his identity and to be funny]

[Laughter]

NICHOLAS: Very straightforward.

BRAD: But very true though.

NICHOLAS: Yeah, well, I don't, uh, I don't know that I would use the exact language to say the same thing. I mean, I am in Health right now, too. And for me, it's ninth period and I—I don't mind—

KARINA: We are in the same class.

KELLY: But it's Health the last period of the day so it's like chill.

NICHOLAS: Yeah, but I really—

KELLY: We are totally off topic!

BRAD: I know I could be doing something better with my 40 minutes [than spending it in Health with *those* kids].

KARINA: But it has like that reputation, like state English. Like, I haven't been in state English in like a long time, but the essays, like I will see my friends' essays and they will get like a 100 on them and but like I'll look at it and be like "Seriously?" I feel like I was writing like that in eighth grade. And then it's like we are graded so much harder in AP and then it's just, well, this is completely different, but our school [grades] is unweighted which kind of sucks for our average but—

NICHOLAS: No—

KARINA: Whatever.

NICHOLAS: I am not even going there. . . .

NICHOLAS: But, I would have to say, I mean a lot of them, like if you are taking [grade] 7 Honors, [grade] 8 Honors, you are just expected to take [grade] 9 Honors, and then [grade] 10 Honors, and 11 AP, and then 12 AP.

ALL: Yeah, yeah.

NICHOLAS: I mean this is just the next path, like if they don't offer Honors you like you move up to AP; it's just sort of the steady progression upward.

KARINA: And it would be like you failed if you went from AP last year into a state level this year, you know, you are just like "Oh, did you do really bad last year?"

BRAD: It's like a drop down. It's like all your peeps [people who surround you; friend group and family], all your parents went to college and whatnot and you didn't, it's like, "What's wrong? You were in Honors and now you are not."

NICHOLAS: Although I like Health. Last semester of Leadership, I would have liked a different teacher but we won't go there but—

BRAD: Yeah can we chat about that afterward?

KARINA: Callahan?

NICHOLAS: I didn't have Callahan, I had your teacher . . . [dissolves momentarily into a conversation about how much they love Craig Callahan] but most of the electives I have taken when I have been in with all the, I have been intermingled with all the rest of the—

KARINA: Normal people.

NICHOLAS: I would just consider them, I guess normal, but I would just say the rest of the class of 2010, I liked—I didn't mind. I considered it a nice change of pace because I am in the same classes like four periods, no five periods, with the same crew of people, the same 10 to 15 people which is nice, I mean, I like them, they are great, don't get me wrong—I sound like Joe Biden right now—but um, but it's, but like spending time in Health now or like in Leadership last semester with those students that I don't get to normally interact with, I am enjoying.

This lengthy exchange between Brad, Nicholas, Karina, and Kelly is particularly revealing, specifically as related to the ways in which schooling helps to structure student identities and perceptions. The conversation highlights three main points that we comment upon here:

1. Non-Honors/Non-AP/Non-IB classes are perceived to be less rigorous.
2. How students in the less-selective courses are perceived and simultaneously how focal students perceive themselves in relation to the "normal" students.
3. The progression into the advanced courses has been naturalized.

Brad and Karina are perhaps most direct when talking about state-level courses, classes they perceive to consist of mostly "common sense" and where the standards are framed as considerably lower than what they experience in their AP and IB classes ("I feel like I was writing like that in eighth grade"). Taking state-level classes, particularly after one has been on an accelerated track, is perceived as a step down and therefore an embarrassment, a common sentiment among focal students. When asked to compare how state-level courses compare to AP courses, Melanie Gruzina and Marley Swanson offer the following assessment:

MELANIE: Um, like I think they [AP teachers] are less lenient. They don't take excuses and stuff and they just expect you to do better and they don't follow up with you as much if you aren't doing well and they like say, well they are like there if you need them but you have to be more proactive because they won't try to find you. Which, teachers have been saying that they won't do, I don't know, since like eighth grade, but a lot of them still do, like, if you are in a lower level class or whatever. Like, if you are in a class that is required, usually those people will come and try to find you and catch up with you. In an AP class, I feel like they are more like, "You should probably come find me sometime" and I feel that that's more like it [college] and that's how it will be different.

KRISTIN: Wow, well that's, like, a big difference, like, a big jump. I mean if they are doing that in the AP classes and not in the state-required courses . . . why do you think that is?

MARLEY: Because the AP students *are willing to work* whereas I feel that the state students are more just like going through the day just to get out of school and do whatever they have that day. I feel like they are just, I don't know, they don't, *they won't put in the extra mile. . . .* [emphasis added]

Similar to the sentiments raised by Kelly, Karina, Brad, and Nicholas, Melanie and Marley express the notion that students in state-level courses are "lazy," less willing to work hard. By positioning students in state courses in this way, the focal students simultaneously affirm their *own* identities as hard workers who go the "extra mile" to achieve. They take the AP and IB courses because they want to challenge themselves and "feel good about themselves," whereas other students are perceived to be "going through the day just to get out of school." Focal students, then, fashion their own position within the academic hierarchy (as well as the lesser status of their peers) largely in relation to their own efforts, giving them a sense of superiority and entitlement (Yonezawa and Wells 2005).

Last, the exchanges demonstrate the extent to which students' course-taking patterns have become completely naturalized. Given that they were accelerated early on, it is only *natural* that they continue into the most advanced coursework. Further naturalized is their clear discursive and physical separation from those students who are constructed as "normal" or "regular." Such academic and social distance not only enables the construction of students' perceptions of themselves as academically inclined/motivated/able—and therefore highly "distinctive"—in contradistinction to their "lazy" peers in less rigorous courses, but additionally encourages this construction to remain relatively unchallenged, as focal students are surrounded by students *just like themselves*. In the final analysis, focal students deem themselves worthy of "special" academic treatment within the school and logically worthy of "special" and distinctive college admissions outcomes. In fact, it is only in their senior year when focal students are in courses required by the state in which they experience *any* face-to-face academic interaction with a critical mass of those deemed "less worthy."[16] Such broad-based course attendance, however, while perhaps pleasurable to some, does not fundamentally challenge the constructed binary. Bishop (2008, p. 6) explains:

> Social psychologists had studied like-minded groups and could predict how people living and worshiping in homogenous groups would react: as people heard their beliefs reflected and amplified, they would become more extreme in their thinking. What had happened over three decades wasn't a simple increase in political partisanship, but a more fundamental kind of self-perpetuating, self-reinforcing social division. The like-minded neighborhood supported the like-minded church, and both confirmed the image and beliefs of the tribe that lived and worshiped there.

Similar to what Bishop (2008) sees happening in communities across the United States, student separation in the highest academic track has led to a self-reinforcing vision of who they are as students, which serves to divide them from all others. The school's tracking practices construct an exclusive space for students at the academic top, not unlike what Peshkin (2001), as well as others studying privileged, private school spaces discover (Cookson and Persell 1985; Gaztambide-Fernández 2009; Howard 2007; Khan 2011). In the case of the elite privates, "the school's exclusivity . . . convinces pupils of their superiority" (Hayes 1994, p. 114, as cited in Peshkin 2001, p. 95). While elite private schools, as commented upon by

Gaztambide-Fernández (2009) and others, provide a sense of distinction that reaches *across* the student body, Cannondale, like other large public high schools, separates and rewards the select few, who in turn, internalize their placement in the exclusive classes and subsequently deem themselves more worthy than all others (Allat 1993).[17] In this sense, Cannondale's practices are not entirely unlike the "star high schools" that Attewell (2001, pp. 267–68) spotlights:

> My central thesis is that star high schools are caught in an assessment system in which top students vie for entry into selective colleges. Many schools adapt to this system, seeking to maximize the chances of their strongest students. *Some* of these schools have developed polices that resemble "winner-take-all" markets: Their strongest students benefit at the expense of those below.

While CHS does not appear to resemble a "winner-take-all" market, we can see how those in the top academic tracks are best positioned for admissions to the most highly selective colleges ("Most Competitive" and "Highly Competitive+"), partially through the policies and practices of the school itself (e.g., tracking). Unlike others, these students have access to the most highly valued academic curriculum, being additionally imbued with a strong sense of entitlement that provides further edge in the college admissions process. Such edge, however, must be understood as relational. Although students in the top track may be far better positioned than other students at Cannondale with respect to the college admissions process, the reach of such distinction may be far more circumscribed than students and parents anticipate, a point that we take up more fully in both chapters 4 and 6.

Conclusion

This chapter demonstrates the ways in which parent, community, and school expectations and actions coalesce around student identity processes. Students in the top 10% at Cannondale assume identities as highly selective college-goers, identities that have been primed by their parents from birth and reinforced by their status within the most prestigious academic tracks. Because students assume this specifically located identity, they aspire to the most prestigious postsecondary institutions and become heavily invested in the work it takes to position for such institutions.

Key to students' assumption of this identity is course placement. Very early on, parents invest heavily in students' academic lives. First, parents make very strategic (non-Bourdieun sense) decisions about where to purchase homes. Parents then provide opportunities for students to develop their interests and intellects, normalizing involvement in a plethora of activities. Later, parents intervene to ensure that students are placed in the most rigorous courses and marked with "distinction" (i.e., "gifted and talented") to ensure access to the most rigorous courses in high school. Inside these accelerated tracks, the school reaffirms the students' identities and aspirations, and much of the college culture of the school and associated resources are directed toward these students.

As a result, parents in Cannondale feel that they can refrain from micromanaging the minutiae of the college process and instead "lead from behind" (Lizza 2011).[18] "Lead from behind" describes a strategy in which one takes a back seat to others in the implementation of a particular mission, yet still has a (or the) defining role in shaping the aims and overarching goals of the mission (Lizza 2011). Nelson Mandela describes the philosophy as follows:

> I always remember the regent's axiom: a leader, he said, is like a shepherd. He stays behind the flock, letting the most nimble go out ahead, whereupon the others follow, not realizing that all along they are being directed from behind. (Mandela 1994, as cited by Lizza 2011)

To successfully lead from behind, significant groundwork must be laid. For example, one needs buy-in from those carrying out the mission. In other words, those carrying out the mission must see their values as being in line with those orchestrating the mission. There also needs to be a significant amount of trust and respect built into the relationship.

Thinking about *leading from behind* in this way makes it an apt metaphor for describing Cannondale parental actions in regard to the larger college process. As demonstrated, parents spend a great deal of time and effort laying a foundation for their children. Parents put a tremendous amount of effort into cultivating particular identities and skill sets early on (often before children were even born—e.g., housing choices), which result in the normalization of these values and identities and, ultimately, the adoption of selective college–oriented identities that importantly, students embrace *as their own* (passing on what Ball [2003] refers to as the "transgenerational script").[19] This latter part is key; students see their actions—their *choice* to take, for example, AP, IB, and other advanced classes; to pursue several extracurricular activities; to seek out leadership roles; to volunteer—as theirs. While they acknowledge consistency with their parents' goals—for example, often stating that their parents want them to go to college for the same reasons they want to go—they ultimately take ownership of their decisions and actions. *They* choose their courses, *they* choose their extracurricular activities, and *they* choose the colleges to which they will apply. In this context, parents can sit back and refrain from the day-to-day micromanaging that is so often assumed to characterize parental involvement among the privileged in the college process, partially because they have successfully prepared students to adopt these goals as their own.

We take up discussion of the actual outcomes of the college admissions process in chapter 6, turning now to a discussion of the positioning work engaged by parents, students, and school personnel in an iconic elite private day school.

Micromanaging the College Admissions Process: Leaving Nothing to Chance at Matthews Academy

By the end of September I was on Lexi's back about getting started. She, being a kid, didn't want to get started. . . . She mentioned it to Dave Henderson who then said, "Tell your mom to take a deep breath," which very much frustrated me because the dates were coming in October [for Early Action and Early Decision]. — (Cynthia Willard, Matthews parent)

I'm sure his English [grades] probably [worked against him], cuz although he wants to go for mathematics, there are still schools that focus on the liberal arts. — (Julie Marino, Matthews parent)

As we suggest in chapter 3, students in the top 10% of their graduating class at Cannondale High School assume identities as highly selective college-goers, identities that have been primed by their parents since birth and subsequently affirmed by their placement in top academic tracks in secondary school. Because students internalize this identity, they aspire to the most highly valued postsecondary destinations in the nation, constructing themselves in juxtaposition to all other students who, they assume, will attend far less-prestigious institutions. It is within this context that Cannondale parents exert a somewhat "hands off policy" with regard to the highly intensified postsecondary admissions process, as parents feel that their children are themselves heavily invested in positioning for entrance to a particular strata of schools and that they have been prepared to do the work. As we argue in chapter 3, parents in the affluent public school engage a very distinct form of "up-front class work," taking great care to purchase homes in particular catchment areas while subsequently working to position their children for accelerated or gifted and talented programs at the elementary and middle school level under the assumption that such early designations will translate into later accelerated placements.

This particular form of "class work" is engaged under the assumption that once marked "distinction" is accomplished, schools themselves, and particularly the secondary school, will work to position their now appropriately designated children (the top 10% of the secondary school class; those taking the AP and/or IB courses) for entrance to the most highly valued postsecondary destinations. Such parent formulation rests upon the earlier and successful "concerted cultivation" of their children, who are now expected to be fully capable of taking on this work themselves, as they have been primed to do so. In this context, parents are largely satisfied with curricular opportunities available to students (which can be converted into capital vis-à-vis the selective college admissions process), as well as with the college counseling services within the public suburban high school. This is in contrast to the shape and form of positioning work engaged in the elite private sector, a sector that we explore in this chapter.

Although Lareau (2003) and Lareau and Weininger's work (which follows parents and students into the college admissions process, 2010) on "concerted cultivation" as a trademark of middle-class childrearing practices is highly provocative, evidence presented here, like that of Roksa and Potter (2011), drives toward a more class-nuanced and institutionally linked set of understandings with regard to current positioning for class advantage.[1] Such "class moves," we argue, are tied to distinct differences in the discursive and *material* practices that become *normative* in a particular school sector. In the case at hand, differentially located parents and students (those in elite/affluent private versus elite/affluent public secondary schools) conceptualize and enact noticeably different "class work" at the point of college admissions, even when parents' socioeconomic status is largely comparable. Here we focus on the ways in which and the extent to which students and parents in an NAIS coeducational secondary day school build upon and extend parentally induced advantages, particularly as tied to the most highly valued postsecondary destinations in the United States.[2]

Although "concerted cultivation" may well characterize parental childrearing patterns that set the stage for continued class privilege, such childrearing patterns must additionally be understood as concretized via linkages to a very specific set of educational institutions.[3] In the case of the affluent public school, for example, parents work to purchase homes in highly privileged school catchment areas, ones in which the schools are known to be "good," and usually stellar. Once "good" schools are ensured by virtue of home purchase in particular areas, many affluent suburban public school parents attempt to further mark their children with "distinction" via entrance to existing elementary school "gifted and talented" programs and linked accelerated opportunities at the middle school level.

In this chapter, we extend the notion of materiality and institutional location by focusing on students in the private secondary school sector. As we will argue, the practices through which privileged parents in *this* sector attempt to maintain and/or augment class privilege are explicitly tied to the *micromanagement* of the postsecondary linking process, a process that extends far beyond consequences of early childrearing patterns and is differentiated, in key ways, from what goes on in the affluent secondary public school.[4]

Fractures in the Middle and Upper Middle Class: The Case of Matthews Academy

Like parents in affluent suburban schools, parents who send their children to elite private schools invest "up front" in their children's future class position. Attendance at a private school reflects both parental "work" involved in accessing such schools, as well as the underlying work and accompanying sacrifices of having enough disposable income to pay for them. Importantly, the current class circumstances of parents in the schools discussed in chapters 3 and 4 are, by and large, quite similar, comprised of families with largely equivalent tertiary-level educational backgrounds, occupational status, and, to a notable extent, levels of disposable income. Rather than upper class in the sense of being able to live entirely off investments, families at both the private and public schools detailed in chapters 3 and 4 are largely professional and/or upper managerial, constituting the top 20% of the US class structure, with enough disposable income to indirectly and directly invest in their children's future via access to particular schools.[5]

In spite of the fact that our suburban public and NAIS private school serve largely comparably capitalized students and parents, there are notable differences in what becomes normalized "class work" in the two sites.[6] What is not starkly revealed in terms of background characteristics is clearly exposed with regard to form and duration of class positioning, wherein private school parents *intensify* their explicit efforts at class positioning at one and the same time as parents in the privileged public sector, for a range of reasons highlighted in chapter 3, largely *retract or redirect* their explicit involvement in the process. Data clearly suggest that privileged parents in the private sector notably intensify their involvement at the point of the postsecondary admissions process, a response that is specifically shaped by the *organizational habitus* of the school as well as the ways in which parents internalize such habitus and make it their own.

A notable proportion of students who attend elite private day schools attended private secular or independent (nondiocesan) Catholic elementary and/or middle schools, with important implications for what becomes "normalized" as positioning work within the private school sector. As we see in chapter 3, the majority of parental work in the affluent public school sector is done early on—homes are purchased in areas known for having "top schools," and students located at the top of the academic hierarchy in secondary school are generally those who were earlier marked with "distinction" through placement in accelerated programs. Parents recount stories of extreme vigilance and even pressure, when necessary, to ensure that their children are appropriately designated at an early age.

Among privileged parents at the private school, however, such positioning work takes a different shape and form, involving both the initial and subsequent selection of a *particular* institution each step of the way, rather than a single school district in which all subsequent education occurs. Importantly, once admitted to a private elementary school, there are no *formal* or long-term designations, such as "gifted and talented," that offer explicitly accelerated curricula to select students beginning at the elementary level. Although "ability groups" in reading and math certainly exist in the elementary privates, such group and individual classifications are relatively fluid, enabling movement up and down the ability group spectrum depending on progress during any given year. Unlike elementary "gifted and talented" programs that strive to offer special and markedly different curricula to those designated worthy of early "distinction," it is largely the *pace* of the curriculum rather than the substance that marks difference in elementary school ability groups.[7] Initial ability group placements do not, then, map neatly onto AP and/or IB curricula in the way that "gifted and talented" designations tend to pipeline into accelerated middle school placements and eventual placement in AP/IB courses or tracks.[8] Although parents sometimes challenge early ability group placement, the stakes of such placement are understood to be considerably lower than formal designations such as "gifted and talented."[9]

A key aspect of "class positioning" in our sample drawn from the private school sector revolves around the selection of a *sequence* of institutions (elementary school; middle school; secondary school) rather than a district.[10] In this regard, parents of private school children become accustomed to assessing and selecting a school based on cost, institutional mission, and "fit" for their child, a "skill set" that is honed by parents throughout the school selection process and slowly transfers to their children. Matthews student interviewees, for example, report that by the end of grade 4, they were invited to speak their mind with regard to what middle school they wished to attend. Options included staying in their current private pre-K through 8; transferring to a private combined middle/high school; and/or taking the entrance examination to a "star" urban public middle/high school with the hopes of gaining admission.

In grade 8, students are fully in the loop with regard to secondary school selection. As retrospective data demonstrate, although such decisions are never wholly located in children's portfolios, private school children are expected to engage in a serious and detailed assessment of the "self" in relation to all possible secondary school options, ultimately justifying to their parents why they prefer one school over another.

Such expectations and skills become normalized over time for private school parents and children, and are well practiced prior to the postsecondary admissions process—a process that rests, in large part, on a similar "skill set." Although children may engage such middle and secondary school "choice" largely in terms of where their friends are going, they are nevertheless expected to articulate to their parents why they come to the conclusion they do, a conclusion that may or may not, in the final analysis, be accepted by those who pay the tuition.[11]

Beginning with Secondary School Entrance

Beginning with selection of a middle school, and markedly intensifying at the point of secondary school entrance, students are primed to locate themselves in the broader field of available options. This culminates with students spending a full day at all potential schools during specifically marked out "Visiting Days" for eighth graders. Parents, in the meantime, participate in a variety of "See Us in Action" programs on a different set of designated dates at these same institutions.

Thinking back on the secondary school selection process, students at Matthews Academy reveal great sophistication with regard to their choice. Brandon Cowan is one example:

BRANDON: It was a decision between Matthews and Deacon. They were the two choices. And I visited both. I wouldn't say it was a "no brainer," but it was pretty close.

LOIS: And why is that?

BRANDON: I just really liked the atmosphere of the classes [at Matthews]. Just the kind of interaction between teacher and student. . . . I like the co-ed thing. That definitely appeals. But the classes at Deacon were more traditional. The teacher talks, he tells you what to know. But here, it's more interactive, I think, and that's the best way to learn. . . . Teachers can become students every once in a while.

LOIS: And did your parents agree with your decision?

BRANDON: They did. They . . . my dad did a couple of those "See Us in Action Days" here [Matthews Academy]. He kind of visited and saw what the classes were like, and he just kind of told me about what he saw as well. Just the way he felt. And he didn't push me either way, but I think he felt the same way I did. We thought it would be a better place to learn.

Not all students in the top 20% at Matthews are from privileged backgrounds.[12] Ron Tomlinson, a White working-class father who struggles hard to position his son for class advantage, states:

RON TOMLINSON: I wanted my son to be someplace where he could, well, you know. . . . That's why I shopped around at high schools [Matt Tomlinson attended a first-ring—nonprivileged—suburban public middle school], and they had an entrance test for Matthews and we were on the waiting list. . . . So then when they ended up calling [to admit him], I ended up sending him there.

LOIS: How did you know about Matthews?

RON: You know, Matthews just has a great reputation in the area for being one of the best high schools around, and every year they publish, like, you know, the list of their students and the colleges they went to, and I mean that's really what it's all about. . . . Like Forest Hills [the only other coeducational NAIS school in Blair] . . . thought about sending him to Forest Hills too, and they've got a good reputation, but their kids aren't going to the same places [colleges] Matthews's are going to. Why would you want to pay the same money? You know what I mean?

Recounting his son's friends who remain in the first-ring public school sector, Ron Tomlinson is clear that sending Matt to Matthews was a good choice, despite the sacrifice.

He's done well there. I see a lot of some of the other kids that were smart in the eighth grade with him, and these kids, you know, I see them around. Sometimes he keeps in touch with some, and a lot of them ended up exactly like I figured he would end up, you know, where they got bored in school and then grades suffering, and they did poorly and they graduated, and yeah, they'll do OK because they're smart enough, but they are probably doing nowhere near as well as they could have at this stage, and they don't have, like, the grades or the SAT scores they probably would have had to get into the top colleges.

Choosing to send a child to Matthews, irrespective of the class background of the parent, is all about admittance to a "top" college, a point that we expand upon when we discuss the experiences and practices of low-income self-identified Black students and parents in chapter 5. As Ken Sanderson, a well-known professional in Blair, emphatically states, sending his son to Matthews after completing middle school in an affluent suburban public school was "to try to prepare him as best we could to go to college . . . to get into the best college he can." Recognizing the centrality of this goal, Matthews devotes an entire office to college counseling,[13] and college counseling takes center stage in the life of the school during junior and senior year.

Entering the Postsecondary Search Process

By junior year, the college search process is in full swing, and Matthews students, like those in Cannondale, are expected to make explicit moves toward actualizing their cultural, social, and economic capital so as to obtain returns on parental investment. Although parents are expected to help facilitate the process, the actual work associated with postsecondary admissions, at least from the perspective of the school, lies entirely in the hands of the students.

The particular position that Matthews Academy occupies in the larger field of economic and educational privilege is critical to an understanding of the postsecondary admissions process as produced and lived out in this specific classed location. Matthews is not comparable in prestige or privilege to St. Paul's (Ivy/MIT/Stanford pipeline: 30%), Trinity School (Ivy/MIT/Stanford pipeline: 41%), Horace Mann (Ivy/MIT/Stanford pipeline: 36%), Phillips Academy Andover (Ivy/MIT/Stanford pipeline: 33%) (Laneri 2010), or other comparably located day and boarding schools that draw the vast majority of their students from highly capitalized communities. Matthews Academy, in contrast, draws its student body from Blair and surrounding environs—a tier-2 city whose occupants have relatively weak linkages to the most highly valued economic, cultural, and social capital in the nation. Furthermore, as the Head of Counseling at Matthews Academy points out, "relatively few parents of Matthews students" compared to parents at more prestigious day and boarding schools, "matriculated at Ivy League institutions," even when competition for entrance to such institutions was far less intense.

As such, the social networks of Matthews Academy parents are not comprised largely of individuals who attended the most highly valued postsecondary destinations (Ivy/MIT/Stanford), nor can they be considered members of the (transnational) capitalist class (Sklair 2001). Although highly economically and socially privileged in the context of Blair, parents have considerably less capital—economic or social—than comparably located parents who reside and work in close relation to cities of greater concentrations of capital and wealth. This, in addition to other key factors, has consequences for student ability to access the most highly valued postsecondary destinations. For example, 11% of Matthews Academy students matriculated at Ivy/MIT/Stanford in 2010, compared to 41% and 36%, respectively, from Trinity and Horace Mann. (Eleven percent is actually very high for Matthews, as its five-year average for 2007 to 2011 is 6%; see chapter 6.)

Importantly, parents, students, and the school itself sit upon markedly shifting ground with regard to the accumulation of capital and wealth over the past two to three decades. Although economic and social disparities between tier-1 and tier-2 cities have always existed in the United States and elsewhere, the magnification of such social and economic inequalities (Aron-Dine and Shapiro 2006; Piketty and Saez 2003; Reich 2001) means that privileged families in Blair are increasingly less privileged relative to comparably located families in centers of greater concentrations of wealth.

At a very practical level, this means that although parents who send their children to Matthews are highly privileged in the Blair context (and perhaps increasingly so, given the intensification of inequalities within the city itself), they are increasingly *less* privileged than parents in elite private schools that draw students from communities that are increasingly more highly capitalized.

This has clear implications for allowable tuition costs at differentially located schools ("what the market can bear"), as well as relative endowment levels over time.[14] As more robust endowments enable additional targeted special programming, facilities, and college counseling services that can be expected to translate into marked advantage with respect to the college admissions process, it is arguably the case that students who attend privileged private NAIS secondary schools in tier-2 cities are increasingly less privileged in the postsecondary admissions process than they were twenty years ago,[15] a sentiment often expressed by the Head of Counseling at Matthews Academy during the course of this research.

In addition, the most highly valued postsecondary destinations in the United States have worked to expand their admissions base, both geographically and with regard to student background characteristics (Bowen and Bok 1998). No longer largely comprised of White male progeny of the northeastern (Yale, Harvard) and/or southern (Princeton) elite (Karabel 2005) who attend private day, boarding, and/or "select sixteen" boarding schools (schools that formerly functioned as a pipeline into a range of Ivy League institutions [Cookson and Persell 1985]), the most valued postsecondary destinations in the United States now sit in a national (Hoxby 1997) and increasingly international marketplace for admissions. This renders acceptance at such institutions increasingly competitive, and the long-standing *stranglehold* (Cookson and Persell 1985) of elite secondary privates over the Ivies is no longer in evidence.[16] The 30-year veteran head of college counseling at Matthews affirms this point. He notes that while he and the headmaster "could formerly pick up the phone and call Harvard (which they did on a regular basis) on behalf of their students," thereby *ensuring* acceptance for a particular student, this is no longer the case.

This altered set of economic and social structural drivers renders the "effects" of parental "concerted cultivation" and explicit/intensified moves toward "class positioning" increasingly partial, as parents, irrespective of their own class advantage in any given location (or *field*, in a Bourdieuian sense) now sit on shifting terrain of power, privilege, and postsecondary admissions goals in a now national and increasingly international market-place of higher education.[17] As a consequence, privileged parents exhibit markedly increased *anxiety* over their children's future—anxiety that centers squarely on, while simultaneously seeking resolution in, admissions to particularly located postsecondary destinations. In response to notably deepened anxiety among both parents and students, the college counseling staff works to exert an increasingly heavy hand with regard to what they call "controlling expectations," while simultaneously working to keep parents at a clear distance in the admissions process.

College Counseling: Managing Expectations

For whatever reasons, it still astounds me sometimes that we as parents can't sort of step back from a lot of this process, which is, in effect, related to our genetic confirmation. I think everybody would be better off if they were able to do that, but we can't. They [parents] bombard us from all sides. When I use this phrase [genetic confirmation], you get a few laughs every once in a while, but it's fewer than when you remember back in the day. We get some [laughs] but we get fewer now than ever before. — (Dave Henderson, Head of Counseling)

A veteran elite school college counselor, Dave Henderson states: "One parent is a 'poster parent' for the issue at hand. The parents have spent $7,500 already and are prepared to spend $1,500 more on SAT prep courses." He continues:

What these parents focus on is what they think they can control—test scores and the like—what they do not realize is that there is so much they don't control—and this is what makes the difference. The parents do not understand what colleges are looking for—you really need a "hook" to get into the top schools now. That hook can be a variety of things—it can be the area (geographic location) you are from; race/ethnicity; gender in some cases; athlete and what sport you play; and so on. In other words, you have to have something that the college needs. It is not just about being good, or even stellar—you need something that fills a need.

In light of increased parental pressure in the wake of generalized anxiety with regard to their children's future, the college counseling office takes steps to accomplish the following: (1) keep parents *out* of as much of the process as possible at one and the same time as parents must stay connected to the process so as to facilitate and pay for all aspects of college admissions/attendance; (2) empower students to make the process their own, as they simultaneously position themselves in relation to current contextual realities by continuing to take the most challenging courses available; and (3) encourage students to embark upon a rigorous assessment of "self" with regard to academic and extracurricular strengths and weaknesses, as well as desired type and location of postsecondary institution.

In the middle of junior year, the college counseling office instructs students, in an all-class meeting, to set up appointments with the counselors, after which time parents are officially brought into the process, albeit with a well-circumscribed role. As Dave Henderson notes:

> I'd much rather bring parents to the process after we [he and the student] have done some work beforehand. So [I'm] trying to announce to parents: *"We're not meeting with you, this isn't your agenda,"* and many times parents think it is. But we're trying to send the signal, *"Your daughter's my client; you aren't."*

Parents at Matthews, however, are not keen to be sidelined in an increasingly competitive admissions environment. In response to what they perceive as blatant marginalization, parents push back, demanding *more* time and a *more* intense role with regard to the process than ever before, a move that the college counseling office does not appreciate. As Dave Henderson notes, parents now come in earlier than junior year and even demand meetings with him before they enter the upper school:

> We had the parents in here [college counseling office] yesterday of an eighth grader. I sort of attacked him, nicely, I hope. I said, "What is your goal? Is it Ivy League? Because if that's why you're sending your daughter here, that's the wrong reason.

Despite the fact that college counselors feel the need to routinely warn parents that "your child must drive the process, not you" and that "college is a match to be made, not a prize to be won," parents stand their ground, insisting on being intimately connected to each stage of the process, often micromanaging the process as if they were their children's personal college counselor.

At the most basic level (and not unlike their counterparts at Cannondale), privileged parents pay for and facilitate college visits, and ultimately pay, in most cases, for the cost of attendance, which is exceptionally steep, even at public institutions. Parents prod; remind their children to meet deadlines; stay on top of and seek feedback on their college essays; study for the SAT/ACT and SAT subject tests, as relevant; and so forth. They also support their children emotionally as they go through the increasingly arduous admissions process that spans approximately two years.[18] As many parents note, "breakdowns" are common, and it is a rare student, male or female, who goes through the process emotionally unscathed.

As mentioned in chapter 2, in the middle of junior year, students are instructed to set up individual meetings with their counselors as soon as possible, to be followed by a collective family meeting before the end of spring term. From this point forward, children are encouraged to meet with counselors one on one, as necessary, and without parents present. In contrast to this explicitly stated expectation, it is not at all uncommon for Matthews parents to schedule additional and not infrequent one-on-one meetings with the school counselor and, from there, to take over the process.[19]

In fact, and in contrast to privileged parents in the affluent suburban school, Matthews Academy parents continually monitor and assess their children's strengths and weaknesses, with an eye toward their chances of acceptance at particular institutions. Despite the fact that this set of tasks is distinctly marked by the counselors as being in the "student responsibility" column, parents, based on their own felt understanding of the importance of grades, difficulty of course load in relation to what is available in the school, SAT/ACT test scores, type and extent of extracurricular activities, and the like, routinely engage such assessment.

This vigilance extends well beyond parents who are themselves highly privileged. Ron Tomlinson, a White working-class parent who has no prior connection with private schools and did not attend university until later in life, is, according to Dave Henderson, "hunting big game" (specifically Harvard, Yale, Princeton), after which comment Dave Henderson notes, "He is not going to get it." The struggle between son and parent is palpable, as Matt wants to go to Rensselaer Polytechnic Institute, as per his own assessment of his strengths, weaknesses, and where he "fits best," and Ron Tomlinson wants him to attend one of the Ivies, specifically Harvard.[20]

Ron Tomlinson's desire to situate his child in an Ivy League institution is certainly understandable, particularly in light of the sacrifices that he continues to make in order to send his son to school. Matt, however, wants no part of his father's scenario, making it clear that he wants to go to Rennselaer Polytechnic Institute, an institution that he sees as perfectly suited to his strengths. In response, Ron Tomlinson drives even harder toward Ivy League colleges, a push that Matt largely ignores. Ron Tomlinson recounts discussions with his son:

> "Take your pick [of colleges to visit]. Here's my schedule." And I offered it before the application process. I said, you know, when he was at Harvard over the summer (for a sports camp), he really didn't get to see the school. You know, cuz at first he's like, "I'm not sure (why I didn't look at the school). I was at practices." "Why don't I take you back there in the regular school year?" . . . Nothing, ever, you know, and I was trying not to pressure him too much, and there were times where I was like, pulling my hair out. . . . One of the reasons why I told him I was hoping he would apply to Harvard was income-wise, it's free for me to send him there (tuition pricing is tied to income levels and Matt, by his father's calculation, would attend tuition-free).[21]

As we will see later in the chapter, Ron Tomlinson is by no means alone in his attempts to script and ensure his child's future via postsecondary admissions.

Students Assess Strengths and Weaknesses

As part of the Matthews-based process, students are encouraged to engage in frank assessment of their strengths, weaknesses, and desires with regard to what kind of postsecondary institution they wish to attend, a task that students generally take quite seriously.

Notably, this becomes part of the habitus of this particular kind of institution—wherein a *specific* set of actions and activities around the college admissions process becomes normalized for both parents and students. Such actions and activities are largely enacted in relation to the school. Even when explicitly asked in the interviews about activities and friends external to Matthews, students talk virtually entirely about Matthews. With few exceptions, Matthews comprises their entire world during the academic year, particularly as students approach and engage the postsecondary admissions process. Their friends attend Matthews; they play on Matthews sports teams; their work experiences, if they have them, are largely linked to positioning for college; their discussions with their friends, senior year in particular, are comprised of discussions about college and the admissions process; and their parties are almost wholly with friends from school, wherein postsecondary admissions inevitably surfaces as a topic of conversation.

In this regard, the postsecondary admissions process becomes a *shadow curriculum* in that it embeds its own totalizing actions, activities, and set of external experts such as tutors, expensive test prep courses (often suggested by the counseling staff), and so forth.[22] Although an individual may be somewhat shielded from this barrage of Matthews-centered activities if he or she participates in an out-of-school drama performance, dance company, hockey team, or vocal or instrumental ensemble, for example, such experiences additionally feed into performance opportunities at Matthews. Inevitably, all such activities become part of the postsecondary admissions dossier, as students and parents drive toward "distinction."

Little social or academic interaction, in fact, takes place outside the bounds of the school, with students arriving at 7:45 a.m. and generally returning home after 7:00 p.m. Those who engage in both sports and drama (this is not unusual) do not return home until after 9 p.m., since sports and drama practices run back to back after school. Finally arriving home, juniors and first-semester seniors inhale a quick dinner, often do homework and college admissions activities until 3 a.m., only to get up the next morning and repeat the cycle. As students in the top 20% generally select the most rigorous courses available so as to "make colleges see that they are continually challenging themselves," it is not unusual for the top 20% of students to take five or six APs per semester during their senior year, courses that they take seriously at least first semester, as first semester grades are included in the admissions dossier and students are specifically warned that they do not want to make it look as if they are "slacking off."

Increasingly, and as routinely noted by teachers, students, and college counselors, students in the top 20% are doubling up on math and science courses with the expressed aim of making themselves more competitive in the admissions process. Such doubling up is *rarely* construed as positioning for admittance to STEM fields, but rather a bold move designed to mark "distinction" wherever and whenever possible, particularly with regard to the most highly valued postsecondary destinations wherein evidence suggests that top math courses, in particular, are valued in the admissions process.[23]

Although weekends are ostensibly for "fun," such fun is peppered and constrained by the ever-present "shadow curriculum"—extensive study sessions, SAT prep courses, course tutoring to up their grades and make them more competitive in postsecondary admissions, and so forth. Although teen partying is a ubiquitous part of the landscape, it is difficult to engage a steady stream of hard partying and simultaneously engage all activities necessary to make oneself competitive for "top" colleges.[24]

In the midst of what one focal student refers to as a "marathon," students are instructed to engage in a serious assessment of the "self," building upon and extending skills that were learned and activated four years earlier when "choosing" a secondary school. Embedded in this process is an analytical assessment of *the field* (here defined as a dynamic social arena where exchanges and struggles take place involving particular forms of capital) of postsecondary admissions, wherein, as we see later, students are instructed to come up with an explicit strategy for maximizing one's strengths in relation to the broader field of action.[25] Below we hear from iconic students Matt Tomlinson, Ryan Dougherty, Samantha Singh, and Stephanie Larkin, all of whom thoughtfully addresses their strengths and weaknesses:

MATT: Strengths, I would say definitely lies in my extracurriculars, because I do soccer, hockey, and lacrosse. . . . Another student and I started a chess club here, which is doing really well. . . . Any clubs that I wanted to do, I've started. Most are not anything major, but I also did really well on my SATs (scores confirmed with college counseling office: 670 verbal; 780 math)

LOIS: Did you prep for them?

MATT: I am just one of those really good test takers (he did no SAT prep courses and took the test only one time, unlike other students).

LOIS: And with those kinds of test scores, you still think you'd say your strengths lie in the extracurriculars?

MATT: I would say that my test scores are certainly a big thing, but there are a lot of kids out there who did really well on the test, so extracurriculars are going to *make me stand out a little more* than just good SAT test scores and good (high level) classes.

RYAN: I think a lot of kids who apply to college are scholar/athlete, scholar/musician, but one of the things that's kind of given me a bit of an edge is that I have both scholar/athlete and the scholar/musician aspect. So I kind of have all three of those areas (the third being his academics), and because I've had so many experiences, and sports and academics: baseball, tennis, cross-country. . . . And I actually ended up doing this for a lot of my [application] essays, playing to my strengths, you know, talking about physics and music. . . . In general I do not like to think of myself as having weaknesses. . . . I think I was across the board pretty strong.

SAMANTHA: I always thought I was pretty strong because I have one of the highest GPAs and I do a lot more school activities than almost anyone else, and I've always played sports and . . . I don't know. I guess I was always pretty confident.

LOIS: If you got in Caltech [California Institute of Technology; which she did], you're very strong in math and science. What about humanities and social sciences?

SAMANTHA: I'm not taking history this year, but in the past, I've always had to put a lot into history. I did fine, but it was my worst subject. But in English . . . it's one of my favorite classes. I do really well in that.

LOIS: How would you describe yourself in relation to the college process?

STEPHANIE: I'm one of two people in that class [AP Calculus BC class, the most rigorous mathematics course available] who's not taking AP Physics. . . . I don't think I'm bad at science necessarily, it's just that I'm not that interested in it. I really don't put that much effort in. . . . I think overall I'm pretty academically strong. [I'm] OK at standardized testing. I probably do bring something to the table because *I do have an international background.*

Students in the top 20% at Matthews generally apply early to select colleges, whether Early Action (nonbinding) or Early Decision (generally binding), attempting to maximize possibilities of admittance to particular institutions since selective colleges take a relatively high proportion of students from the early application pool.[26] In consultation with the college counselor, students are encouraged to develop a strategy that takes into account their self-assessment, desired type and location of institution (e.g., small versus large; urban, suburban, rural; university versus liberal arts college), and expected "chance of admission" based on published admissions data.

With the "self" firmly etched at the center of this analysis, students hone and engage a very specific set of skills that layer on top of personal, academic, and extracurricular "work": (1) self-assessment of strengths and weaknesses; (2) self-assessment in relation to the larger marketplace, or *field* of action, within which this all plays; and (3) strategic intellectual and practical deployment of accumulated academic and cultural capital. The latter includes, among other things, grades, SAT/ACT scores, number of AP courses and scores, difficulty of course load relative to what is offered, personal and academic experiences, extracurriculars both in and outside of school, and notable awards, all of which are strategically deployed in the admissions dossier. Particularly critical to such dossier is the personal statement, a piece of individual writing (usually read and commented upon by teachers, parents, and at times the college counselor) that further enables applicants to create "distinction" in the admissions process, thereby maximizing the chances of acceptance at a range of top institutions in an increasingly competitive marketplace.

The Applications

After completing on-site visits to between 10 and 20 carefully selected institutions, students assemble a final list of colleges to which they will apply. With college counselors fully in the loop, such list embodies a well-thought-through strategy with regard to the odds of admittance at a range of institutions.

Such strategy comprises "safeties"—institutions at which they would almost certainly be accepted; "probables"—those that would most likely accept them; and "reaches"—those that would probably *not* accept them, but might possibly accept them.[27] Our interviews with focal students—once in the fall and once in the spring of senior year—clearly reveal such an embedded strategy. Below we hear from representative students Brandon Cowan, Joe Marino, and Ethan Sanderson:

LOIS: Where did you end up visiting, and then applying?

BRANDON: Let's see . . . [I visited] Northwestern, Amherst, Bard, Oberlin, Tufts, Swarthmore, Harvard, Princeton, and Carlton. I didn't apply to Northwestern or Amherst, so those dropped off the list. I applied to Bard early and got in there. I also applied to Middlebury.

LOIS: And why did you apply to Bard Early Action?

BRANDON: I think that Bard, I knew for sure, that that was a definite possibility, and it was going to stay my top two or three no matter what. So it was almost kind of a time thing. I knew I was applying anyway, and they have Early Action, so I thought I might as well do it in October rather than wait 'til December. And then the other ones, I think I really wasn't sure yet which ones I was going to apply to. . . . I hadn't really made a final list yet by mid-October, so I kind of knew that Bard was definitely going to be a frontrunner, so I spent a lot of time on reviewing that application and making sure everything was right. And then I just said, "Now I'm going to start focusing on the Common Applications." So it just worked out well that way.

LOIS: When you were deciding on your initial list [of colleges you were going to apply to], how did you do that?

JOE: I kind of just went online and looked up the college, saw how they were, kind of imagined if I could see myself going there, and then from there, I said "OK, This one I'll be looking at. This one, it didn't wow me. . . ."

I did receive the Caltech [California Institute of Technology] medal last year from Matthews, so I have a scholarship there, so I do believe that I will get in pretty easily. . . . I applied to Columbia, Carnegie Mellon, Caltech, Harvard, and RIT [Rochester Institute of Technology]. . . . And so I never doubted that I wouldn't get into RIT and Caltech—and from there, I kind of thought I *could* get into everything else, and Columbia and Harvard might be a little bit of a stretch. So I set up my list in that way, that I would have a couple safeties, a couple that I should get into but you never really know, and then one that's a reach [Columbia], and then one that's an even further reach [Harvard]. . . .

I think every place that I went to, I visited either the head of the math department or a math professor. I emailed them and my mother e-mailed them, and we set it up and we asked "Could you possibly meet a prospective student?" And they said, "Sure, I'd be willing to." My mom actually suggested that and so I said "OK." I'd be willing to meet with the math professors, just because we wanted to get a greater sense of the faculty. Because me, I go to every math professor after school [Matthews]. I have questions that are not at all part of the curriculum. . . . I do all those things, so I wanted to know that I could do that at college.

LOIS: So, what happened at Lake Forest College? [He said he had had a bad experience there when he visited.]

JOE: I got in and sat down with the professor. He asked me about myself. About two minutes into the interview, a student knocked on his door and asked when he would be free and he turned to us and he said, "This isn't gonna take more than a couple more minutes, will it?," and I'm like, "I guess not." And so he also asked me how I did on my SAT math, and I said I received an 800, and he said, "Well, any idiot can get an 800 on the math. That doesn't really say much about your math knowledge" . . . and I'm like . . .

LOIS: How did you decide where to apply?

ETHAN: I was in contact with my college counselor about the choices I had made about colleges, and he told me whether he thought it was a good idea or not. He agreed with me on my choices. It was a mixture of sort of touring and seeing if I felt right there, and academically what I was looking for, which is strong humanities and languages.

LOIS: So where did you end up applying?

ETHAN: I applied Early Decision to Stanford and was deferred, and my strategy was, sort of, apply early to Stanford, but also get a good list. I applied to 11 schools and I have my reaches, middles, and safeties.

LOIS: OK, let's go through them.

ETHAN: I'll do it in order: Stanford, Yale, Princeton, and University of Chicago; Williams, NYU, Tulane, Johns Hopkins; Vanderbilt, Trinity, and American. My safeties would definitely be Trinity, Vanderbilt, and American; my middles would be the Tulane and NYU group; and then my reach is the obvious [Stanford, Yale, Princeton, University of Chicago].

The above students, like virtually all students in the top 20%, reveal a well- articulated admissions strategy. Only Briana Kenney admits that her applications were driven by fear rather than strategy.

LOIS: So where did you end up applying?

BRIANA: I applied to quite a lot of schools.

LOIS: Did you apply early to anywhere?

BRIANA: I applied Early Action to Cornell. I was deferred. I actually had a big dilemma about applying early. I kind of wish I would have applied Early Decision to somewhere. It would have so much easier, but I wasn't ready to make a decision.

LOIS: So where did you end up applying?

BRIANA: Brandeis, Middlebury, Williams, Hamilton, Case Western, American University, Skidmore, NYU, George Washington, Colgate . . . I applied to like 16 schools, Duke . . . I can't even remember now. . . .

LOIS: Why did you apply to that many?

BRIANA: I was scared. I mean, I sort of went for breadth and tried to hit as many schools as possible so I wouldn't end up not going anywhere. I was kind of freaked out about it. . . .

Although Briana confesses that she is not aware of any strategy with regard to her applications, her final list clearly embeds such a strategy, a move orchestrated by her parents and school counselor Dave Henderson. American University, for example, although an outstanding school, is less difficult to get into than Duke, and her list, whether consciously acknowledged or not, reflects comparable strategic thinking to that of other students.

We now turn to the role of privileged parents in this site, a group that flat out refuses to adopt any kind of circumscribed role in the process.

Thinking, Plotting, Planning

In spite of the fact that the college counseling office positions parents as ancillary players in the postsecondary admissions process, Matthews parents, particularly mothers, insert themselves into the process *every step of the way*. This is less connected to parental desire to "get their money's worth" at the postsecondary level than to a strong sense that Matthews will not work hard enough to maximize their children's chances of acceptance at the very top institutions. In light of parental perceptions of being sidelined in the process by being told that it is largely "out of our control" (referring to both parents and the school), parents reconceptualize the admissions process as one that is under *their* control, even if not under the control of the school. As a consequence, they intellectually and practically construct the necessity of "working" the process in spite of direct edicts from the school counseling staff that they should get out of the way. Such parental "working" becomes normative practice in this sector of schools, unlike what we see at Cannondale in chapter 3.

As we point out earlier, many components of the college admissions process do lie outside of the control of counselors, parents, and students. The number of applicants to particularly located institutions ("Highly Competitive+" and "Most Competitive," in the case at hand) in the United States has skyrocketed, while the number of admitted students at these same schools has remained largely the same. This means that a greatly increased number of applicants are competing for largely the same number of slots that were available 30 years ago, especially at highly prestigious "name brand" institutions.

Even in the face of this reality, privileged parents in the private secondary sector will not be deterred, and counselors are not at all successful in confining parents to any kind of narrowly prescribed role. Rather than backing off direct "class positioning" work, thereby trusting the school to work on behalf of its students, privileged parents in elite privates do exactly the opposite—they intensify their strategizing (in a non-Bourdieuan sense) at the very moment that the school insists that they *back off* such strategizing. As increasing numbers of parents in this sector intentionally work to strategize around the postsecondary admissions process, it becomes much more difficult for those not initially engaged in this practice to confine themselves to the sidelines.

Susan and Robert Larkin, who experienced their own schooling in Europe and whose two older children attended European institutions of higher education, cast their uniquely positioned "outsider" eye on the process in the United States.

SUSAN LARKIN: . . . So I would say the last 8 to 10 years, I've heard parents talking about it [college application process and entry]. Parents of the older children, I would say, maybe even into middle school, parents are contriving or conniving.

ROBERT LARKIN: From my point of view, in a real sense, it [the conniving and contriving] started in sophomore year. Became much more apparent. So we had heard, Susan probably more than I had, we'd heard the noise, some of the sure things [one had to do to get ready for the applications process], but it didn't have anything to do with us, things that we had to do. And I think it was at that level, we began to realize that it was competitive, and . . . maybe you could've started sending your child to this place [a specific institution] to do extracurriculars and you would tell your colleagues [other parents of children in the class] afterwards, to show how good you are, but you wouldn't actually bring them all up and say, "Why don't we all send our children to [the local cancer research facility] to do cancer research" . . . because everyone wanted to get a step ahead with their children, was my impression. . . .

So I think that sophomore year onwards, we began to realize it was a game, and that we were perhaps a bit late in the game, and that we're still a bit late in the game, and we're realizing that. Even if you put down your name for mock trial and you don't even appear or do anything, at least you can put on the form [college application] . . . I did mock trial at sophomore level, even if you had only turned up to one meeting, and we go "shoot," we didn't do that, because *we* thought honor was pure. . . . It's just a bit unfair, you know, that sort of, well, most people are probably behaving entirely honorably, but there's some sense of competition, and do anything to get your child well positioned, and I think we've been swept up in it because at the end of the day, the person who loses if we stand our ground is Stephanie.

Succumbing to what they come to understand as normative practice among similarly positioned parents, Susan and Robert Larkin begin to encourage Stephanie to maximize her deep international roots, thereby distinguishing herself from others in the college competition.

SUSAN LARKIN: I did say to Stephanie, it's all well to say you've traveled, but further down the line, this may be mistaken for colleges thinking, "Here's a rich kid, driving around in expensive cars, you know, [staying at] the Best Western overseas." I said maybe you have to demonstrate you can do more than that.

I mean, I knew she could, so I put it to her that [she should] volunteer at this home in Bogotá. And it was started and run by a former colleague of mine from [the firm where Susan is employed] because otherwise it might have been hard for us to get there because of her age [17]. But there were 170 boys of all ages, and just under 20 girls. She spent two weeks with them and was a little tearful when she left. And she did say that she might well go back and volunteer. And I thought again, that if one wanted to demonstrate her adaptability that it was the perfect testing ground for her.

Although initially disdainful of such "game playing," the Larkins, and others who harbor similar feelings, ultimately "connive and contrive" to ensure that their own children seek out activities that mark them as "distinctive," hoping to maximize the possibility of acceptance at the most valued postsecondary destinations. Activating her social capital, Susan Larkin arranges for Stephanie to work in a children's home in Bogotá as a way to demonstrate that she is not just some "rich kid" who is well traveled, that she is, in fact, "adaptable." Susan Larkin, while not initially on board with "conniving and contriving," eventually succumbs to this aspect of the process to ensure that her daughter stands out to admissions committees.[28]

In addition to activating their own cultural, social, and economic capital to create "distinction" in the postsecondary admissions process, parents (usually mothers) intentionally work toward *reconceptualizing* the entire process as being under *their control*, becoming *highly* involved at every turn. This includes engaging the research on potential institutions, drawing up lists of criteria for admission, keeping spreadsheets with regard to admitted student test and class rank data for schools under consideration, informally or formally assessing the probability of admission at institutions in the prospective application field, engaging in the continual "self-assessment" of their children even though their children are specifically instructed to do this themselves, drawing up fine-grained plans with regard to family trips to visit postsecondary destinations across the country, and so forth.

In spite of this high level of activity among parents, there are in fact few complaints about the work of the college counseling office, and parental actions should not be read as any kind of generalized critique of counselors. Rather, parents unambiguously assert, via their actions, that they *can* exert control over important aspects of the process and that they are, in fact, going to do it, despite being instructed not to. Donna Kenney is clear as to her justification for not backing off:

DONNA KENNEY: I don't know how many other parents feel this way, or who you [Lois] already talked to, but it was really hard to get the kid to focus and to get off of their rear ends and pay attention to it. So I was doing all the stuff on the Internet, and before we would plan a trip, we would figure out which schools to go to, and which we could handle on a given [college-visiting] trip. And there were schools we had to eliminate because we couldn't get to all of them. And then, I do sheets with getting the most important information. I get language about their English Department, whether there is field hockey. At some point, she seemed interested in sororities. We wrote down whether they had them and what percentage [joins], so that we could see at a glance as she was going through. Then we would have information on how to find the admissions offices at each school and directions, and then Kenneth [husband] would take it and MapQuest . . . you know. . . .

Switching from "we" when referring to keeping track of which schools have club field hockey teams, sororities, and so forth, Donna Kenney ultimately embraces "I" as she shares her own emotional involvement in the process.

DONNA KENNEY: I think . . . for me . . . it has been a little bit of a nail biter [laughter]. I would tell you that we [my husband and I] have kept our hands off with helping with any schoolwork, but we changed that process with the college thing. We read her essays and we realized she needed help.

LOIS: It sounds as though you did an immense amount of work.

DONNA KENNEY: I did. The school should have done more, they—they being Kenneth [husband] and Briana [daughter]—they kept telling me to back off a bit, but it had to get done. We had to organize it.

While the Larkins, Donna Kenney, Ron Tomlinson, and other private school parents may have somewhat different motivations for their actions, nearly *all* parents of focal students in the top 20% of the class express the necessity of taking a *very* strong hand in positioning their children with regard to the admissions process. Despite the counselor's edict to be "hands off," the clear majority of these parents are involved every step of the way, from helping their children to conceptualize and carve out "distinction" *as an applicant*; proofing and often editing college essays; planning and executing road and/or plane trips to visit potential colleges; and weighing in on and facilitating final decisions once accept, reject, and wait-list letters are received. Reconceptualized as a family activity, parents use any and all capitals at their disposal to help to position their children in the college admissions process, a process and set of commitments that does not stop when all applications (generally between 8 and 16 full applications) are finally submitted.

Admissions decisions begin to come out in December for Early Action and Early Decision applicants; all regular admission decisions are communicated via letter or e-mail by the second week of April. For this group, the receipt of final dispensations from colleges and universities involves a *second* full round of on-site visits—generally in mid-April—where students spend up to several days at each college in a carefully conceived and often elaborate "Admitted Students Program." Again, parents, and almost always mothers, take full responsibility for planning and executing this second round of visits after they themselves engage further research on strengths and weaknesses of the now "live" options. Parents inevitably hover in range of each "Admitted Students Program," preparing to "grill" their children as to pluses, minuses, and generalized thoughts with regard to "their decision."[29] Of course, the results of this final round of parental research and visitation are clearly reported out to their children, with an eye toward influencing the college to which their child will matriculate in the fall.

Class Positioning and Elite Privates

We argue that largely privileged students and parents at an elite private secondary school engage a particular form of "class positioning" in the context of altered market realities linked to both the global knowledge economy and broadly construed postsecondary admissions processes in the United States. Parents and students now engage a very specific form of "class warfare" via explicit attempts to gain and maintain control of "Highly Competitive+" and "Most Competitive" postsecondary institutions, particularly the privates. Such "class warfare" acknowledges, whether stated or not, the growing importance of the "college linking process" in new global circumstances, where one can no longer assume that a "four-year college education" will ensure advantage.[30]

As noted in chapter 1, "the key question about educational expansion is whether it reduces inequality by providing more opportunities for persons from disadvantaged strata, or magnifies inequality by expanding opportunities disproportionately for those who are already privileged"

(Shavit, Arum, and Gamoran 2007, p. 1). As numerous scholars argue, educational expansion does not serve, in and of itself, to reduce class-linked inequalities in education (Raftery and Hout 1993; Shavit, Arum, and Gamoran 2007, among others). What is not known, however, are the ways in which qualitative distinctions are struggled over and produced, on the lived-out ground of differentially located class actors at the point of the increasingly pivotal college admissions process. As we see here, such lived-out struggles enable qualitative distinctions to take hardened shape and form, as those with privilege now engage all available capitals to drive toward particular college locations in a space of objectively broadened opportunities (see also chapter 3). This sets in motion on a day-to-day and week-by-week basis what Lucas calls "effectively maintained inequality" (EMI).

Such day-to-day and year-by-year struggles can only be picked up ethnographically, of course, as the "stuff" of daily life breathes substance into a range of important quantitatively linked structural drivers and analyses. Putting such qualitative work into conversation with important quantitative work enables us to more clearly understand the lived-out and complex mechanisms through which inequalities are produced and maintained. The struggle over class is now unequivocally a struggle over particularly located postsecondary destinations, and privileged families are mobilizing harder and faster to consolidate position for their children in new global and postsecondary circumstances.

The observations in this chapter additionally forecast the particular role that gender plays and will continue to play in new class productions, a topic to which we return in chapter 7. Although largely uninvited and even denigrated at times by the school, such self-embraced "class work" in relation to the postsecondary admissions process at Matthews is largely "mother work," comprised of a set of intellectual and practical actions and activities that often, although not uniformly, sit side by side high-level professional and managerial commitments.[31] Although fathers certainly participate in this process and go on virtually all college visits that have been arranged by mothers, they generally script themselves as having to worry about "paying for it," rather than taking full or even primary responsibility for all aspects of the intricate planning process.[32] For the most part, the conceptualization and actualization of the day-by-day and month-by-month "work" associated with the almost two-year postsecondary admissions process sits in the hands of a group of highly educated and often professional and/or upper-managerial women who deploy their time and energy toward this end. As such, the actual parental work involved in struggles over postsecondary admissions is highly gendered, reminiscent of Ball and Vincent's (2006) work on middle-class women's role in child care and school choice with regard to their young children.

This particular moment of deepening "mother work" as it plays out with regard to struggles over class advantage is quite ironic, given that women across race/ethnicity were locked out of top institutions, particularly the Ivies, for well over a century. Now centrally located in newly conceptualized and enacted "class warfare," women take the lead in positioning both their sons and daughters for class advantage in a context where such advantage can no longer be assumed. Although it can be argued that such work is still women's work and therefore reflective of deep patriarchal division around home and workplace patterns of labor and childrearing (and it most certainly feels that way to many women), our analysis presses toward a different conclusion. Rather than reflective of any particular historic form of patriarchy and attendant relationships and responsibilities in home and workplace, *the stark insertion of gender and gendered labor into new class processes and productions* arguably and fundamentally alters the fulcrum of class struggle and "class warfare" as it takes shape in the current historic moment. Where men comprised the center of class analysis and class struggle of the not-too-distant past via industrial workplace struggles and so forth, it is now women, via the kind of class positioning we see here, who now sit at the epicenter of new class productions and outcomes that will have long-term consequences for twenty-first-century class structure. We will briefly return to this topic in chapter 7.

In the next two chapters, we focus on what Cookson and Persell (1991) call "outsiders within"—in this case, low-income self-identified Black students who enter private secondary schools largely through special intake programs. As we will argue, although parental and student motives for entering the elite private school sector broadly mirror those of students and parents discussed here, their frame of reference, initial definition of valued postsecondary destinations, and experiences with college counselors and the postsecondary admissions process more generally differ markedly.

"Outsiders Within": Relative Opportunities for Low-Income Black Students in Elite Private Secondary Schools

I wish I would have had a lot more help, even from my parents. They kind of just sat back and let me [handle the college preparations]. But I wish someone would have at least stepped in and been like "this is what you could do"; "this is what you should do"; "there's any easier way to do this or that." It was [just] me, kind of researching and finding stuff on my own. You know, how I need to do things, like even for my FAFSA [federal financial aid] form, I did it all by myself. I just asked my mom for her [tax] sheets. But I wish I would have had someone to help me. . . . I had to remember, I have a paper due today, oh, but I have to remember to go home and ask my mom to file her taxes [so I can apply for financial aid].
— (Breanna Daniels, Bradford student)

I think I am setting an example for other kids like me. I mean, to be the first in my family to go to a good four-year college. No one really has done that yet. One of my older brothers started a two-year school, but he dropped out and never went back. I've even inspired my mom to go back to school. She wants to be a pharmacist! — (Steven Jones, Matthews student)

As we see in chapter 4, for students in the top 20% of the Matthews Academy graduating class, the college applications process is an intensive and carefully orchestrated endeavor, one collectively engaged by in-school college counselors, parents, teachers (who read and comment upon college essays), and students. Although our data reflect the experiences and practices of students and associated parents who are in the top 20% of the graduating class, we feel confident that parental input into this process as detailed in chapter 4 characterizes a notable proportion of the privileged Matthews population. Having said this, the degree to which one reaps the desired benefits from the process depends in large part on the quality of the students' academic portfolio (GPA, position in the opportunity of the school, degree to which students challenge themselves as evidenced by course taking patterns, SAT/ACT scores, and so forth) and the degree to which the student is, him- or herself, invested in the process. Despite parents' best efforts in this regard, student investment in the process obviously differs.

Parents and students at Cannondale exhibit a different experience, wherein what becomes normative practice around the college admissions process manifests in a somewhat dissimilar fashion from Matthews. Most notably, the parental micromanagement of the process, which is so clearly evident at Matthews, is not as blatantly evidenced at Cannondale. Rather, parents "lead from behind," assuming their children, who have distinguished themselves by being in the top 10% of the class, have the skills they need to "drive the process." Although ready and willing to "step in" as required, normative practice among Cannondale parents is to let their children do the work of college admissions, as they have been groomed to do, rather than micromanage the process as Matthews parents do.

In contrast to Breanna, then, not a single privileged student states that "[I] wish . . . [I] would have had a lot more help, even from my parents." Noting that her parents "kind of just sat back and let me [handle the college preparations]," Breanna is largely left to her own devices. This is in sharp contrast to privileged focal students at Matthews and Cannondale, whose parents have invested a great deal of time, effort, and resources (monetary and otherwise) with an eye toward positioning their children for particularly located highly selective colleges. As the schools largely cater to those at the top of the track structure, such "doubly privileged" students reap the benefit of their own located class position coupled with their location at the apex of the opportunity structure of the school. In contrast, Breanna and the vast majority of low-income Black students are "doubly disadvantaged" in the context of the privileged institution, both by virtue of class background and their position at the bottom of the opportunity structure, given that the preponderance of low-income Black students are initially placed in the lowest-level classes, a position that tends to take on a caste-like quality as they move toward graduation.

In this chapter, we shift our focus to the college-related experiences and practices of low-income Black students in the elite private secondary school.[1] Like other groups in such schools, low-income Black students and their parents explicitly intend to use elite private schools for social and economic advancement. However, unlike privileged parents in both affluent public and elite privates who have consciously engaged the preparation and packaging of their children with an eye toward competitive college admissions since they were very young, low-income Black parents operate from an entirely different structural location and accompanying set of perspectives. As data make clear, both parents and children conceptualize attendance at elite private secondary institutions as constituting an escape from poverty *and* a virtually guaranteed opportunity to enter the four-year (in contrast to two-year) postsecondary sector, a sector to which they do not see themselves as having access had they remained in underresourced, predominantly Black and Latino urban public schools. Data presented in this chapter are drawn from the two NAIS institutions detailed in chapter 2: Matthews Academy, a coeducational day school, and Bradford Academy, a single-sex day school for girls.

In many ways, despite entrance to the elite private sector, Black focal students and their parents remain outsiders to the school culture and normative practices that define the school space. This "outsider within" status has marked material and practical consequences for how the college process is engaged and the extent to which students feel comfortable approaching the college counselors. On the one hand, students largely operate *outside* the purview of the college counselors, often taking on the college admissions process alone with little direct school-based or outside assistance. On the other hand, by virtue of attendance at schools like Matthews and Bradford, where college preparation is embedded into the very fabric of the school, a basic level of college knowledge is distributed and absorbed simply by being part of the school space, thereby providing focal students with enough information to navigate the college applications process from a stronger position than might be expected of students who largely "go it alone." Most important perhaps, low-income Black students possess greater knowledge about the college process than they would have had they remained in their predominantly Black and Latino low-income public schools, a fact that they comment upon frequently.

Six of the focal students found their way to elite private secondary schools by way of City Prep, a nonprofit education organization. The role City Prep plays—and, more importantly, does not play—in regard to students' college processes is important to consider. A significant part of the organization's mission is to prepare low-income, academically talented Black, Latino/a, and Native American students for entrance into and success in private Catholic and elite private secondary schools in the Blair region and, ultimately, in competitive colleges and universities. City Prep includes Primary and Secondary Prep programs to help students in grades 5 through 8 prepare for entrance into highly regarded private secondary schools. The Postsecondary Prep component was initiated after the Secondary Prep Director and the Executive Director shared their concerns with the Board of Directors regarding the type and quality of college counseling that City Prep students were receiving in their private secondary schools—both independent and Catholic. Both Jane Evans (Postsecondary Prep Director) and Claudia Harrison (Secondary Prep Director) state, on separate occasions, that City Prep students, and most likely other students of color, were being counseled into two-year rather than four-year colleges, and/or that the specific needs of this population were not being met by the counselors in their schools. Claudia Harrison notes that this was based on conversations with students about their college counseling within their respective institutions. As City Prep's ultimate goal is to facilitate success in four-year colleges and universities, the organization began its own college counseling program to help their students to access four-year colleges.

Jane Evans currently works part-time as the City Prep college counselor. Her role mainly focuses on organizing weekend, in-state college visits, bringing college representatives to City Prep, organizing financial aid workshops for students and parents, setting up SAT preparation courses, and paying close attention to students' high school GPAs. However, despite the stated intentions of creating a comprehensive college counseling program for City Prep students, Jane Evans does not engage in such counseling and advisement—this is simply not built into the structure of the Postsecondary Prep program. While she provides opportunities to access help with SATs and to hear from college representatives, she does not provide students with targeted guidance on creating their college lists and/or locating schools that would be a good fit for them. Further, unlike the college counselors at Matthews and Bradford, Jane Evans does not have any professional background in college counseling. Thus, while City Prep students have some advantages over non–City Prep students in regard to preparation for private secondary school, they do not have much of an advantage over non–City Prep focal students in regard to the college process.[2]

Private Secondary Schools and Imagined Future Opportunities

Focal parents and students are very clear about their decision to enroll in elite private secondary schools; such schools are seen as a pathway to college and long-term economic opportunity. Putting their capital to work (not unlike privileged Cannondale and Matthews parents), low-income Black parents engage "up-front" work designed to mobilize their children academically and socioeconomically. However, the type and scope of this work differs from that of the affluent Matthews and Cannondale parents, as low-income Black parents put their work into accessing elite private secondary schools with the specific understanding and expectation that such schools will prepare their children to access "good" four-year colleges, a sector to which they do not see themselves as having access prior to private school entrance.[3] In this regard, parents rely on information from others (personnel at City Prep, middle school counselors, Black parents with older children) and the generalized reputation of the schools (Johnson 2011) to steer them toward the best institutions and subsequently help them navigate the complicated private school admissions process. Lacking relevant social and cultural capital and explicit college knowledge, these parents believe, based on their interactions with others, that attending private secondary schools, as opposed to urban public secondary schools, would result in competitive postsecondary entrance. These parents did not seek out Matthews and Bradford based on personal in-depth knowledge of these institutions, but rather ended up applying to these particular schools as part of a generalized desire to pursue better options for their children than those currently available in the urban public sector, a sector beleaguered by sharp disinvestment, high levels of surveillance, and extensive testing regimes that result in scant "real" education for students (Anyon 1997, 2014; Lipman 2011). Focal students experienced a great deal of academic success in elementary and middle school, and, in many cases, school personnel took it upon themselves to advise parents of secondary school options that included elite private schools. Once able to envision private secondary schooling as an option, parents rely upon community reputation to select the best available secondary school for their children.

Reputation Matters

Enacting the capital at their disposal, focal families, like those in chapters 3 and 4, rely on information embedded in their own networks to choose schools. While not possessing deep personal knowledge about particular private school options, parents are aware of what schools are considered the best in the Blair area. Some focal students and parents were advised by City Prep staff as to which private secondary schools would be a "good fit" for their children; others were advised by their middle school counselors (who routinely are contacted by private school representatives, seeking to recruit students of "diverse" backgrounds, for recommendations as to who might be appropriate private school candidates). Based on these recommendations, parents and students then attend open houses, set up shadow days, select their top schools, and engage in the arduous elite private secondary school application process.

Importantly, every low-income Black student and parent states that he or she ultimately chose Matthews or Bradford because of the schools' respective reputations, reputations that are linked to exclusivity and academic excellence. Informed by Prep that these particular schools serve as pathways to high quality four-year colleges and universities, both parents and students stress the outstanding education offered at Matthews and Bradford. In making her high school decision, Anna Nalin notes that she ultimately chose Bradford over a public school because "it has a great reputation and it is well known to colleges." Anna's comments are in line with those of other students who similarly suggest that the reputations of their high schools will serve them well in their quest for entrance into a "good" four-year college.

Fundamentally motivating parents' "up-front" work on behalf of their children is a strong desire for a rigorous academic school environment. Breanna notes that for personal and social reasons she would rather have attended the public secondary school that all of her middle school friends were attending, but she acknowledges that she would not have received the same level of academic preparation for college—and therefore access to a graduate program in economics or accounting—had she not attended Bradford. While most of the focal students applied to what are considered to be the "better" of the Blair public high schools, they did so only as a "backup" in the event that they did not gain admission to one of the privates. In contrast, Leila Martin (Matthews), who attended a predominantly immigrant/refugee public middle school, did not apply to any of the local public high schools. As Leila's mother explains, it was her personal knowledge of the public schools in Blair that prompted this decision:

> When she [Leila] was in [middle school], I see the high school students a lot on the street. My eldest son went to [a predominantly Black public high school in Blair], and I been there all the time, and I see what's going on with public schools. And at some point, not because I hate public schools, but we were looking for other options for a better education.

The choice to enroll in elite private secondary schools is driven by a clear desire for social mobility. Students aspire to attend "good" four-year colleges and universities and, ultimately graduate programs, and attendance at elite private secondary schools is conceptualized as a pathway to success. Yet the choice to attend Matthews and Bradford comes with notable trade-offs. Both students and parents highlight, for example, the negative aspects of students' secondary school experiences, particularly the lack of diversity and/or the lack of Black adults and students, with attendant consequences on overall school culture. It is at the lived-out juncture of reputation and sociocultural environment that we begin to see the inherent conflict these schools present to low-income Black students. In spite of the drawbacks, the perceived opportunity for social mobility and long-term economic security triumph, as parents and students chose Matthews and Bradford over urban public schools.

OUTSIDERS WITHIN.   Although this group of low-income Black students is advantaged by virtue of access to privileged private schools, their own located economic position and prior academic preparation in poorly resourced elementary and middle schools sets limits on the extent to which these students can realistically hope to compete with the broader population of largely privileged attendees. This linked economic and class/race marginality instantiates this group as "outsiders within" (Cookson and Persell 1991), although *formally* possessing all rights, responsibilities, and privileges held by other students. This does not mean that all students of color in privileged educational sectors function as "outsiders within," a point that we take up at some length in chapter 6. In point of fact, there are students of color (economically privileged multigenerational Black students as well as other students of color, largely the children of "flexible immigrants") who function exceptionally well within the academic and social mainstream of the school, but as we make clear here, they are situated far differently in the academic opportunity structure than the vast majority of low-income Black students.

As Zweigenhaft and Domhoff (1991, 2003), Cookson and Persell (1985), and others note, elite private schools (particularly elite boarding schools) have historically functioned as pipelines to Ivy League and other highly selective colleges and universities. On the heels of the civil rights movement, such secondary schools endeavored to diversify their student populations (Zweigenhaft and Domhoff 1991, 2003), and a high proportion of low-income Black students who entered private schools through programs such as ABC (A Better Chance) were initially well positioned to enter Harvard, Yale, Princeton, and other Ivies (Bowen and Bok 1998). Even in the face of the steady, quiet reversal of civil rights gains (Bell 2004; Orfield and Lee 2005), strong growing opposition to affirmative action (Bowen and Bok 1998; Tierney 1997), and shifts from scholarships and grants to high-interest loans (Gladieux 2002; McPherson and Schapiro 2002), most highly competitive postsecondary institutions are still somewhat diverse, holding out at least the possibility for the most talented and well-prepared low-income Black students to enter America's most prestigious colleges and universities.

Here we enter the habitus of low-income Black students' respective elite secondary schools, with specific focus on how such habitus shapes their engagement with the college application process and their thoughts as to what constitutes a "good" college and *the right fit for them*. This is followed by an examination of student access to and use of their schools' college counseling resources, interrogating both the structure of the schools' counseling opportunities and student activation of their own agency. Clearly acknowledging students' status as "outsiders within" the highly privileged school space is critical to understanding how low-income Black students approach the college process. While in many ways they feel marginalized from the formal structures of the college process as initiated by the school (and the school counselors, in particular), students still markedly benefit from the college-going culture that saturates the institution. As explicitly college preparatory in nature, Bradford and Matthews provide students with a great deal of college knowledge on a day-to-day and week-by-week basis. In this respect, low-income Black focal students know what they need to do to position for and apply to college; however, unlike their largely White and privileged counterparts whose parents often micromanage the process on their behalf, Black focal students often receive little formal guidance. They are left on their own to figure out *how* to do this work.

College Knowledge and School Culture

At elite private secondary schools like Matthews and Bradford, preparing for and seeking entrance to competitive colleges and universities is intimately tied to the culture of the school. As discussed in chapter 2, the school cultures of Matthews and Bradford are shaped by and explicitly linked to four-year college admission. College planning begins early, in the form of course planning (selecting courses with college aspirations in mind) and general information sessions. Visits from college representatives comprise an essential component of the college culture at Bradford and Matthews, particularly junior and senior year. Students, from grade 9 forward, understand that representatives from a variety of competitive postsecondary institutions routinely visit their schools to hold informational meetings and answer students' questions, and students attend these sessions to learn more about potential college choices.

While the college culture is certainly reflected in the resources made available through the schools' college counseling offices, it is also embedded in curricular and extracurricular offerings. As noted in chapter 2, over the past several years, both Matthews and Bradford have changed their curricula, particularly in regard to math and science offerings, to provide all students with an array of upper-level and elective courses to give them an "edge" in the college admissions process. For example, curricular reorganization, coupled with intense effort on the part of math teachers to ensure that all students have the relevant math prerequisites by the time they are seniors, now enables every student to take an advanced-level mathematics course such as AP Probabilty and Statistics, AP Calculus, or Regular Calculus before they graduate. Additionally, for those students in non–AP English courses, drafting, editing, and revising one's college essay is embedded within the twelfth-grade curriculum, ensuring that all students will have prepared and vetted essays before submitting application materials to colleges. In this sense, attending college information sessions, revising college essays in English classes, and taking high-level math and science courses become a fundamental part of the college-going habitus.

As college preparation permeates all areas of school life, the schools have increased the number and type of extracurricular offerings, particularly in regard to student clubs and activities. For example, over the past five to ten years Matthews added such clubs as Book Review Group (in which students write book reviews to be published in a national magazine) and Young Research Scholars Club (a club dedicated to cultivating research scholars and connecting students with veteran researchers in Blair). Although a college-going habitus permeates the very fabric of these institutions, and a great deal of information is distributed about the college process through group college informational sessions, visits by college representatives, and so forth, it is not necessarily the case that all students know what to do with this information once they receive it. They do not necessarily know, for example, how to organize their work with regard to the process to get it all done in a timely fashion, nor can it be assumed that they know how to use the distributed and admittedly extensive knowledge to their advantage.

Reflecting back on privileged students and parents in chapter 4, it is quite clear that parents, usually mothers, take a strong overall hand in conceptualizing the entire process and helping students to organize their time so that they can get it all done. Although the school wants the students to "drive the process," it is questionable whether any student can accomplish the array of necessary tasks on his or her own. These tasks include (1) pinpointing, studying for, and taking an array of the most relevant and required college entrance tests (e.g., PSAT, SAT/ACT, SAT subject tests); (2) visiting colleges to view potential college choices; (3) putting together a potential application list that spans safeties, probables, and reaches; (4) engaging all aspects of admissions forms and relevant application essays; (5) obtaining recommendations from teachers, after figuring out which ones to approach for recommendations; (6) riding the emotional current of accept, reject, and wait-list outcomes; (7) visiting the now "live" college options once all accept, reject, and wait-list notifications are received; (8) making a final choice in light of all "live" possibilities; and (9) pulling together parental tax materials to fill out FAFSA and additional community and college-based loans and grants. Importantly, this must all be accomplished at the same time students are keeping up their grades in highly challenging courses, engaging all extracurricular activities, and so forth.

This dizzying array of required actions and activities must be conceptualized, handled, and kept track of, and it is therefore not surprising that privileged parents exert a strong hand with regard to many aspects of the college process. Low-income Black students have no such metaphoric mini-CEO conceptualizing, managing, and helping to produce all required tasks. Although they know the nuts and bolts of the college process simply by being immersed in the college-going site, it cannot be assumed that they know what they need to do with this information or how to use it to their advantage in the college application process. Stated differently, low-income Black students do not necessarily know how to *enact* this knowledge and, as "doubly disadvantaged," do not have parents who understand the intricacies of the college process and therefore can help them. Thus focal students are certainly highly privileged compared to their peers in predominantly Black public schools where college knowledge is a scarcity at best. In important ways, however, they are left to muddle through the process largely on their own without important activation strategies. They remain "outsiders within."

Shaping Students' Perspectives about "Fit"

As detailed in chapter 2, college counseling offices at institutions like Matthews and Bradford run like well-oiled machines, with full-time, veteran college counselors at the helm. Matthews and Bradford counselors emphatically state that the primary goal of their highly individualized counseling process is to help students find a match between their personal and academic backgrounds and a given college or university. Across the board, college counselors maintain that selecting a college is about "a match to be made, not a prize to be won" (Gayle Johnson and Dave Henderson, personal communication). The academic and sociocultural habitus of the two schools under consideration intersect with family-based habitus to produce desires with regard to how students think about *the right fit*. Students are provided the opportunity to work with counselors to create college lists, have veteran English teachers (many of whom hold PhDs) review college essays, and visit with admissions personnel from some of the best colleges in the United States. As detailed at length in chapter 2, the college process formally begins in January of junior year, followed by constant college process meetings, seminars, and reminders about deadlines, until spring of senior year as students begin to make their college choices.

While this college-going culture undergirds the life of the school, it is not, in practice, necessarily equally available to all students. Those students, who are "outsiders within," thereby lacking certain kinds of relevant capital, do not always know how to go about gaining access to or feel entitled to seek out the plentiful college-related resources ostensibly available to everyone. In other words, just by virtue of being students in these schools, focal low-income Black students have access to the basic college process information (e.g., writing strong college essays, applying to a mix of probable, reach, and safety schools, asking teachers for letters of recommendation, filling out various financial aid forms if seeking need-based support); however, lacking certain active strategies and not having parents who are well versed in how to do some of these things means that the college process for "outsiders within" is not as seamless as it is for their more privileged and largely White peers.

Before delving into the factors that shape focal Black students' thoughts about *fit*, it is critically important to point out that these students initially conceptualize "good" colleges and universities differently than the privileged Matthews and Cannondale students. Low-income Black students, with an eye toward their community of origin, measure their success and what constitutes a "good" college against the successes and college options of their peers who attend predominantly Black urban public secondary schools, as opposed to their predominantly privileged, largely White elite private school peers. As these urban public schools have limited academic resources and lack college counseling and advisement, Black students attending these schools have very limited postsecondary options. Thus, for the low-income Black students and parents who are linked to private secondary schools, attending *a* college that grants four-year degrees is itself a measure of success, and they do not necessarily view attending a less selective and/or local four-year college as a failure. In short, being "outsiders within" and having a different frame of reference produces, with one eye, different ideas about what are acceptable college options, at least initially.

The conception of what constitutes a "good" college shifts for the majority of these students as they engage the college process. Although they still have one eye on their community of origin and continue to compare themselves to those "left behind" in urban schools, they *simultaneously* absorb explicit discussions of the postsecondary hierarchy that circulate nonstop among privileged populations and in privileged secondary schools. By way of example, ubiquitous discussion of safeties, probables, and reaches imply hierarchical locations of postsecondary institutions with respect to competitiveness index and "quality" of education. Although low-income Black students often work hard to remain an integral part of their community of origin, as this is their home, their own absorption of this hierarchy leads many of these students to different understandings of what constitutes a "good" college—understandings that go far beyond the initially evidenced two-year/four-year distinction.

Creating "The List"

When thinking about possible colleges to put on their lists, students consider the most positive and negative aspects of their experiences at Matthews and Bradford, and select colleges accordingly. Students think very carefully about the academic and social habitus of their schools and use these factors to create their college lists. Given that these students are well aware that Matthews and Bradford are highly regarded in terms of academics, it stands to reason that they seek out colleges and universities that are also well known for their high academic standards and rigor. In line with the habitus of their schools, focal low-income Black students do not ever consider two-year schools; however, when weighing a given four-year school's viability, they begin to measure its academic reputation against that of their secondary school's reputation, reflecting a shift in their own definition of "good" college, as noted above. Black student participants, most pointedly Nathan Vasquez and Lucy Vargas, state that to attend Matthews (or Bradford) for four years and then attend a less competitive or noncompetitive college or university is "a waste." Attending a noncompetitive local school, which, by and large, would be a "reach school" for their peers in predominantly Black public schools, is now barely considered a "backup" for these students, as their thinking about college has been shaped by the elite private school habitus.

Importantly, the postsecondary schools that students consider and where they ultimately apply depend heavily on where they, as individuals, are situated within the opportunity structure of the school. Black focal students understand that if their SAT scores and GPAs do not match what a given college lists as normative for its current freshman class, then that particular school may be out of reach, This again reflects absorption of the myriad distinctions embedded within postsecondary classification and ranking systems—understandings that now go well beyond the two-year versus four-year distinction that they employ when reflecting on the options of their public school peers.

Just as focal Black students analyze the academic cultures of their school in creating their lists, they additionally analyze the social and cultural context of their school. As will become further evident in chapter 6, low-income Black focal students spend a significant amount of time scrutinizing their school's raced and classed cultures. Students discuss feeling a sense of "culture shock" transitioning into these schools, and grapple with loneliness and awkwardness on a day-to-day basis. Living as "outsiders within" for four years (and perhaps even longer, if they entered in middle school), they collectively seek to attend colleges and universities that are not only academically rigorous but also racially diverse, thereby offering ample opportunities to be around other Black people. When looking at schools' websites or attending college representatives' presentations, they routinely ask questions about the racial diversity on various campuses and whether particular schools have cultural- or diversity-related clubs and activities. Schools with low percentages of Blacks (or people of color more broadly) and/or that do not seem to place high priority on diversity-based student activities are not looked upon as favorably as those that fare better in these areas, while simultaneously known to be "good" schools academically.

Seeking "Good" Colleges

Black focal students are clear that attending a private secondary school that is well known for its academic caliber exerts a profound impact on their thoughts and decisions with respect to college. As stated earlier, all low-income Black focal students focus on gaining entrance to "good" four-year schools, and there is no discussion of the two-year college sector. While students state that they would have had similar desires had they attended predominantly Black urban public schools, they simultaneously insist that their academic preparation, access to information, determination and focus, and potential financial support were strongly enhanced by attending a private secondary school. Student college choices further reveal how attendance at elite private schools has shaped their perspective with regard to viable colleges. For example, schools such as Sarah Lawrence, which send college representatives to Matthews and Bradford, rarely show up on the lists of students in the predominantly Black/Latino urban public schools of Blair. Once students experience Matthews or Bradford, however, Sarah Lawrence, Skidmore, and the like often surface as possible and even likely postsecondary destinations.

In discussing her friends who attend a predominantly Black urban public high school, Breanna reflects on her preparation for college and the extent to which her nonprivate school peers are being prepared:

BREANNA: Sometimes I tell my dad I can't wait to get out of here [Bradford]. I feel bad, and it's kind of like I don't appreciate what he's doing (by sending me here). But, one thing I can say was the education was definitely worth the money. They [teachers] prepared me so much. My friends [outside of school] are like "I got an A." I'm like "Do you do any papers?" they say, "No," and I'm like "Oh, well, I get As and I do *lots* of papers [emphasis hers]."

HEATHER: Your friends at public schools in the city?

BREANNA: Yeah. I know when I need to get my stuff done; I know how I need to do it. I've become more organized and I think it's definitely prepared me for college, 'cause a lot of the courses that I take are like college courses. Like I told you [during a previous conversation], my anatomy class, it's definitely like college style, and so I think it's definitely prepared me.

HEATHER: And the writing was one of the things that you . . .

BREANNA: Yes, definitely the writing. I never had to do so many essays, like five-page or ten-page essays. I know some of my friends [who are in] college, are like "Oh I have to do a five-page essay," and I'm like "Oh, I'm doing that now!" . . . If I went to [a predominantly Black urban public school] I probably would have gotten maybe, *maybe* an essay a month, whereas I get between two and five essays from different classes in a month here.

HEATHER: So you feel that your preparation is a lot stronger than your friends?

BREANNA: Yes, definitely!

Several students—most pointedly Breanna (Bradford), Mark (Matthews), and Lucy (Matthews)—suggest that their peers who attend predominantly Black urban public high schools have a "different mindset" about college and their future opportunities. When asked specifically if they feel that the above noted lack of preparation and "different mindset" is attributable to the students as people or the schools as institutions, students overwhelmingly locate core explanatory factors within the institutions themselves. Marie Thompson (Matthews) sums up this point most succinctly:

MARIE: The students, I mean, in the public schools, want to go to college, but I don't think they set as high of expectations for themselves as someone that has a better background in school.

HEATHER: So, do you think it's the students or the schools?

MARIE: I think it's the schools.

HEATHER: Why do you think that?

MARIE: I just don't think they have as much materials. I don't know how to word it. The teachers probably care (in the predominantly Black urban publics), but there's so many more people that they have to look after, and then there's some people that slip through. . . . Like there are some people there that are so smart, smarter than people at my school, but it just seems like they get so much negativity from their schools. . . .

Given these data, it is not surprising that when responding to questions regarding how their high school years shaped their thoughts about college, students most often reference the academic reputation and prestige of the colleges and universities on their lists, and the extent to which this is related to the reputation and prestige of their secondary school. Angela Simmons states that her top choice, Sarah Lawrence College, "parallels Bradford in a lot of ways. [It is] a very old accredited institution [with] really good academics." When Angela notes that Sarah Lawrence "parallels" Bradford, she is measuring the reputation of Sarah Lawrence against that of Bradford, and the degree to which offerings at Sarah Lawrence will complement and extend what she has already gained academically by virtue of her current secondary school. As such, those institutions considered less competitive and noncompetitive are not considered to be viable options by Angela and her peers. Likewise, Steven concurs:

> Well, at Matthews I get an academically challenging education. And you have to keep your grades up. They offer so many AP classes that you're immersed in all this work, and all these extracurriculars. I'm the head of five clubs . . . and I'm in chorus. And just being at Matthews, and the competition available, has just pushed me so far. Now I'm looking back, and I'm like, I can get into some of the best schools in the country, and it's because of the atmosphere here and everything they offer, everything they push you to do, that you're able to get yourself into, and then go further with it. . . . It's all that combined with all the academic stuff, and that makes me see that *the sky's the limit* for any place I want to go.

Steven later explains how Matthews shaped his college outlook and options:

> I think there are two factors to this, one being the academic course load that's available for me. I'm in five AP classes and I've been in all Honors classes since my freshman year. And that, combined with how the teachers teach you, and how well they know what they teach, and how well they can teach it to you, and the reputation of the school, helps a lot. I always hear people say, "You go to Matthews, you can get into any college that you want to." My friend from church, that was actually a direct quote from her. So, I think everything inside of Matthews, and the aura associated with Matthews, will help get me into any school I want to go to, as long as I keep my grades up and I'm a well-rounded student.

Steven, however, is very clear that these are *his* advantages and opportunities (with regard to course offerings and placement), and that such advantages are not uniformly available to all Matthews students, particularly low-income Black students. In fact, he repeatedly notes that there are few students of color, and virtually *no* other low-income Black students, in his AP classes. Even so, the majority of low-income Black students in this study, including those with far less stellar academic records than Steven, maintain that the reputation of their school, in conjunction with the basic college structure that helps to facilitate the process, will enable entrance to the postsecondary destination of their choice. Nathan states:

> You have a lot of people [at Matthews] who are familiar with and close to the college process, like Dave Henderson. The school and the teachers are known in the college world. They have strong reputations. So when [college admissions] people look at my record here, they know I've come from a quality school. . . . And, like, I'm gonna compare all the academic and extracurricular stuff [at a given college] to all the Matthews stuff. If they [a college] don't have somethin' that's similar to what I have at Matthews, I won't really look at the school.

In a separate conversation, Nathan talks at length about reviewing his college essay, several times, with his English teacher, Dr. Reynolds. According to Nathan, Dr. Reynolds spent significant time in discussion with Nathan, prompting and guiding him through the process of crafting a thoughtful, thought-provoking essay related to a critical childhood event. Based on this and similar experiences, Nathan and his peers firmly believe that they have a clear advantage in the college process in relation to those "left behind" in underresourced urban high schools. Although they largely feel that "they go it alone" with regard to the college admissions process, students are clearly aware of the advantage conferred by attendance at an elite secondary school.

Several issues are at work here. On the one hand, low-income Black students objectively constitute "outsiders within." They neither have the economic, social, cultural, nor racial capital nor the status to mark them as *clear* insiders. The fact that they enter the school at an academic disadvantage relative to most other entering students means that they are doubly marked as *academic* outsiders, as they simply do not possess the educational background of most other students in their respective institutions and are therefore placed in the lowest-level classes. This is particularly true at Matthews, which has a more intense track structure than Bradford (where there is no "bottom" group as there are only two levels—Honors and Regular, due to the size of the school).

This placement takes on a caste-like quality for this particular group of students, the vast majority of whom are now visibly situated and continue to be situated in the lowest-level classes through the duration of their secondary school career. As such, a particular combination of race and class is structurally "marked" in and by the school as less academically capable. Although largely due to their prior academic experiences in poorly

resourced public schools, wherein "catching up" is difficult, it is additionally due to the fact that the school does not take seriously enough the
potential of these students to climb the track structure—in other words,
get out of the lowest classes. Given prior academic preparation in relation
to the more privileged student body, this would require that resources be
specifically devoted to this end—extensive teacher time in the form of
extra classes and so forth. Although there are certainly White students
situated in the lowest-level classes, they do not stand out as a visible presence in the way that the Black students do. Additionally, as White students
are dispersed throughout the track structure, there is no sense that Whites
disproportionately populate low-level classes in the way that they are seen
to be populated by low-income Black students. The fact that there are a
notable, but small, number of people of color in top-track classes compli-
cates this scenario, but does not fundamentally challenge it, a topic that
will be taken up at length in chapter 6.

Course placement patterns clearly establish a sustained "bottom
group" that is marked by race and class. This not only further denotes
these students as "outsiders within," but sets up and reinforces a false notion that this group is simply "less intelligent." Clearly this is not an intentional move on the part of the school, but neither does the school make
intentional moves to provide the kind of extra help that would pierce this
particularly located caste form. Although the felt impact of this structural
arrangement is not clear, it is arguably the case that the low-income Black
students—all of whom were marked as exceptionally intelligent and hard
working before entering the school—now question this designation, as
within the confines of the elite private school, they inhabit the "bottom."
This may work to somewhat erode their own academic confidence and
prowess that brought them into the school to begin with. In spite of this,
focal students are well aware of the considerable advantages with regard
to the college admissions process that are conferred as a result of attendance at elite private schools. As a consequence, they express great pride
in being Matthews and Bradford students while simultaneously feeling
clearly marked as "outsiders within."

Such status is made more complex by the fact that low-income Black
students do not compare themselves in a sustained way to those whom
they themselves mark as "other" inside their respective schools. Although
certainly not unaware of differences between themselves and more privileged students who are largely but not entirely White, their *own* consistently constructed "other" must be understood as predominantly Black

urban public schools and the student's Black neighborhood peers who remain in such schools. In contrast to the articulated dampening of expectations and poor academic quality that marks the experience of their friends who still attend urban publics, students at Matthews and Bradford emphatically state that "the sky's the limit" and that they can get into the best colleges in the country based on their attendance at elite private secondary schools. Although they *absolutely* sustain this belief in the face of those "left behind" in predominantly Black urban public institutions, their everyday felt status inside their elite private schools prompts them to think seriously, at least initially, about placing themselves in highly regarded postsecondary schools with sociocultural environments that better match their biographies.

SEEKING DIVERSITY.   When developing the list of colleges to which they plan to apply, students state that their primary concern is the academic caliber of any given postsecondary institution. Secondarily, at least at the initial stages of the college search process, they seek a diverse environment, which primarily means finding an institution that is not overwhelmingly White—an environment that is markedly different from that of Bradford or Matthews, where students can "be comfortable" and interact with people of different racial and ethnic backgrounds. Students at Matthews and Bradford express strong desire to find and connect with other Black students and adults.

LEILA: I'm definitely gonna pick a school that's like racially diverse, one that has an equal number of like minorities and an equal number of [Whites] so I don't have to be isolated. 'Cause in other places, like at home [in my neighborhood], I'm not isolated, and I don't want to feel that way, I want to be friends with everyone. . . . Everyone here [Matthews] is like "Oh, she's really quiet. She doesn't really talk to anyone. She's so focused on her school work all the time, that's why she doesn't want to talk." And that's not the case. I just don't feel comfortable sometimes.

Leila explicitly references the impact of her marginalized class and race status on her school experience. The discomfort and isolation that Leila notes is directly related to being among a relatively small number of low-income Blacks, and this has a profound impact on where she initially plans to apply to college. Similarly, Mark expresses his desire to attend a Historically Black College:

HEATHER: OK, so tell me about applying to a Historically Black College from Matthews.

MARK: I think that I felt that I needed something different from Matthews. My biggest fear for some reason is [going] to a college that's just a bigger Matthews, 'cause Matthews is basically a college-style high school.

HEATHER: You don't want small liberal arts?

MARK: That's like with the same bubble, same filters, same group of people, just a little bit bigger than Matthews. I want a whole different experience. The reason why I liked Howard so much is 'cause there was a bunch of people who looked like me for a change. . . . I liked the brotherhood that's associated with Howard. There's a certain connection that I'll have with my fellow classmates that I really can't get at Matthews, which I was missing from Matthews. So, I think that's part of the psychology behind it.

Mark's desire to attend a Historically Black College, thereby experiencing a sense of "brotherhood," is directly related to his experience at Matthews, where he is one of a very small number of Black males in his class. For similar reasons, Breanna also wants to attend a Historically Black College:

Well, that's the thing, coming out of here [Bradford] I want to go to a Historically Black College, 'cause I feel like I've lost all connection with like, I don't know, not *all* connection, but I feel like I don't have that connection with some of my friends anymore, and I just want to get back into that. So I was looking into a Historically Black College like Fisk because they have a nice accounting program.[4]

In point of fact, all Breanna's self-identified "close friends" are Black and attend an urban public high school. Sadly, she feels that her years at Bradford have served to drive a wedge between herself and her closest friends, wherein many now charge that she acts and speaks like a White girl (a point to be explored in the next chapter). Feeling "lonely and awkward" as one of the few low-income Black students at Bradford, Breanna strategically melds her desire for a strong accounting program with her desire to be around Black students and faculty. Importantly, Breanna and other low-income Black students reflect a much larger felt and articulated desire to mesh academic excellence with access to greater racial diversity and particularly a broadened Black community, a dual sentiment that arguably stems from her experiences in the elite private sector. As Breanna notes, she desires to find a place that will build upon and extend the knowledge she gained at Bradford, while affording her the opportunity to "be around people I would identify with more." She continues:

> 'Cause being here is hard to kind of, you know, I go around seeing people that don't look like me, that don't come from where I come from, that don't have similar backgrounds. It would just be more comforting to be around people who you can identify [with].

Overall, low-income Black students find little common ground with their largely White and privileged counterparts and, in the early stages of applying to college, look for postsecondary environments that offer greater diversity than their current secondary schools. This does not apply to Steven, however; he maintains strong relationships with non-Blacks given his successful negotiation of the dominant academic and cultural habitus of Matthews Academy.

Shaping Students' College Admissions Processes

As McDonough (1997), Cookson and Persell (1985), Howard (2007), Gaztambide-Fernández (2009), and others note, elite private schools, whether day or boarding, employ full-time, highly experienced college counselors who enact college counseling processes that are unrivaled by both affluent publics and less prestigious privates. Such college application and admissions processes (Avery, Fairbanks, and Zeckhauser 2003; Stevens 2007) have been ramped up considerably in recent years, at times kicking off with a freshman year parent meeting, largely in response to demand from the dominant privileged parent population.[5] Overwhelmingly, scholarly literature focuses on college application and admissions processes with respect to White middle- and upper-middle-class students and parents (Avery et al. 2003; Stevens 2007), and little attention is paid to the experiences and practices of other groups. Although Zweigenhaft and Domhoff (1991, 2003) and others focus on Black students in elite privates during an earlier time period, there is scant attention to this group in current context.

Given what we know about the barriers to college access for Black and/or low-income youth more generally (Heller 2002; Perna 2000; Thomas and Bell 2008), it might be assumed that Black students coming from academically impoverished backgrounds, whose families lack financial and/or particular kinds of social and cultural capital, would seek out the expertise of the college counselors and that the counselors would actively work to ensure that these students have access to their considerable resources. For the majority of low-income Black students, however, this simply is not the case.

Role of the College Counselors

College counselors at Matthews and Bradford stress that one of the goals of the college application process is for students to exercise their own sense of agency and "drive" and subsequently "own" the process. As Dave Henderson states: "Matthews seeks to empower students to control, or own the process, if you will. So it's *their* process, and not someone else's, i.e., parents or grandparents."[6] Likewise, Gayle Johnson of Bradford notes: "Whatever I can do to empower a young woman and help her make decisions about her future, that should be my goal." Under this scenario, the college counselor serves only as a guide, preparing students to navigate their own paths toward college and beyond.

In contrast to the college counselors' stated expectations, low-income Black students are in fact the *only* group for which this is actually the case. Other than the basic information about the college admissions process available and distributed to all students in the school via all-class meetings and visits from college representatives, low-income Black students in fact *do* "own" the process, unlike their more privileged counterparts as we see in chapter 4. Ironically then, they are the only group to enact what the school expects of *all* students, but does not, in fact, get. In a context of deep privilege where parents seek to micromanage the college admissions process so as to ensure maximum advantage for their own children, it is the "outsiders within" who feel marginalized by the process in light of the actions and activities of their more privileged counterparts, while being the only group to actually comply with expressed school expectations.

Specifically referring to students from relatively low-income backgrounds, counselors at Matthews and Bradford maintain that the college admissions process for low-income Black students, other than the need for more financial aid and fewer Early Decision applications, does not differ markedly from that of the dominant group. Data from student and parent interviews, however, suggest otherwise. College counselors maintain that they, as individuals, as opposed to school-related counseling resources and services more broadly, figure prominently in dispensing information and advice that shapes students' lists of possible colleges and subsequent college-related decisions, irrespective of student background characteristics or academic position in the graduating class.

In striking contrast to data reported in chapter 4, where students highlight the role of both their parents and the college counselors, when asked where and how they gather information as they create their initial college lists, focal Black students note the following, in order of importance: (1) college representative visits to their schools; (2) conversations with faculty and other students; (3) books and literature found in the senior lounge or college office; (4) online research conducted alone and/or with a parent or parents; and (5) conversations with alumni of color. When asked directly about the role of their college counselor, resultant data reveal an interesting paradox: While students maintain that their schools employ high-quality college counselors, and they, in fact, articulate in great detail the expertise of these counselors, low-income Black students overwhelmingly note that they have little interaction with them. Lucy, for example, touts the positive function of the counselor, who is specifically devoted to the college admissions process:

> I feel like they make it very well known that you have a plethora of options. I don't know how college counselors work at public schools and other schools. I don't know if they, I don't know how they work, so it's nice to have a college counselor who's *just* a college counselor and dedicated to that. . . . And [they] can give you advice and can say, maybe you should go to this school, 'cause it seems really good for you. It's nice having that. I don't know if other schools are like that, but it's helpful having that here [at Matthews].

Yet when asked where she obtains information about possible colleges and advice about "fit," Lucy does not reference the counselor at all but rather a White peer whose father went to an elite college, a peer who informs and reminds her of forms and deadlines, visits by college representatives to the school, and various college and university websites. This is not to say that all other students in the class have vast amounts of the time and attention of the college counselors that could and should be devoted to low-income Black students, but simply to point out that, for a variety of reasons, low-income Black students do not consistently access counselor expertise, even though they are highly aware of and express great respect for it.

In this regard, it is possible that low-income Black students do not feel entitled to demand the attention and time of their college counselors, unlike far more privileged students who have been groomed to seek out and expect the attention of powerful professionals. This is reminiscent of Lareau's (2000, 2003) research on class-linked patterns of childrearing, where, based on long-term in-depth ethnographic investigation with families across social class and race, poor and working-class families—White and Black—do not impart a sense of entitlement and comfort with powerful and privileged professionals. This is in sharp contrast to comparably gathered data on middle- and upper-middle-class families—White and Black—who explicitly raise their children to expect the attention of those in authority and to feel comfortable in the presence of those who possess it.[7] Given that these students do not experience the elite educational institution as *their* space—but rather as "outsiders within"—the fact that focal students do not routinely interact with their college counselors is not surprising. In point of fact, many focal students felt more comfortable interacting with Heather, directing questions to her about the college process during the interviews, rather than approach their counselors directly.

Lucy's experience is comparable to that of most students in our low-income Black sample, almost all of whom note that while they recognize the expertise of the college counselors, they do not avail themselves of this expertise by actually meeting with them. Steven, a highly successful low-income Black student who has been consistently placed in all top-track courses since freshman year, is the only low-income Black student to tell a markedly different story. Responding to a question about his meetings with the head of college counseling at Matthews, Steven states:

> They've been going well. I had my third meeting with him [Dave Henderson] last week and I have my top 13 schools I'm applying to. I'm only applying Early Decision to one school. My grades are solid. My course load, he [Dave Henderson] said, looks solid, 'cause that's important. He wants me to get all As this semester to show "intellectual promise" 'cause colleges prize that. He wants me to take the ACT and the SAT subject test. . . .

Steven maintains that while his mother is very supportive and involved in his life, and has lots of *opinions* regarding the college process, it is Dave Henderson, with his 30 years of full-time college counseling experience, who is central in shaping his search and application process. Notably, Steven is the *only* low-income Black student from Matthews or Bradford who narrates this level of guidance and support from a college counselor. Perhaps by virtue of his position in the opportunity structure of the school, he is the only low-income Black student who feels comfortable enough to demand Dave Henderson's time and energy. The majority of low-income Black students do not meet one on one with their counselors at all (outside of the initial meeting required of all second-semester juniors), in spite of the fact that they are encouraged to meet on a regular basis.[8]

Steven recognizes that his experience in the school, both academically and socioculturally, is vastly different from that of other low-income Black students. He speaks at length about the lack of Black students in his Honors and AP courses and how this and other sociocultural factors (the fact that he is, as he states, "the un-Black male," a point to which we return in chapter 6) positions him differently in relation to the dominant culture of the school. Looking at Steven's considerable accomplishments at Matthews and his academic promise moving into college, it is no accident that he both seeks out and obtains intensive and sustained college counseling. As a Black, low-income male who performed exceptionally well in all Honors and AP courses at an elite secondary school, Steven is positioned toward the top of his class, which both privileges him over many other students, Black and White, with regard to the college process and makes him feel relatively more comfortable than other low-income Black students with respect to the overall habitus of the school.

Based on his academic standing and personal accomplishments, Steven has the confidence as well as the personal cultural, social, and academic capital to effectively navigate the college counseling process, thereby turning himself into a high priority for Dave Henderson, who seeks to place students in the best possible postsecondary destinations both for their sake and to further the reputation of the school as a center of academic excellence and outstanding college matriculation outcomes. By and large, however, Matthews and Bradford low-income Black students do not access the college counseling office to the same extent as their economically and socially privileged peers. In point of fact, many low-income Black students do not feel comfortable approaching the counselor at all.

As noted in chapter 4, not all students at Matthews are from privileged backgrounds, nor does social class map neatly onto academic standing in the school, as there are many students of privileged background who are not in the top 20% of the class. What is clear, however, is that *all* students across class and race/ethnicity with top academic standing feel comfortable in accessing the college counselors on a regular basis, as this both becomes normative practice within this top group (not all of whom are White and/or privileged) *and* such students feel more than comfortable approaching the counselor given their academic success.

It is also clearly evident that low-income Black students, with the exception of Steven, do not access the college counselors at all. While it is certainly true that not all privileged students use the college counseling services to the same extent, such privileged students, irrespective of their position in the academic hierarchy of the school, have highly educated parents who can help them through the process. Low-income Black students, in contrast, are largely left to their own devices with regard to figuring out *how* to actualize the increasingly complex college admission process. Their expressed feeling of being substantially adrift embodies, in contradictory fashion, their deep respect for the institution with regard to strong academics and impressive counseling services at one and the same time that they sense that they are not really part of it.

Although a number of students, like Mark, Sarah, and Marie from Matthews, assert that they and their parents (only one of whom attended a four-year college) have the college process well under control, it is clear that they are doing this absent explicit guidance from the college counselor. For example, in spite of the fact that Marie and her mother state that they have the process fully under control, when asked to speak about her experiences with Dave Henderson, Marie indicates that she does not have a relationship with him at all and that both she and her mother are dissatisfied with the few interactions Marie has had with him. She indicates that her meetings feel rushed—that Dave Henderson "threw" large chunks of information and materials at her, and sent her on her way to make sense of it on her own. In spite of having to "go it alone," Marie and her mother draw upon information obtained from college representative visits, college websites, and the plethora of college resource materials and lists of available scholarships that are posted in the counseling office. Although Marie and her mother have amassed a great deal of information with respect to the college process, neither she nor her mother know what to do with this information once they get it. Marie has no connection to the counselors and her mother did not attend college, leaving them collectively adrift with regard to how to actualize the process so as to be advantageous to Marie.

To be fair to Dave Henderson, he repeatedly states that students must "own the process." It is also arguably the case that Marie is not the only student who does not get all of the handholding that they want or need from their college counselors. For example, after discussing her relationship with Dave Henderson, Marie asked Heather about the difference between applying Early Decision and Early Action, a topic that is often discussed during both college advisory meetings and the college seminar course. It is noteworthy that Marie, who is still unsure of the difference, feels more comfortable asking Heather during the interview than explicitly seeking out Dave Henderson to ask for further clarification.

Rather than approach their college counselors directly, several other Matthews and Bradford students direct questions to Heather about the college process, such as Nathan's inquiry about what his SAT scores mean (whether they are average or below average). This suggests that the vast majority of low-income Black students, who are indeed "outsiders within," are unsure *how* to go about gaining access to an array of resources inside their resource-rich elite private schools without making themselves look uneducated or creating more discomfort for themselves and their parents. Unlike their more privileged and largely White classmates as well as the Cannondale students, they do not have the advantage of highly educated parents who routinely clarify points that students find confusing. As a result, low-income Black students, with the clear exception of Steven, flounder when trying to execute the intricacies of the college admissions process virtually alone.

As noted above, Lareau (2003) suggests that low-income parents, both Black and White, neither explicitly groom their children to advocate for themselves nor teach them how to negotiate with a broad-based adult community. While White and Black middle- and upper-middle-class parents engage in the concerted cultivation (Lareau 2003) of their children, prepping them to demand access to resources and information and to enter into negotiations with adults in positions of power, lower-middle-class, working-class, and poor parents do not cultivate such skills in their children, given that they themselves do not engage them on a routine basis. It is possible, then, that many of the low-income students and parents do not know how to access information or gain clarification from their college counselors and, most important perhaps, do not possess a deep sense of comfort or entitlement to do so.

Additionally, unlike privileged Matthews and Cannondale parents who engage in direct negotiations with school personnel on an "as necessary" basis, low-income Black parents do not engage direct negotiations with the school, nor do they intervene in the ongoing work of the institution on behalf of their children.[9] Similarly, they do not pick up the phone and call the college counselor, an action routinely engaged by privileged parents as they and their children collectively engage the college process. In light of the fact that their children feel like "outsiders within" even though they attend these schools every day for ten months of the year, it is certainly understandable why low-income Black parents are reluctant to approach the college counselor themselves. Regardless of student and parent comfort level with the college counseling apparatus, there is no question that the school should take more responsibility for this population of students, as students should not be punished for their "outsider within" status by a school that overtly celebrates their acceptance.

Based on his work in a predominantly White affluent suburban high school, Demerath (2009, p. 163) similarly suggests that Black students "did not adopt many of the same instrumental strategies oriented toward individual advancement as their White peers—especially the 'adult handling' and self-advocacy skills that could serve as effective negotiating tools." In both Demerath's case and our case, the status of "outsider within"—the status of having all formal rights, responsibilities, and privileges without commensurate cultural, social, and economic capital to navigate as a full insider—works to marginalize low-income Black students with regard to important aspects of the institution. Significantly, this is not the case for Steven, a low-income Black student who is positioned very differently in the opportunity structure of the school than all other low-income Black students in our sample.

In the final analysis, *formal* access in the guise of "making services available to everyone" does not guarantee comparable lived-out privilege. Although accorded access to elite private schools via special intake programs and funding linked to such "diversity" initiatives, the vast majority of low-income Black students do not reap benefits comparable to those of largely White and privileged students, given that maximum benefits of the site are increasingly dependent on the activation of particular forms of parental and familial capital and linked prior academic advantages, which low-income Black students do not have. Given the ramping up of the competition to the postsecondary sector, and the perceived centrality among privileged parents of the now hyper-competitive admissions process in their drive toward "locking in" advantage for the next generation, it is arguably the case that the "outsider within" status renders low-income Black students, with the exception of standouts like Steven, *increasingly marginalized at an on-the-ground level,* in the ever-intensifying race to postsecondary destinations. Although far more prestigious private secondary schools such as Trinity, Horace Mann, and the like may have greater resources to devote to college counseling services wherein counselors have enough time and resources to stay on top of everyone, this is not the case in schools like Bradford and Matthews, where resources are far more limited due to relatively low tuition (what the market will bear) and notably less robust endowments (see chapter 4).

Although justifiable in relation to available evidence, this argument must be rendered more complex by the fact that, as noted earlier in this chapter, low-income Black students do not compare themselves or their educational/college search experiences to those of their privileged classmates, but rather to those of the friends they left behind in increasingly underresourced public schools. Thus, in spite of their clear status of "outsiders within," low-income Black students by and large do not consistently focus on what they do *not* get in elite privates, but rather on what they *do* get by virtue of escaping schools that they would have attended had they not entered Matthews or Bradford.

There is, however, a glimmer of sustained critique of privilege with regard to what others get in the school that they don't. Breanna, for example, explicitly fingers the assumption of wealth and class/race privilege as embedded within the elite private school:

> Like, with our [Bradford college] counselor, we've needed help, but because they [the college counselors] assume that everyone has hired a private college counselor, that other people don't need help.[10] I know a lot of people in my class have hired college counselors, and I was talking to one of my [Black] friends, and we don't have that, and she [the college counselor] has stacks, literally stacks, of fee waivers for SATs and she hasn't told anyone about them, you had to ask for them. She's had fee waivers for college applications that would have really helped me if I would have known beforehand, but she hasn't told anybody about that. And I could have been applicable for a scholarship for [local state university], but because she didn't hand in my transcripts on time, they received it late [and] it didn't go in for the scholarship. I just don't think they really care too much.

Unfortunately, Breanna missed several class meetings on the college admissions process due to her part-time employment. However, this too has a distinctly class/race referent, as Breanna's need to have a part-time job means that she generally leaves school after her eighth-period class on Friday, as ninth-period Friday is often a free period, and she needs to take two metro buses to get to work on time. Unfortunately, ninth period is when Gayle Johnson gathers the class to discuss the college process, and such meetings are generally not planned far enough in advance for Breanna to adjust her work schedule. Breanna undoubtedly missed pertinent college information in her efforts to get to work, a demand clearly linked to her low-income status and expectation to help her family. The extent to which we can fault Gayle Johnson for holding impromptu meetings on the college process during regular school hours when all students are expected to be in attendance, however, is questionable. Unfortunately, as stated earlier, City Prep is not filling this gap for their students, and many low-income students enter private secondary schools via this program.[11]

In this chapter we detail the produced and lived-out marginalization of low-income Black students with regard to the college counseling process. As argued, this is linked both to the degree to which students seek out the college counseling services, as well as the fact that college counselors expect students to own the search and application process. Although this charge is leveled at *all* students in the school, low-income Black students are the *only* group, in fact, that explicitly actualizes this charge. The extent to which adolescents across the board can or will engage the process with vigor is, of course, questionable, but students from privileged backgrounds, like our privileged Matthews and Cannondale participants, have an arsenal of help if they fall short of expectations, including, as we see in chapter 4, an enacted willingness among parents, and particularly mothers, to step in and *themselves* own the process by metaphorically acting as their child's personal college counselor.

Beyond this, privileged parents routinely push their children: they drive them about on college tours often two years before the more formal process begins; activate their own educational and cultural capital by calling the college counselors on a regular basis with any and all concerns regarding their children's search and application process; and, if necessary, given substantial economic capital and accompanying discretionary income, hire a private college counselor in case their children still do not function at the "appropriate" and expected level.[12] If all this fails and children still do not engage the college admissions process with the expected attention and energy, privileged parents can and do use any and all available funds to arrange for a fifth year of secondary school at any one of a number of elite boarding schools that now offer, at a steep price, of course, a postgraduate year wherein students are specifically helped to assemble college admissions packets, receive extensive tutoring before taking the college entrance test for a third, fourth, or even fifth time, and/or generally be given the time and space necessary to "mature."[13]

Low-income parents are obviously not in a position to do any of this, as it takes a certain combination of cultural, economic, and educational capital to be able to accomplish this set of tasks. In the final analysis, it is low-income Black students who are left to engage the process, *as individuals*. The fact that low-income Black students handle the process themselves, rather than as surrounded by a larger privileged family and community that steps in at every turn, is made more acute by their particular status within elite institutions. As "outsiders within," this group of students does not feel empowered to approach school authorities so as to maximize advantage already embedded in their attendance at elite private schools. Thus, ironically, although "pushed ahead" by virtue of attending elite schools, they are potentially "left behind" (relative to their peers in privileged institutions), as fundamental class processes take over within the school itself, particularly in relation to course-taking patterns and the day-to-day and week-by-week work related to the college admissions process.

The sheer materiality of all this must be taken into account also. The college visits routinely made by privileged students and their parents, for example, cost money and require the types of professional and managerial jobs that allow parents control over their own work schedules.[14] So too there are myriad additional expenses, which can be considerable: application costs are high, and students from these schools apply to a large number of institutions (generally between 8 and 16); SAT prep courses, also routine in this sector, cost anywhere from $1,000 to $5,000, and many students take one or more such courses, dependent on their innate ability to score well on the SAT and/or ACT college entrance tests; and numerous sittings of the college entrance tests escalate already skyrocketing costs. Beyond this, privileged families monitor the grades of their children over their secondary school career, standing ready and willing to pay for private tutoring if students show any hint of falling behind in one or more courses. If all else fails or anxiety is sufficiently high, privileged families hire a private college counselor to spend targeted time on a student's dossier (student essays and so forth), a move clearly out of reach for low-income families. Ultimately, the "outsider within" is left to negotiate on his or her own, rendering the lack of connection with the college counselors particularly troubling.

Conclusion

The role of the elite private secondary school in the lives of low-income students warrants further attention. Despite their expressed frustration going through the process, these students continue to see themselves as highly privileged in the college search and application process, as they compare themselves largely to those left behind in schools that have undergone severe disinvestment over the past two decades, rather than to their more privileged counterparts in their current institution. Elite private schools remain highly classed and raced (Gaztambide-Fernández 2009; Howard 2007), in spite of the fact that students who were formerly not allowed entrance into these schools by virtue of class and race exclusionary processes are increasingly sought out, albeit in small numbers. Although members of the elite school community, possessing all formal rights and privileges comparable to those of their more privileged counterparts, it is worth remembering that the vast majority are not *fully* participating members, in that they do not have access to all highly valued academic and personal resources within the institution. While varying position in the internal opportunity structure is a key component here, in that placement in AP Calculus, AP Literature and Composition, and so forth becomes critical in terms of access to the best of what the school has to offer, it is also important to conceptualize this as a set of accumulated advantages that begin much earlier.

It is always possible, of course, to scale the track structure and earn the right to be placed in AP Calculus BC senior year, even if one attended an impoverished middle school. We must recognize, however, that this is highly unusual, as knowledge is cumulative and it is difficult to individually overcome the inadequacies of past preparation. Only systemic interruption of past academic inequalities via an extensive system of extra classes would even begin to address this issue. Similarly, although it is possible to feel empowered enough to routinely approach the college counselor with either complex or relatively mundane questions related to college admissions, as we see in this chapter, low-income students often do not necessarily feel entitled to do so (Lareau 2003).

That all students do not receive equal amounts of the college counselor's time is due to the fact that low-income Black students do not feel empowered to engage the counselor in this fashion, as well as the fact that the college counseling office expects all students "to own the process."

This lack of lived-out parity reveals the inherent limitations embedded in notions of equal educational opportunity in highly stratified societies, no matter how well intentioned such initiatives may be. This is particularly the case, perhaps, with respect to special intake programs that place students in private secondary schools, where it is fair to interrogate the extent to which students admitted under such programs can ever be full participants in a highly privileged environment. This does not come down to who skis on the weekend, who is able to wear pearls at graduation, who travels to the Caribbean over break, and so forth, which, quite frankly, has few long-term consequences with regard to leveraging educational benefit in relation to future class position (in using these examples, we do not mean to deny the *felt* consequences of such linked class/race marginalization among adolescents in elite secondary schools, which can be considerable). Rather, we draw attention to who, in current circumstances, possesses the accumulated social, cultural, and educational capital that enables and promotes full use of academic and personal resources in environments of deep privilege.

Although traditional notions of equal opportunity serve to open the access door—and this is not inconsequential—being physically present in a given institution does not guarantee equal access to resources and information. This is particularly the case as both movement through the structure of opportunities in any given institution and, more specifically in this case, the ability to *activate* broadly distributed college knowledge via what Bourdieu calls "know how" is highly linked to an architecture of capital accumulation wherein some have more relevant capital than others. The individual low-income Black student can always make it, of course, and Steven provides one example here. However, individual and collective logics are markedly different, and although an individual can always "make it," the class can never follow.

Peter Demerath's (2009, pp. 167–168) work usefully affirms this point:

It is possible that minority students in particular were ill-served by the school's assumption that ceding control to students and accommodating their preferences would help them succeed. This well-intentioned means of supporting student success positions the student as the arbiter of judgment with regard to how to go about garnering the credentials and distinctions necessary for educational and occupational success. In the case of African American students, such logic presumes that all students have an adequate familiarity with the explicit and implicit rules of academic success.

While the students in Demerath's study and the students in our study have equal access to resources as per a traditional definition of equal opportunity, the architecture of capital accumulation as linked to class and race privileges accorded since birth serve to stratify, in a highly on-the-ground fashion, what we call differentially located *opportunities in practice*, particularly in highly privileged institutions.

At both a concrete and visceral level, elite schools know that many of these students do not bring with them the implicit and explicit rules (Delpit 2006) for academic and college admissions success that is necessary for full membership in such schools. As we indicate in chapter 4, although all students are told to "be drivers of their own college admissions process," privileged students are enveloped in a set of human- and capital-based relations that scaffold an arsenal of capital and privilege, thereby serving to encourage and enable already advantaged students to (over) perform in competitive environments.

This is not to take anything away from the hard work of privileged students, many of whom work very hard to gain advantage in increasingly competitive circumstances. Indeed, no prior generation of Americans has had to work as hard as our current youth to gain or maximize advantage as they attempt to position for the now "global auction" (Brown, Lauder, and Ashton 2011). Our point is not that privileged students do not work nor that such students do not deserve what they get, but rather that they are deeply enveloped by their own located forms of already existing class privilege that take on particular meaning and significance in the early twenty-first century. As struggles for the production and reproduction of privilege become ever more contentious and brutally waged within secondary schools via attempts to position for postsecondary admissions, "outsiders within," although allowed access, have more difficulty in finding ground to academically compete.

The particular shape and form that this takes in the elite private secondary school sector deserves further consideration. Low-income Black students, as well as low-income Latino, Native American, and other groups, enter elite secondary schools through a combination of proactivity (e.g., City Prep, various foundations that support such ventures, and so forth) and the schools' own internal measures to recruit a more diverse student body, as such schools both want to temper the charge of elitism and simultaneously offer genuine opportunities for low-income individuals, particularly students of color. With regard to the issue of access, then, the goal of the school and that of the students and parents converge. This is the case, however, for arguably different reasons: Private schools want to increase their systemic diversity with regard to their "bottom-line" admissions profile, and students and parents seek to enhance their educational and social mobility, a point that comes through clearly in the data presented in this chapter.

However, once the access barrier has been pierced, relevant primary group goals no longer converge. Students and their parents retain their original goal of garnering a top education both at the secondary and postsecondary level. Significantly, the definition of a "good" college perceptively shifts during the course of their secondary school career, at least among the students. Absorbing the much discussed hierarchical ranking schemata with regard to a range of postsecondary destinations, low-income students no longer focus only on the two-year versus four-year distinction, but now employ a more complicated set of qualitative indicators much more in line with privileged students and privileged populations more generally. In this sense, the goals of the students are brought into even closer alignment with the matriculation goals embedded in the overall culture of the school.

In contrast, once elite secondary schools augment the diversity of their student body, which is arguably a subgoal, they largely return to their *primary* goal, which is to maximize postsecondary outcomes with regard to the institution in such a way as to enable them to build upon and retain the reputation that served to attract its student body to begin with. In so doing, they work to reinforce their position as *elite* institutions, a goal that largely rests upon a proportion of their student body entering apex and "Most Competitive" postsecondary schools. As a consequence, elite secondary schools end up placing *their focus less on the individual student* and his or her movement through the track structure and use of college counseling services than on maximizing overall institutional matriculation outcomes, while making certain that apex institutions continue to be represented.

We see in this chapter, for example, that it becomes the student's responsibility to optimize the voluminous opportunities offered at Matthews and Bradford with respect to college counseling, rather than the school's responsibility to make certain that *each* student enters the most prestigious institution that he or she can. In this sense, whether intentional or not, from the school's perspective, once students gain access to the institution, the question of equal opportunity is moot, as all students are now in the same institution and theoretically possess the same opportunities.

In this volume, we challenge in key ways the notion that equal access automatically leads to equal opportunities. To begin with, privileged parents, as we see in chapter 4, now micromanage their children's press toward class advantage, leaving nothing to chance. Whereas in the past, sheer attendance at elite secondary schools was often enough to ensure entrance to Harvard, Yale, Princeton, and other Ivy League institutions, this is no longer the case. As we suggest earlier, the current struggle over entrance into a broader range of "Most Competitive" and "Highly Competitive+" institutions has, for a variety of reasons (as detailed in chapter 1), become increasingly intense. In light of the ramping up of the college admissions frenzy, privileged parents work harder than ever to position their children for selective college admissions from a very young age. This works to disadvantage low-income populations generally and, most particularly in this case, low-income Black students who attend elite secondary schools, such as those in this volume, who now find little ground to compete.

Second, as mentioned above, the primary goal of elite schools, aside from offering a challenging curriculum, is to get their students into the best colleges possible while achieving continued representation at apex postsecondary institutions. Achieving such representation enhances the bottom line of the college process as seen from the schools' perspective, in that parents will continue to send their children to these schools only if such attendance works to their children's clear advantage in the college admissions process. For this reason, it becomes imperative that such institutions keep up their profile of top college acceptances. To accomplish this, schools work to maximize possibilities via highly challenging curricular offerings for top-track students and, increasingly, school-based linkages with prominent faculty members at local universities that enable students to participate, in delimited fashion, on funded research teams. In the latter instance, students, can, at times, engage joint presentations at national conferences that are orchestrated by university faculty members and/or participate on multiauthored scientific papers that are ultimately published in peer-review journals. Needless to say, all such experiences are strategically woven into college admissions dossiers, thereby enhancing possibilities for acceptance at exceptionally competitive institutions. Such opportunities tend to be reserved for students positioned at the apex of the secondary school opportunity structure.

Attewell (2001) makes a similar point with regard to public schools that serve affluent students. Such schools, he argues, which he refers to as "winner take all" institutions, work to maximize possibilities for those students at the very top of the secondary school academic hierarchy, leaving all remaining students unable to access opportunities even close to what these high-end students receive by virtue of their position in the opportunity structure. Privileged institutions, then, arguably work to position a top group for possible entrance to the most valued postsecondary destinations, a finding that is additionally confirmed in the Cannondale example in chapter 3. For this reason, low-income Black students who are almost entirely placed in the lowest-level classes become a much lower priority for the college counselors and the school more generally. This is in spite of the fact that such private secondary schools seek out such students to diversify their populations.

To be clear here, this outcome is certainly not intentional on the part of the school, the college counselors, or school personnel more broadly. These practices, in fact, sit at the juncture of competing institutional goals. As it is arguably the case that expensive private schools would cease to exist if parents did not see value in sending their children to such institutions by virtue of top college placements, the goal of enhancing the college admissions profile and, in particular, landing a respectable number of acceptances at top Ivy League institutions each year takes precedence over all others, no matter how worthy they may be.

Steven, of course, is a great success story, while simultaneously confirming the above analysis. It is Steven's academic standing in the AP/Honors classes that bring him to the attention of the counselor and other relevant school personnel. That he is a low-income Black student is important in one sense, as he represents the success of this particular diversity initiative. However, it must be understood that Steven, in spite of the fact that his mother does not micromanage the college admissions process in the way that parents of privileged students do, would gain the attention of the college counseling staff no matter who he was, as his anticipated success in the college admissions process will bring great credit to the school. In contrast, the vast majority of low-income Black students will attain no such stature with regard to college admissions and therefore do not constitute an obvious priority for the school's college counselor. As students are expected to "drive" the college admissions process themselves, the fact that they do not regularly seek out their counselors only reinforces suspicions that they do not work hard enough to maximize their own possibilities. In this sense, a standout student like Steven serves to symbolically indicate that if one works hard enough, any and all personal, academic, and economic handicaps can be overcome.

Given the above analysis, the assumption that "access," in and of itself, promotes equal opportunity must be called into question. Our data press toward the conclusion that by exercising facially neutral policies and

practices (in other words, a policy or practice that is neutral toward all affected groups; e.g., each student gets a college counselor and then the onus
is on the student to take the college process and "make it his or her own"),
we perpetuate race/class inequalities within elite schools, as such policies
do not acknowledge or take into account that a particular "class" of students is negatively impacted by virtue of prior background. Although this
is certainly not the intent of such schools, neither do they work to seriously
interrupt these eventualities.

We turn now to chapter 6, where we addresses issues of institutionalized
and peer racism from the perspective of the low-income Black students
themselves, specifically exploring the most overt messages of racial difference that affect students' individual experiences within the school. In addition, we take up the differences between privileged parents and students
of color—multigenerational and/or "flexible immigrants" of color—and
low-income Black parents and students, subsequently theorizing the critical intersection of race and class in privileged educational sites. In so doing, we consider the extent to which particular kinds of diversity initiatives
in elite schools unintentionally instantiate a narrow and stereotypical construction of Blackness—one from which low-income Black students feel
compelled to distance at one and the same time as they find little common
ground between themselves and an increasingly visible population of students of color whose class habitus mirrors that of the school. At the end
of chapter 6, we detail the matriculation outcomes of students across our
three school sectors and student populations.

CHAPTER SIX

Race and Class Matters

I am a Black Girl nothing more, nothing less. — (Christina Gibbons, Matthews student)

In chapter 5, we focus on the unintended consequences of facially neutral policies and practices embedded within elite private schools. Although elite private secondary schools now work to enhance the racial and ethnic diversity of their student body via particular kinds of diversity initiatives (in the case at hand, working with local scholarship programs so as to enable competitive low-income racial minorities to attend the school), once the students access the schools, there is little attempt on the part of the institution to engage remedies that could address student lack of academic preparedness as compared to the academic preparedness of students across race and ethnicity from far more privileged backgrounds.

Additionally, and as we see in the case of college counseling in chapters 4 and 5, there is virtually no attempt on the part of the institution to address the extent to which facially neutral policies and practices with regard to college counseling (e.g., each student receives a college counselor and is told to make the process "his or her own") fundamentally advantages students of privilege and, with few exceptions, disadvantages everyone else.[1] This combination of individualistically driven policies and practices as opposed to collective attempts to address large-scale gaps in social, cultural, academic, and economic capital works to create a context in which low-income Black students are "outsiders within." The consequence of such practices, although not intentional, is to perpetuate, *at an institutional level*, racial and class differences. As a result, although *formally* possessing all rights, responsibilities, and privileges held by other students, low-income Black students at Matthews and Bradford do not participate as full citizens within the community.

A clear exception to our point on facially neutral policies and practices is that both Matthews and Bradford, to their credit, have recently taken explicit and conscious steps to make it possible for this group of low-income Black students to take a high-level mathematics course in their senior year. It is here, in fact, where the schools address systemically induced differences in academic preparation, thereby going beyond policies and practices that purport to treat everyone the same. Given that high-level mathematics—Calculus, AP Probability and Statistics, and the like— strongly predict entrance to top postsecondary institutions, it is admirable that the schools have stepped in to make this possible. They do so through a combination of curricular rearrangement in grade 9 that enables all students to meet the prerequisites for high-level mathematics (specifically Calculus), coupled with extra classes and substantially increased teacher time. This enables the schools to directly address particular weaknesses in prior mathematics preparation. This represents the type of initiative that addresses our concerns noted in the previous chapter. As we argue, access can never, in of itself, challenge substantial inequalities, as simple access does not take into account that a particular "class" of students is negatively affected by a lack of resources and language that would enable them to individually maximize access to opportunities in these resource-rich schools.

In this chapter, we focus more directly on individualized and felt treatment of low-income Black students in a context in which difference manifests itself in the school's environment in particular kinds of ways. To be clear, we address *felt peer racism*, but we do not have evidence from White and/or privileged students of color or participant observation data that validate such treatment directed toward this group. Significantly, however, the topic surfaced strongly among low-income Black students, making such felt treatment as linked to the nature of their "outsider within" status important to unpack. As part of this discussion, we additionally take up the position of privileged multigenerational Black students and the privileged children of "flexible immigrants" of color in elite private schools.[2]

Notably, in spite of the above detailed limitations with respect to institutional access as a mechanism to address social and economic inequalities, it is important to point out that low-income Black students ultimately do very well with regard to college matriculation outcomes. In point of fact and given their own reworked sense as to what constitutes a "good" college, as detailed in chapter 5, low-income Black students at Matthews matriculate at highly selective and selective four-year colleges roughly on par with the majority of Matthews students. Although we do not have comparable data for the entire Bradford class, we would expect similar matriculation outcomes. In fact, then, although there are issues related to the unintended consequences of facially neutral policies and practices and, as we will see in chapter 6, felt treatment in elite schools, their "outsider within" status seemingly has more psychological impact than practical consequences with regard to college admissions. As we suggest here, however, such psychological impact should not be dismissed.

As noted in chapter 1, this chapter will have a somewhat different feel to it than chapters 3, 4, and 5, as we begin to speculate and theorize around the rich ethnographic work presented in earlier and more explicitly data-driven chapters. Here we more intentionally "plunge beneath the surface of ethnography in a more interpretative mode" (Willis 1977, p. 119), a move that we sustain throughout chapter 7. Although ethnographic data are embedded within this chapter, we intentionally break from strong ethnographic form to probe, at a more deeply analytical and theoretical level, the meaning behind data reported here and in earlier chapters. At times, then, we go well beyond the actions and words of the participants themselves to theorize, in new ways, class and race productions. We do so with an eye toward challenging the scholarly community to think more deeply about issues related to race and class productions and their meaning in the twenty-first century. As stated in chapter 1, our analytical work around race, class, "ideological whitening," and children of "flexible immigrants," in particular, falls into this category.

Low-Income Black Students in Elite Schools

Most of the literature on Black students in private schools addresses students' social-psychological and sociocultural transitions from "integrated" or predominantly Black public schools into predominantly White private secondary schools. The students' class backgrounds and their experiences within their former institutions are often not fully discussed, and the dominant narrative is of the low-income Black "inner-city" student who enters an elite private school, followed by an Ivy League college (see Thompson and Schultz 2003; Zweigenhaft and Domhoff 1991, 2003).

As we suggest in the previous chapter, only one Black student in our sample fits this model, and data press toward expanded understanding of the current experiences, practices, and outcomes of low-income Black students in elite private secondary schools, as well as the extent to which this population of Black students are positioned as "outsiders within" by virtue of a very particular set of race/class interconnections that do not characterize more highly privileged students of color, whether children of "flexible immigrants" or children of social and economically privileged multigenerational Black parents. As we suggest later in this chapter, more highly capitalized students of color have very different experiences in elite schools than do their low-income Black counterparts.

Our data were collected 25 years after Zweigenhaft and Domhoff (1991, 2003) first interviewed individuals who were graduates of the ABC program in the 1960s, a program designed to increase the number of students of color in elite preparatory schools. At the point of their first interview, graduates of the program were close to 40 years old; the second interview was held 10 years later, when most former ABC graduates were close to 50. Our data were collected approximately 50 years later than the first group of Black students entered these elite private schools—a period within which the broader class/race landscape of America has changed markedly, at least in some respects. Self-identified Black students now enter the elite private school sector and/or predominantly White institutions at different points in their educational careers, with some having no educational experiences in predominantly Black institutions, or even public schools more generally.

So, too, the category "Black" in elite private schools, as well as highly competitive colleges and universities, has become increasingly complex, blanketing students of varying class and national origin, including the children of "flexible immigrants" whose parents possess cultural, social, academic, and economic capital vastly different from that of low-income multigenerational Black students and their parents. Economically privileged Black students, whether of "flexible immigrant" background or not, exhibit key class commonalities with children of "flexible immigrants" who are of diverse race, ethnicity, and national origin, as well as similarly privileged US born White students, rather than low-income Black students who comprised the intake programs in the 1960s and 1970s. In contrast to a time when nearly all Black students were brought into the elite private school sector by virtue of special programs for low-income minorities, the biographies, national origins, and school experiences of today's Black students are varied. This is not to deny the racially charged and predominantly White environment within which Black students of varying economic and social background now experience privileged institutions. It is simply to acknowledge that Black students in privileged schools have become an increasingly diverse group since the 1960s, a point made by Henry Louis Gates and Lani Guinier (2004) in their critical reflection upon intake patterns at Harvard and other elite universities.[3]

This chapter begins with a brief discussion of low-income Black students' varied sociocultural middle to secondary school transitions, subsequently moving through student reflections on the nature of racial segregation in the elite private sector. We follow up with an examination of the ways in which students navigate, challenge, and/or negotiate stereotypes and assumptions that they bump up against in the elite school environment, simultaneously addressing the extent to which students both "prop up" and work to distance themselves from racially charged discursive constructions. At the end of the chapter, we turn to college matriculation patterns of the three student focal groups that sit at the center of this volume, addressing the ways in which "class and race matter" in today's privileged institutions and the altered class structure of the twenty-first century.

Before proceeding to these important transitional experiences, we clarify what we mean by the sociocultural habitus of a school and consider Bonilla-Silva's (2006) notion of the ideology of color-blind racism. Both are relevant as we work to understand the ways in which racial differences manifest themselves in privileged institutions and student responses to the felt effects of peer racism. By sociocultural habitus, we mean the social and cultural context, or actual and perceived milieu of any given educational institution. With regard to low-income Black students, the sociocultural habitus points specifically to the dominant-raced and -classed culture of the elite private secondary school. As "outsiders within" who attend these schools but are not full members of the community, low-income Black students' biographies bump up against the sociocultural habitus of the institution, one that is tied, in key ways, to Whiteness and privilege. In this regard, low-income Black students, most of whom come from predominantly Black and Latino schools and neighborhoods, not only must make an array of academic adjustments entering their secondary schools, but they must also make marked adjustments socioculturally.

Bonilla-Silva's (2006) notion of color-blind racism is critically important to our analysis. Here we sketch the components of this current ideology, as they provide a basis for working through some of the ethnographic interview material presented in this chapter. Although we do not go point by point between framework and data, we refer to these components as we discuss the felt effects of peer racism, in particular. According to Bonilla-Silva (2006), the racial ideology of the Jim Crow era (overt, intentional, unapologetic racism) has been replaced by "a powerful ideology" that acts "to defend the contemporary racial order: the ideology of color-blind racism" (p. 25). Color-blind racism, he argues, is a subtle, insidious form of racism based on the belief that *good* White people *don't see color* and *treat all people as individuals*. Such *framing* of race systematically downplays the legacies and current manifestations of institutional racism, while simultaneously holding people of color responsible for their social position (Bonilla-Silva 2006). Whereas during the Jim Crow era of de jure segregation, the low status of Blacks could be explained by the presence of oppressive and regressive laws, color-blind racism, in contrast, operates under the guise of meritocracy, holding each individual responsible for his or her social and economic status:

> Color-blind racism serves today as the ideological armor for a covert and institutionalized system in the post-Civil Rights era. And the beauty of this ideology is that it aids in the maintenance of white privilege, without fanfare, without naming those who it subjects and those who it rewards. (Bonilla-Silva 2006, pp. 3–4)

Color-blind racism comprises four frames that are not mutually exclusive: (1) abstract liberalism, (2) naturalization, (3) cultural racism, and (4) minimization of racism. Abstract liberalism "involves using ideas associated with political liberalism (e.g., 'equal opportunity,' the idea that force should not be used to achieve social policy) and economic liberalism (e.g., choice, individualism) in an *abstract* manner to explain racial matters" (Bonilla-Silva 2006, p. 28). Here, Whites and others can use the principles and "language of liberalism" to perform a "reasonable and even moral" identity, while simultaneously "opposing almost all practical approaches to deal with de facto racial inequality" (p. 28). Under this frame, affirmative action, as a measure to address long-term historical and contemporary racial inequality, becomes rearticulated as *preferential treatment* and *reverse discrimination* (Bonilla-Silva 2006). Bonilla-Silva notes that this frame is the most pervasive, often encompassing all others.

Naturalization, his second frame, "allows whites to explain away racial phenomena by suggesting they are natural occurrences. For example, whites can claim "'segregation' is natural because people from all backgrounds 'gravitate toward likeness'" (Bonilla-Silva 2006, p. 28). As will be seen in this chapter, the prevalence of this frame, and that of abstract liberalism, exerts a profound impact on the student participants in this study in regard to their discussions of racial identity, affinity, and racism.

As per Bonilla-Silva's (2006) argument, the third frame, cultural racism, "relies on culturally-based arguments such as 'Mexicans do not put much emphasis on education' or 'blacks have too many babies' to explain the standing of minorities in society" (p. 28). Bold biological claims regarding race and racism (e.g., that Blacks are inherently, biologically less intelligent than Whites) have been replaced by cultural claims, such as those above that serve to explain *lack* of achievement in regard to educational and socioeconomic mobility among Blacks and other oppressed groups (Bonilla-Silva 2006).

The fourth and final frame, the minimization of racism, suggests that "discrimination is no longer a central factor affecting minorities' life chances ('It's better now than in the past' or 'There is discrimination, but there are plenty of jobs out there')" (Bonilla-Silva 2006, p. 29). As we will suggest in this chapter, these frames are woven into the very fabric of US society and elite private schools, and work to shape low-income Black focal students self-perceptions and racial identities in significant and disheartening ways. Although Bonilla-Silva focuses on color-blind racism as being under the ideological control of Whites, it is, as we suggest here, reinforced and elaborated by low-income Black students in privileged institutions. Although we do not address this point directly, we can expect that color-blind racism at least partially permeates the mindset of many privileged and nonprivileged people of color in the United States, whether multigenerational or "flexible immigrants."

Middle School to High School Transitions

Similar to earlier studies (Cookson and Persell 1985, 1991; Zweigenhaft and Domhoff 1991, 2003), students from predominantly Black/Latino urban public and predominantly Black/Latino diocesan Catholic schools focus on the "culture shock" they experienced moving from schools and neighborhoods that are predominantly low-income Black/Latino into schools that are predominantly White and highly privileged. Students talk about their first years inside an elite private secondary school as ones in which they, as visible racial minorities, felt socially "awkward" and "uncomfortable." Breanna, for example, states:

> Here [Bradford], it's hard to kind of adjust 'cause there aren't many like us, many African Americans around, so it's kind of hard. My one friend Marissa, she's African American too, we were in SATs [in separate rooms] and there's

part of the SATs that says if you're African American check this, and she was the only African American in the room. Everyone was like, "Oh Marissa, that's you!" and she felt awkward. Some moments are just awkward. Like when I was in Anatomy, we were studying blood and certain kinds of diseases and the teacher [said] that it [a particular disease] occurred mostly in African Americans. I could just feel everyone staring at me.

Kenneth Daniels, Breanna's father, notes that her experience at Bradford was "a social disaster":

> The students are very clannish, they're very snobbish . . . flaunting their wealth and talking about how much money they're allowed to spend on their mother's MasterCard, and stuff like that. And Breanna's not used to that, you know. . . . So, making friends, the kind of friends she had in public school, wasn't possible.

Comments from low-income Black students and their parents suggest that the often touted "multicultural intimacy" associated with such programs in elite private secondary schools is rarely realized in practice, rendering such broad-based intimacy a chimera.[4] Given steep class/race-linked inequalities among students in these schools, who both sit in different classrooms and travel back and forth on a daily basis to starkly different homes and communities (and by starkly different visible means of transportation), papering over such deeply entrenched class/race inequalities becomes implausible. As we will see later in this chapter, the situation with respect to privileged students of color, including privileged Black students, is markedly different in this respect.

While Kenneth Daniels holds the most critical view of this sector of schools, other parents share his perspective. Clare Nalin states that her daughter Anna had to get used to being the only person of color in her Bradford classrooms. She recalls that Anna often came home freshman year frustrated at not being able to get along with many of the girls and felt "out of place." Lucy similarly notes the differences between the sociocultural habitus of her middle school and Matthews Academy, specifically calling attention to her minority status:

LUCY: . . . There are a large amount of differences [between middle and high school], 'cause I didn't feel like a minority in middle school, nor did I feel like a majority. *I thought I was just there.* Here, *I know I'm the minority*—here, it's obvious; it's already made obvious.

HEATHER: How? What do you mean?

LUCY: Just, I mean . . . it's not like when I looked around the people beside me [in middle school] I was like, "Wow, there's a lot of people that look like me." It's just like, "Oh, there's that person [whom I know well or grew up with]." But here, there are a lot of people that aren't like me at all; they're very much from a different racial background; they're different economically; they speak differently than I do, like this is a total other world in comparison [to my middle school].

Many low-income Black students refer to their elite secondary school as "a different world," particularly those who spent their formative years in predominantly Black/Latino public and diocesan Catholic schools and reside in predominantly Black and Latino neighborhoods. Such students report few prior opportunities to interact with Whites (other than teachers) and narrate greater struggles in their adjustment to a predominantly White and highly privileged school environment.[5] This, coupled with circulating and not always unfounded stereotypes and assumptions about elite private institutions and Whites more generally, prompts low-income Black students to enter the elite private school sector with caution, "naturally" seeking out other people of color and, more specifically, other low-income students of color.[6]

When asked about sociocultural transitions from middle to secondary school, Black students who attended predominantly White Catholic and secular elite private middle schools narrate smooth transitions. Helene, one of our focal students in the top 20% of the Matthews graduating class, is the only Black student to attend an elite or predominantly White Catholic school since she was four years old. She recounts that the school culture in middle school closely mirrored that of her secondary school, making the transition to Matthews Academy very easy. Jennifer Williams, who spent the second longest duration in a predominantly White private school, concurs, indicating that her middle school was similar to Bradford, so she was "used to it." Transitioning in the third grade, she notes that although she perhaps had some difficulty adjusting at the time, it was too long ago for her to recall.

In contrast, Mark and Christina transitioned into elite private schools during their middle school years, recalling quite vividly their heavily raced and classed experiences. When asked whether she felt that her transition from eighth to ninth grade would have been similar or different had she remained in her predominantly Black urban public school through eighth grade, Christina responds:

It would have been much harder. It goes back, I think, to the race issue. Since [my urban public middle school] is predominantly Black, it would have been harder adjusting and adapting. 'Cause when I went to [elite private middle school] I mean our [referring to herself versus the other students'] lifestyles were totally different, so like [elite private middle] prepared me for what to expect [at Matthews].

Mark concurs, speaking passionately about his transitional struggles moving from sixth to seventh grade:

MARK: It [his racial background] has impacted it [his transition] a lot, because that is the first thing I identify, 'cause it's hard not to, coming in here and you're different from everybody else. . . . Your identity is based on that 'cause you're reminded of that every day. So, every day I come in thinking from that perspective: "I'm an African American male, how should I respond to [racism]?" And, over time, I realized that I should respond based on what I feel is right, not what . . . people think I should do. . . .

HEATHER: Are you saying that you think people expected you to say and do certain things as an African American male?

MARK: Yes, especially when I was younger. I had these expectations that I was supposed to do certain things 'cause I'm an African American male. . . .

HEATHER: You're supposed to play basketball. . . .

MARK: Right! And, I'm supposed to respond to everything racial that somebody says, you know, I think you understand that [to Heather]. Like somebody says something racially insensitive, I'm supposed to automatically respond in some kind of way. And for males, it's supposed to be angry and whatever. . . .

HEATHER: You're supposed to go and beat somebody up?

MARK: Right! And I was kind of confused about that, because they already pushed that on me, and I didn't even feel that. But they expected it from me.

From Mark's perspective, transitioning in middle school was much easier than doing so in secondary school. Here we see that Mark's experiences were shaped, in large part, by deeply entrenched social stereotypes, images, and perceptions of Black males. Mark maintains that he was expected to perform certain stereotypical behaviors and attitudes, in his case, as embedded in a certain form of Black masculinity.[7] To further illustrate his point about transitioning at a younger age, Mark speaks about a Black female friend who entered Matthews from a predominantly Black public middle school in grade 9:

I mean, she had friends here, but she kinda felt a little bit more, I don't know how to say it, she liked people here, but it felt more awkward coming in here. She didn't really break a social curve until her sophomore or junior year, and I broke it freshman year 'cause I was already going to the middle school. 'Cause she'd tell me, most of her social activity was outside of school. And I think I would have been more like her [if I hadn't gone to Matthews middle school].

Like Mark's friend, Leila expresses the loneliness and isolation linked to being a race/class outsider:

LEILA: I identify myself as African (Leila is a refugee from an East African nation), and I don't know, it just seems, I just seem to isolate myself with other African people. I don't know, I just don't feel comfortable. I just have a tendency to go with other Africans and feel more comfortable . . . with African American students too, or like foreign students.
HEATHER: OK, so how has that impacted your school experiences here [at Matthews], with less African, African American, or international students?
LEILA: It's definitely forced me to sort of isolate myself, because there's so many people here, and I don't know that many people except for in the [diversity club], or other African or African Americans. . . .

Further into the conversation, Leila reveals that she did have a few White affluent friends during her freshman year; however, it was very difficult to maintain those friendships because "they want to do things that I can't do, like go to parties. And they want to go to the movies like every day, and I can't afford that, and I can't keep up with them." Leila's move from a public international school that predominantly serves recent immigrants and refugees to Matthews was overwhelming, prompting her to surround herself with African American and "foreign" students. Sarah, who also attended a predominantly Black middle school, similarly comments on her "natural" drift toward minorities when she entered Matthews:

It was actually quite a shock. I mean, I was just used to everyone being accepting of everyone and stuff like that, and then, so when I came here, I drifted toward minorities. I mean, obviously, 'cause that's what I'm used to.

In spite of these narrated difficulties transitioning into highly privileged environments, students work to "fit in," whether consciously or unconsciously, and may find themselves increasingly distanced from their home communities. For example, Sarah describes herself as barely recognizable since the start of her Matthews career. She notes, "I was a totally different person than I am now," primarily describing this transformation via consumer class markers:

SARAH: It was just like kind of a tough time for me because when I came in, I was a totally different person than I am now. . . .

HEATHER: How do you feel you are totally different now?

SARAH: Well, when I came in like the style of how I dress totally changed. I used to dress more urban and now I'm like wearing UGGs and stuff [laughs], so that changed. . . . I don't know, that's mostly the transformation, my physical appearance basically. . . . I think it's mostly because of the environment, I guess people do things to fit in. Like before [coming to Matthews] . . . none of us [she and her peers of color] would wear UGGs and stuff like that. So, I guess it's like more of a transformation of making myself more a part of this environment.

Many students acknowledge changes in dress, speech, and mannerisms since entering the elite private school, changes that invite charges of "acting White" from friends and family, a topic that we take up later in the chapter.

Zweigenhaft and Domhoff (1991, 2003) and Thompson and Schultz (2003) report similar findings with regard to sociocultural experiences among ABC students at elite private boarding schools and students at independent day schools, respectively. Low-income Black students in both studies, all of whom appear to come from low-income Black neighborhoods and middle schools, express feelings of social awkwardness, denoting complexities associated with being *racially visible and simultaneously socially invisible* within the elite private school sector. Interestingly, Black students in majority-White schools in Carter's (2012) multisite study that spanned the United States and South Africa felt similarly. As noted above in the case of Sarah, students nevertheless work to become part of their new spaces, with only partial success, while simultaneously distancing themselves from their communities of origin.

Parents are not unaware of the social-psychic demands placed on their children by virtue of attendance at an elite private secondary school. Kenneth Daniels, for example, conceives of sending Breanna to Bradford as a "trade-off," one that is specifically linked to her poor academic experiences within the Blair public schools. He repeatedly states that he does not care for the sociocultural habitus at Bradford—one that *exudes* Whiteness and affluence—but that he does not feel that Breanna would be prepared academically for college if she remained in a predominantly Black institution. His decision to send Breanna to Bradford is based entirely on academic excellence, and he is well aware of the social trade-off involved in this decision, a topic that he frequently brings up during the interviews.

The experience of privileged Black students in the elite secondary school environment is notably different. Although Helene's parents, Claude and Sophie Dickinson, are aware of the racially linked social complexities involved in sending their daughter to Matthews, their comments take a markedly different shape and form than those of low-income Black parents, as they themselves are high-profile professionals and live and work within a racially diverse set of environments. Although acknowledging that elite private schools are overwhelmingly White, and certainly recognizing the potential personal and social costs of such an environment, this does not factor into their thinking about school possibilities, as school choice is *all* about academics:

HEATHER: So you said earlier that you were kind of drawing on personal experience and knowing what it was like to be the only non-White person [in a predominantly White school]. Can you talk a little bit about that?

CLAUDE DICKINSON: Well, you know, just from the experience, as a college student, knowing that you may not have the support systems that, and an awareness of what is going on, because you are not always part of the "in crowd." The fact that you're not part of the "in crowd" may affect your performance in the classroom. And to me, that quality of life experience, that quality as a student on a campus, can impact upon your studies depending upon how you approach the situation.

SOPHIE DICKINSON: See, my experience is a little different to [Claude Dickinson's] because again, he went to [a highly competitive, private, and predominantly White university] and I think, just from a financial standpoint, I don't know how many non-White students attend [this university], but I went to [a public, less expensive, diverse college], which, again, one, it's in [a diverse community in the Northeast]. And you had all different people with tuition of $325 a semester with 12 or more credits, and so I think I had . . . I mean, campus to me was no different than if I walked down the streets of [this community].

CLAUDE DICKINSON: To some degree, I also don't know how much the fact that we are not American-born Blacks [both Claude and Sophie Dickinson are from Jamaica], how much of a role it plays in terms of our openness to deal with certain circumstances, because we were looking at more educational value, and not so much whether or not we will be liked, not liked, discriminated against, and so forth. I'm not saying it was never a thought, but it was not the first thing. . . . *It's*

a matter of where we get education, that's the first thing. Will I get accepted [into
the school] and will I get the education I'm seeking. The racial make-up, for me,
was *never* a consideration. *You applied; you got in; you went.*

Noting that their experiences and perspectives perhaps differ from
those of multigenerational African Americans, Claude Dickinson emphatically states: "The racial makeup, for me, was *never* a consideration.
You applied; you got in; you went." In spite of the fact that Claude Dickinson suggests that this is due to the fact that they are not African American
but rather Black immigrants, all Black parents in this study, regardless of
class background, level of education, and/or country of origin, prioritize
academic reputation and offerings when making decisions about secondary schools. He is correct, however, that low-income Black parents often
identify themselves as outsiders to the community in a way that he and his
family do not, attributing this to the fact that they are of upper-middle-
class status and not born in the United States. In marked contrast to the
experience of the Dickinsons, low-income Black parents and their children feel bombarded by messages that they "do not really belong"—that
they are race and class outsiders in a highly privileged environment where
racial differences manifest themselves in particular kinds of ways. Such
felt position does not characterize "flexible immigrants" of color, who may
understand that they are largely racial outsiders, but nevertheless clearly
operate within the institution as fully classed members.

It is worth noting that privileged Matthews and Cannondale parents
(including those of non-White backgrounds, such as the Dickinsons and
Singhs at Matthews, and the Tran family at Cannondale) do not frame
themselves as having to make any kind of "trade-off" when seeking the
best possible education for their college-bound sons and daughters, as the
class habitus of the privileged schools to which they send their children
mirrors that of the class habitus of their family and community. In the case
of the Tran family, who are originally from Vietnam, the fact that they
were highly educated in the United States and are now electrical engineers
renders them class insiders with respect to privileged Cannondale. The
Dickinsons were similarly highly educated in the United States and are
now high-profile professionals—cancer research scientist and ophthal-
mologist respectively—in the Blair area. As per their own rendition, the
fact that their families are not historically tied to the United States additionally enables them to look at US racism somewhat differently, thereby
not feeling quite as personally oppressed by it. The Singhs similarly came

to the United States for graduate-level training in biochemistry, and both currently occupy faculty positions at the Research I university. Bottom line is that privileged parents of color, like privileged White families, do not conceptualize a decision to send their children to schools in which the preponderance of students are White as representing any kind of *choice* between being an "outsider within" and attending a school wherein their sons and daughters will be racially and ethnically like "everyone else."

Unlike low-income Black parents such as Kenneth Daniels, who earlier notes that "the students [at Bradford] are very clannish" and "very snobbish . . . flaunting their wealth and talking about how much money they're allowed to spend on their mother's MasterCard, and stuff like that," privileged parents of color, whether "flexible immigrants" or not, do not envision a choice to send their children to elite private schools or suburban publics as any kind of personal or social "trade-off." Given stark interconnections between race/ethnicity and class in the United States, these parents do not generally conceptualize themselves and their children as sharing linked class and race/ethnic status with the vast majority of parents and students in *any* particular school in the United States, as they understand that the dominant privileged population is likely to be White in the kinds of schools that they would be most likely to select for their children.[8] In the case at hand, the relatively small but notable population of children of "flexible immigrants" of color at Matthews and Bradford spans a range of backgrounds, such as Southeast Asian, East Asian, Caribbean, East and West African, Middle Eastern, North African, Latin and South American, among others. In addition, there is a population of biracial students of color, some of whom share this "flexible immigrant" background.[9] For purposes of the current analysis, when we speak of the children of "flexible immigrants," we analytically focus most closely on those children who would be considered racially Black.

It is worth noting that no matter what school privileged parents of color send their children to, their children are likely to be racially and/or ethnically different from the majority population, in spite of the fact that they share class status. In this sense, the decision to send their children to an elite private institution is not conceptualized as consigning them to being "outsiders within," in contrast to *other* available educational opportunities wherein they would not have this status. Practically and emotionally, then, the "choice" is perhaps not nearly as wrenching as it is for low-income Black parents, whose children sit in a racially *and* economically marginal position within elite private schools.[10]

It is also the case that "flexible immigrants" of color, in particular, are generally connected to comparably positioned members of their own national and ethnic communities of origin (both here and "back home") and/or less privileged members of their own communities of national/ethnic origin that migrated to the United States with the hope of gaining exactly the kinds of privileges embedded within these schools.[11] In this sense, "flexible immigrants" across ethnicity and nation of origin have a *dual or even triple frame of reference*, simultaneously comparing themselves to "flexible immigrants" of comparable national/ethnic origin who live and work in the United States; far less privileged members of their own nationally/ethnically located communities who migrated to the United States; and those they "left behind" in their home countries (Ogbu and Simons 1998). As a consequence, although they comfortably live among and interact with privileged Whites, Whites do not comprise their only, or even necessarily their primary, point of reference as they consider their status in the United States

While any individual child, of course, can experience racially linked loneliness and isolation, privileged families of color, whether "flexible immigrant" or multigenerational US born, exhibit sustained personal and professional interactions with other privileged families across race and ethnic lines. For this reason, their "choice" to send their children to private secondary schools, like that of privileged Whites, is emphatically not conceptualized as any kind of "trade-off."[12] In many respects then, for both the children of "flexible immigrants" of color and children of now privileged multigenerational Black parents, there is no all-encompassing and available class/race educational "home" for their children in which their children would share class/race status with the vast majority of students. For low-income Black students, however, the move to a privileged secondary school is, by and large, a move to a position of "outsider within" in direct contrast to the position that their children would occupy in largely Black and Latino urban schools. Such "outsider within" status leads, from the perspective of low-income Black students, to notable racial segregation within the institution.

"Naturalizing" Segregation

When asked to reflect upon the least positive aspects of their secondary school experience, low-income Black students point to the relative lack of other Black students and the extent to which this shapes both their own school experiences and the overall culture of the school. Students additionally state that their school communities are segregated along race and class lines, offering numerous examples of what they largely formulate as "natural" groupings (Bonilla-Silva 2006; Carter 2012; Tatum 1997). Lucy, for example, states:

LUCY: . . . It's not on purpose, but I am mostly friends with minority students. I think the school [Matthews] is sort of segregated. While I don't think it's something people *try* to do, it is certainly the way that it is.

HEATHER: Why do you think that is?

LUCY: I think because we all [non-White students] come from different neighborhoods and different cultures [than White students], so we look for someone who we think will be similar to us when we come into a school like Matthews, that is so different in so many ways.

While it is certainly the case that this is a highly privileged and largely White environment, it is not the case that there are no other Black students, or students of color more generally, in the school. As Lucy states, however, when referring to low-income Black students, "*We* all come from different neighborhoods and different cultures, so we look for someone who we think will be similar to us when we come into a school like Matthews, that is so different in so many ways." This formulation, although understandable, accomplishes two very important things with regard to the workings of the school and, looking ahead, what is likely to be twenty-first-century race/class structure in the United States

To begin with, it effectively marks those who are racially Black but *not* of low-income background as "less Black" and, more specifically, as individuals with whom they cannot possibly identify. Helene, in other words, who sits at the apex of the academic opportunity structure and is in fact on her way to Harvard, becomes discursively marked as "less" or "not really Black," a point that her father clearly makes at the beginning of this chapter. In this context, economically privileged Black students—whether multigenerational and/or the children of "flexible immigrants"—are marked as "less Black" or symbolically, perhaps, as White, as they are seen to embody White culture and position within the school.[13]

In turn, Black and Blackness become marked as low income, occupying a particular position in the school opportunity structure—in this case, at the bottom of the academic track structure given the relative lack of academic preparedness associated with the prior educational experiences of low-income Black students. In so denoting, high-income Black students are marked by social class, rather than race, whereas low-income Black students are marked by race, rather than class, leading to the discursive dismissal of the new complexities associated with race and class in the United States.

Lee's (2005) and Ong's (1999) work on the ways in which and extent to which certain groups of immigrants are ideologically Whitened in the dominant imagination is very useful here. Ong, for example, states, "middle and upper-middle class Chinese immigrants have been ideologically whitened in the dominant imagination" and "lower-income Southeast Asian refugees have been ideologically blackened in the dominant imagination" (Ong, as cited in Lee 2005, p. 6). In this sense, and as Tuan (1998) argues, the economic success of particular Asian immigrant groups has led to the ideological whitening of select groups and subsequent "honorary" status as Whites. Lee's (2005) important ethnographic work on the Hmong similarly suggests that the Southeast Asian Hmong have been ideologically blackened, subsequently occupying a very particular racialized space within the US imagination. Under such racialized construction, the extent to which members of ideologically blackened groups become economically successful and conform to White middle-class modes of conduct and speech determines the probability that the individual and/or group will be ideologically Whitened (Lee 2005).[14]

In this sense, we can expect that a student of color such as Kelly Tran, in highly affluent public school contexts like Cannondale, would be ideologically Whitened given her position at the top of the academic opportunity structure, coupled with her upper-middle-class status. Although race functions as an "absent present" in almost entirely White educational contexts due to its seeming normativity and invisibility—its "unmarked, unnamed status that is itself an effect of dominance" (Frankenburg, 1993, p. 6; Fine et al. 1997; Fine et al. 2004)—Kelly's story suggests that her presence as an upper-middle-class and highly successful "other" of color would result in similar processes of ideological Whitening.

Lee (2005), Tuan (1998), and Ong (1999) focus specifically on Asian immigrants, arguing that in spite of the process of ideological Whitening with regard to certain Asian groups, Asians are not *really* White and discursively occupy the status of "perpetual foreigners" in the United States (Lee 2005, p. 6). Although not occupying comparable discursive status, similar processes of ideological Whitening are in evidence at the elite private school. Low-income Black students in the elite sector are discursively constructed as a particular kind of "Black," both by themselves and by others. High-income Blacks, in contrast, whether of "flexible immigrant" origin or multigenerational status, are discursively constructed as "less Black," "not really Black," or even "honorary Whites" by a range of members of the school community, including low-income Blacks, high-income Blacks, and White faculty and students. As Lee (2005, p. 3) notes, within "this racist discourse, ideas regarding race and class are conflated. Whiteness is associated with economic self-sufficiency, independence, and self-discipline, while Blackness is associated with welfare dependency, failure, and depravity."

As noted above, in the privileged school context, similar processes of ideological Whitening take place, with attendant discursive consequences as noted by Lee (2005), Ong (1999), Feagin (2000), and others. In this sense, and as in US society more broadly, Whiteness is conceptualized as desirable, while Blackness is looked upon as undesirable, with both Whiteness and Blackness defined narrowly, and now clearly constructed in juxtaposition with one another. Black students who do not behave in ways associated with narrowly constructed notions of stereotypical Blackness are ideologically Whitened, and thereby seen "as not really Black."

Such discursive construction is coupled with notions that both within-school racial segregation and neighborhood segregation (which is framed as "choice" to live near others like oneself) are "natural," rather than socially and economically produced. Segregation is something that "just happens"—people "naturally" want to live among and interact with people of their own race (Carter 2012; Tatum 1997). Bonilla-Silva (2006) centrally locates naturalization as an important component of color-blind racism, drawing particular attention to the ways in which Whites naturalize the enduring presence of racial segregation in a range of societal institutions (schools, housing, places of employment, and so forth) in the face of laws specifically designed to eradicate segregation.[15] In the context of the elite private secondary school, we see how this ideology additionally permeates low-income Black youths' discussions about how and why there is racial segregation within their schools.[16] As Lucy notes, "I don't think that it is something that people *try* to do. It is certainly the way that it is."

Several students explicitly reference "the Black lunch table" (see Tatum 1997). Although students at Matthews now refer to what was formerly known as the "Black lunch table" as the "multicultural lunch table," at which one can find some Latino/a and White students, Mark and Christina suggest that it has become a multicultural lunch table simply because there are no longer enough Black students in the school to populate a full table.

Other students, like Marie and Sarah, note that White friends of Latino/a and Black students occasionally "choose" to sit with their peers of color, thereby augmenting its diversity.[17] All low-income Black Matthews students state that they sit at the now "multicultural lunch table" most, if not all, of the time, with the exception of Steven who is the only low-income Black student in all Honors and AP courses, and the only low-income Black student to list White students as close friends, although this exhibits its own set of class complexities, as we will see later in the chapter.

It is important to take note of the language that low-income Black students use when discussing within-school segregation. Students employ phrases such as "It just happened," "It wasn't on purpose," "I just drifted toward . . . ," "Of course," and "Obviously" to discuss why they, and other low-income Black students, seek one another out within the elite private school setting. In using this language, students *naturalize* racial segregation, suggesting that they and their White peers *simply choose* it based on comfort and familiarity. This clearly buries the structurally induced and institutional racism that produces lived-out segregation in neighborhoods and schools. This additionally masks the deeply structural roots of racism, rearticulating segregation as simply a matter of "choice." Black student participants in Carter's (2012) research, those in the United States and South Africa, maintain similar stances regarding segregation, suggesting that students make choices about who to spend time with based on "activities" and "interests" that have little to do with race (or class).

From the perspective of students of color from privileged backgrounds and/or more highly placed within the opportunity structure of the school, this social separation seems less "natural" and more problematic. While this group of students is more critical of the segregated social behavior within the school, embedded within their critique is an unconscious acceptance of negative racial stereotypes. A conversation with Natalie, a Black 2008 Matthews alumnae who was not a part of this study but who sat for an interview with Heather one year after her graduation, is striking. Her comments stem from a question regarding her sociocultural transition from her predominantly White Catholic middle school into Matthews secondary school, wherein she expresses very strong feelings about the Black lunch table and segregation more generally within the institution:

NATALIE: . . . When I was at Matthews, all the Black people clump[ed] together, you know, you've seen that [said to Heather]. And I really felt like a lot of times, especially with the boys, they played up to the stereotypes of Black guys, all the worst [stereotypes], and [they] can't understand why people look at [them] that way, or treat [them] that way [as outsiders]. . . . Or even the complaints of like, you know, there's a Black table . . . and I was like, well, why don't you go sit with any of the White people either. . . . And I think, especially after my class and most of those Black boys were gone, it got better. 'Cause now there's the Black students, the Hispanic students, the cool White kids, whoever wants to sit there, not necessarily the Black table.

HEATHER: So, it's a more diverse table now, but it's still a table?

NATALIE: It's still a table. . . . When I shadowed Matthews, and I shadowed Black people from City Prep and I sat at that table, I was like, I will never sit here when I come here. Never in my four years will I sit here. I will not do this to my image or the image of Black people. . . . I never liked it. . . . It's not just that, I just felt like the Black kids were just so into being Black that they didn't participate in the community enough.

Natalie, who exhibits a high degree of race and class consciousness on a societal level, is highly critical of Black students; these same critiques are often heard from White adults within elite private schools. Like most, if not all, of these White adults, Natalie was in a predominantly White school from kindergarten forward and developed a strong sense of comfort within such an environment. Natalie had a predominantly White peer group at Matthews and found it difficult to understand other Black students' actions and behaviors, particularly among those coming from predominantly Black neighborhoods and schools.

In a more measured approach, Steven raises questions about the internal school processes that serve to produce racial segregation, as he frequently comments on the fact that he is the only African American student in his AP classes. Certainly the academic tracking system, which evidences most low-income minority students placed in the same lower-track classes and results in similar schedules, plays a part in fostering segregated social behavior. On the heels of this prescient observation, however, Steven attributes the overall lack of minorities in the school to the fact that they are not as qualified as majority applicants:

STEVEN: Well, I see a lot of Caucasian kids, especially in my classes. I'm the only African American person in all my classes. . . . Yeah that's it. I mean, I see Matthews like sort of trying to be more diverse, and then I see them not at the same time. . . . I feel like the number of African American males at this school is rapidly declining. Last year's graduating class, there were three [class of 2009] . . . there's two in the sophomore class; there's one in the freshman class. And so is the number of, like, African American or even Latino women.

HEATHER: Why do you think that is?

STEVEN: I can only speculate. I guess the minorities that are applying [to Matthews], they're not as top notch as the other kids that are [applying]. 'Cause, it can't be because of racism, I don't think that exists here. I love everyone; well, maybe with kids, some kids [I don't love so much], but like with teachers and admissions staff, they're so nice, they wouldn't do something like that [intentionally keep out qualified minorities]. Maybe, it's just like the minorities that are applying just aren't as good as the other kids.

What is interesting about Steven's comments is that although he recognizes racial stratification as institutional by noting that he "is the only African American person in all my classes," he nevertheless marks racism solely as constituting an individual and intentional act, rather than systemic and structural. Although Steven describes his middle school and other predominantly Black public schools as providing a highly inferior education, he does not mark this as racism. For Steven, the only form of racism that could account for students not entering Matthews would be that associated with individual and intentional bias on the part of admissions personnel, which, according to Steven, is simply not possible. The triumph of individual acts of aggression as the defining factor of racism is clearly in evidence here. While not dismissing individual acts of aggression as a form of racism, confining our understanding and analysis to such individual acts of "choice" or any kind of individualistically located "sickness" obliterates a deeper understanding of racism as instantiated by structural and institutional mechanisms.

In centering on individual "choice" to explain racial segregation, students do not totally dismiss the ways in which class shapes student social lives, and a few students explicitly take up this point. We hear class intertwined with race when students express feelings of isolation or loneliness. Several students note the dominant class culture of their schools, particularly with reference to consumer markers such as certain types of cars and the ubiquitous presence of UGG boots, North Face jackets, and highly expensive designer handbags. Although Steven is by no means positioned as an "outsider" within Matthews by virtue of his notable academic success at the apex of the academic hierarchy, he is nevertheless clear about the role class plays in creating racially segregated interactions:

STEVEN: Well, socially, [Matthews] is kind of difficult 'cause I can't invite friends over to my house, 'cause I can't accommodate them [as well] as if they were to invite me over to their house. Like, I feel bad inviting them over to my house, you know, and I wouldn't be able to give them the same friendship accommodations that they would be able to give me.

HEATHER: What do you mean when you say accommodations?

STEVEN: Like a nice atmosphere. My atmosphere at my home is nice, but it's not like nice big glass windows, and a pool in the backyard, and beautiful flowers. . . .

Relatedly, some students state that socioeconomic differences between themselves and their more affluent peers constitute cultural differences that make creating friendships difficult. Both Leila, whom we heard from earlier, and Nathan take up this point:

There's the social stuff where everyone's like, "Hey, let's go here," and I'm like, "I only got five dollars. I think I'll go home." And I take the bus [to Matthews], stuff like that. And, *obviously*, I have different interests than a lot of the kids here who are like, you know, rich and whatever, they like skiing and stuff. There's just different stuff that you do that comes from [the economic context in which you grew up]. I would go outside when I was eight and play with my cousins in the street, where they would go skiing.

Breanna also reflects upon class differences between her privileged White peers and herself, and the strain that this puts on her social interactions at Bradford:

When we talk about prom dresses, people talk about going to New York City to pick one up, and I'm like, "Oh, I'm gonna go to the mall and find one I can pay for myself, 'cause I don't want to bother my parents with that. They have my tuition to worry about." And just like getting places, 'cause like my parents have to work all day, and their parents, some girls have mothers that stay at home, so they have transportation wherever they want, whenever they want. I have to schedule it behind buses. . . . I have to wake up [early] just so that I can catch a bus [to come to school].

For most of the students, their own located classed/raced background creates significant gaps between their day-to-day lives and school experiences and those of their highly affluent peers—a gap that substantially serves to create largely racially segregated peer groups. The lived-out interconnection between class and race, however, is rarely subject to analysis or intellectual dissection. For example, when low-income Black students mention "White students," affluence is implied, and when discussing "Black students," economic marginality is implied. Rarely are the class/race signifiers linked, in the sense of individually or collectively locating individuals or groups as "low-income" Blacks or high-income/highly affluent Whites, even though, as noted earlier, there is a population of Black students in elite schools who are of substantial privilege and a population of White students of low-income background.

Under such discursive constructions, Whiteness is normalized and instantiated as privilege and belongingness, at one and the same time as Blackness is instantiated as the lack of such privilege and outsider status. These discursive constructions additionally mark *all* Whites, including low-income Whites in the school, as deserving members of the community, with full rights and responsibilities in a privileged institution, whereas those who are now discursively defined as Black become marked as "outsiders within," thereby not legitimately possessing full rights and responsibilities. As noted earlier, under such discursive constructions, economically privileged Blacks are rendered "not really Black" or "less Black" by virtue of the fact that they are centrally located in the class habitus of the school.

As we suggest here, more highly capitalized Black students, whether multigenerational US born or the children of "flexible immigrants," have very different experiences in elite schools than do their low-income Black counterparts. Specifically, we note that race and class intersect in particular ways such that *social class dictates the salience of race*. Students like Helene, who were raised in upper-middle-class households, or students like Steven, who despite being low-income has been able to adopt the dominant attitudes and habitus of Matthews by virtue of his placement in all top-track classes, are seen less in terms of their race than is the case for the preponderance of low-income Black students. In this sense, students like Helene and Steven are ideologically Whitened (Lee 2005) or, as Steven suggests, seen as the "un-Black" Black. In contrast, low-income Black students who are class outsiders are additionally and vividly viewed as race outsiders, their racial identity magnified in the space of the elite school because of their social class. Such an understanding of the interaction between race and class in this sector of schools contributes to our understanding of the intersectionality of various social identities in particular kinds of classed/raced locations.

While the heavily classed and raced school culture embedded in an elite secondary school certainly works to promote the above set of constructions, low-income Black students discursively "prop up" these renditions, ultimately colluding, for example, in the maintenance of a discursive context in which "becoming successful" means becoming "less Black" or even "ideologically White." This has implications for the ways in which low-income Black students work to contest stereotypical assumptions and stereotypes that take root and are played out in the elite private school sector, as well as the ways in which they are positioned and position one another as having to negotiate the murky terrain around what constitutes "acting Black" and "acting White."

Assumptions, Stereotypes, and Representin'

Within the above detailed context, low-income Black students narrate a sense of obligation to "disprove" negative stereotypes, distancing themselves from such representations while at the same time consciously working to serve as positive representatives of their race. Students report unsolicited negative comments about Black hair and hygiene, as well as Black intellectual and academic capabilities. The felt burden of positively representing one's race is illustrated by Breanna, as she notes that being Black "kind of makes me work harder, you know, 'cause there isn't a lot of us here [at Bradford], so I kinda want to show that [I'm] here for a reason, that I was chosen to come here for a reason." Similarly, Steven explains that his racial identity within the predominantly White Matthews Academy "play[s] an important part in showing how minorities, even though the barriers that they have, if they have them, can still be successful." Mark speaks explicitly about feeling the need to correct assumptions about his abilities, in response to Heather's question about affirmative action and college admissions:

HEATHER: Let me give you an example, someone says to you, you're all seniors now, and you are all talking about college stuff, and somebody says, "Oh Mark, don't worry. You got affirmative action on your side. You'll get into a 'good' school."
MARK: Oh, that one, that one. I would say it might be true that these schools are probably looking at me, you know, I get letters for diversity conferences. I don't really play that [the fact that I am Black] into my résumé, or use that as a crutch or an advantage over everybody else. . . . I would say to them, that I'm competing just as much as you are to get into that school, and they should look at my college essay or my credential rather than my color. Sometimes when the

application says to check that you are African American, like I know there's a little part of me that says, you know, if I check here [it] might [give me] a little advantage, they might need [African Americans]. At first, sophomore year I did think OK, I'm gonna get into college. But over time I was like, no matter if they do accept me because I'm an African American male, eventually they are going to have to realize that I'm a good student, too.

HEATHER: So you would point out to your [White peers] that while schools, for their own purposes, may be factoring that in [to their considerations], *you also have qualifications.*

MARK: Right! *I actually have qualifications!* I'm at Matthews for a reason other than I'm Black.

HEATHER: OK, do you hear that a lot?

MARK: Well, it's not like directly [said], but I know it's there . . . like *I feel it there*, but like, nobody says, "You're into this school [a given competitive college] because you're Black." *But I know it's there.*

Mark, like other low-income Black students in our sample, consciously and explicitly works to contest stereotypes about Blacks' intellectual/academic capabilities—stereotypes that are symptomatic of color-blind racism (Bonilla-Silva 2006). In so doing, he seeks to prove not only that he *belongs* at Matthews, but that he can *earn* a place in a good college rather than being *given* such a place due to any particular institution's stated or unstated desire for Black students. It is worth noting here that the opposite assumption is made about Whites—that they are in elite private schools for a reason and that they *earn* a place in a good college on the basis of their merit. At the same time that low-income Black students feel that their worth to the institution is always questioned, they consciously undertake the burden of representing their race, simultaneously seeking to disprove negative stereotypes about Blacks, particularly with regard to academic capabilities.

Although messages about racial difference flow through these kinds of environments as linked both to systemic impact of institutionalized arrangements, such as tracking, and the individualized felt effects of peer racism, which stem largely from more broadly socialized notions of Whiteness and Blackness, Mark tellingly admits that no one explicitly says that his race has factored into his success; he just "knows it's there." Social isolation such as that experienced by low-income Black students within elite schools arguably fosters feelings among this group that the broader and more privileged population of students harbors genuinely negative stereotypes about them. This perception is certainly understandable. The extent to which such stereotypes are actually voiced or even genuinely felt by the broader population within the schools, is, however, unclear.

Here it is important to remember that the vast majority of secondary school students feel socially invisible and awkward at times, whether by reason of personality, race, sexual orientation, ethnicity, and so forth, but low-income minority students in elite settings are both simultaneously visible *and* invisible, and it is arguably the case that they enter the school primed to experience negative racial stereotypes and constant surveillance. Consequently, they feel that they are both noticed and not noticed. Whether either is objectively the case, their status as "outsider within," by virtue of internal institutional mechanisms and facially neutral policies and practices explored in chapter 5, has significant felt consequences that affect the ways in which this group of low-income Black students interact with the school. Here, low-income Black students are particularly visible, although perhaps not as visible as they feel themselves to be, by virtue of the fact that they are, with one exception, all in the lowest-level classes, a position that takes on a caste-like quality from which they consequently never escape.

In seeking to represent their race positively in light of the particular ways in which racial difference manifests itself in privileged environments, low-income Black students unwittingly reveal their own internalization of such assumptions, particularly as related to Black academic ability and their own presence in elite institutions. Distancing himself from such constructions and, in this case, predominant notions of affirmative action, Mark states: "I see myself as an African American male, not using that as a crutch or anything. I don't believe in that." As noted earlier, Breanna states that being Black "kind of makes me work harder, you know, 'cause there isn't a lot of us here, so I kinda want to show that [I'm] here for a reason, that I was chosen to come here for a reason."

Interestingly, the more overt messages of racial difference that affect these students' experiences lead to a rather universal response from within this group: they want to *prove* that they, on an individual level, are different from other members of their group and that they can distinguish themselves as worthy of competing within a historically White system of elite education. Ironically, this attempt at individually constructing themselves as different from other members of their group partially creates a particular *group* identity in that they universally strive to prove to their largely White peers and the predominantly White institution that they are more than just a token in their school's diversity initiative. What is not clear, however, is the extent to which this individual drive to combat tokenism is openly shared, either among themselves or with others, and therefore the extent to which this does or could constitute any kind of more powerful and collectively shared position.

In such racially and class charged waters, this is further complicated as low-income Black students, at times, tokenize themselves. Steven, for example, states that he "is something of a novelty." Knowing that he appeals to both White students and adults, Steven consciously challenges several stereotypes, taking specific note of the fact that he is involved in the arts, not sports, and is a highly intellectual and self-defined "preppy." In his eyes, this increases his popularity among White students, as they see him as similar to themselves and therefore different from *other* Blacks, in this case, other low-income Blacks. This not only raises Steven's status in the eyes of the school, but also potentially lowers that of all other low-income Black students.

Observational and conversational data with faculty and administrators reveal that Steven is, to quote another low-income Black student, "almost prized" by White people. Steven, in turn, comes to script himself as *different* from other Blacks, self-referentially noting that he is "the un-Black Black," a construction that reinforces culturally racist ideas about Black people and their capabilities, as per Bonilla-Silva's (2006) framework. Although Steven certainly does not "prop up" such culturally racist constructions intentionally, the unintentional consequence of his stance works to do exactly that.

Importantly, no other low-income Black student indicates that Whites in their schools even want to know them. The only participants to similarly comment on the subject of racial identity are Claude and Sophie Dickinson. Claude Dickinson strongly suggests that the fact that they are not American born renders them exempt to some extent from racialized constructions that, as he sees it, are largely directed at and internalized by African Americans:

> I think that because we are also non-American-born Blacks also adds, there's also some benefit that goes along with it. It's one of those unspoken things I think that's out there whereby, like I've had in the past, not at Matthews, but I've had people in the past assume that I'm not Black because I'm Jamaican. "You're not Black." And, I think there's some people who kind of don't connect the dots with regards to that. So, therefore, some of their assumptions they may have about, or prejudice, or presumptions they may have about American-born Blacks, they don't, it doesn't carry over [to non-American-born Blacks].

Sophie Dickinson concurs, noting drawbacks associated with being in their raced, classed, and educated position, as she is often "overexposed," and people are often curious, "too curious" in her opinion, about her status as a highly educated, highly successful Black woman. The Dickinsons assert that being non-American-born Blacks shields them from some of the stereotypes generally associated with African Americans. Clearly stating that it is not "right" or "fair" that they benefit from the assumption that they are "not really Black" because they were born in Jamaica rather than in the United States, they conclude that "it's just the way it is."

Based on their research with independent Black day school students, Arrington et al. (2003) state that "by attending independent [day] schools, [Black] students must also grapple with implicit and explicit messages that the community they represent is not as valued in school" (p. 14), which has a profound impact on their school lives. Based on their work with Black students of varying class background in an elite boarding school, Gaztambide-Fernández and DiAquoi (2010) conclude similarly. Working hard to distance themselves from culturally racist notions of what it means to be Black, Black students, and particularly low-income Black students, unwittingly and yet simultaneously often "prop up" such notions as they attend school in this particular discursive environment. This is linked to the ways in which such distancing shapes how students view themselves, their interactions with White peers, and their interactions with Black peers within and outside of privileged institutions. It is only within a context wherein systemic racism is woven into the very fabric of institutions that ubiquitous and all-consuming notions of "acting Black" and "acting White" can take root and exert real power. To be clear, such notions can be understood only within a broader discursive universe wherein "Black" and "White" have very particular meanings as forged in relation to historic and deeply embedded and racially linked structural inequalities. In this larger context, Black students find it hard to conceptualize themselves, and other Blacks, outside of culturally racist notions of what it means to be a Black person.

When asked about the origins of the assumptions and stereotypes that they navigate within their schools, the majority of low-income Black students pinpoint their interactions with White peers. In looking at student narratives, prevalent social stereotypes, and lack of accurate information and meaningful cross-racial interaction, are seen to underlie these exchanges. What comes through is a sense of fear that White students have learned in regard to Black people, *certain* Black people in particular,

and, more specifically, those who seem (to Whites) to represent or reinforce particular stereotypes. This sense of fear is often replaced by a sense
of confusion and wonderment when interacting with Blacks who behave
and interact in ways that interrupt such stereotypes and who are, in turn,
"ideologically Whitened" (Lee 2005), as is the case with Steven.

Highly privileged Blacks do not, for the most part, take it upon themselves to *consciously* contest the stereotypes that seem to envelop the experiences of low-income Black students in elite schools, both because they
have been *relatively* shielded from such stereotypes given their class position and the fact that they carry the dominant class culture of the school to
begin with, behaving and acting in ways that are entirely familiar to privileged Whites. In addition, privileged White and Black students, whether
multigenerational or the children of "flexible immigrants," have often attended school together since they were quite young, thereby having strong
interconnections and deep friendships. Such interconnections carry over
into parent communities in privileged day schools, where families across
race/ethnicity who share class background often spend a great deal of time
together as they raise their children. It is low-income Black students, with
the exception of Steven, who occupy the particular position elaborated
upon here. Unlike privileged Black students of whatever background,
they consciously carry the burden of contesting racist assumptions and
stereotypes.[18]

Acting White/Acting Black

Embedded within this navigation of stereotypes and representation of
oneself and one's race, and wrestling with various aspects of color-blind
racism, were several students' (and parents') discussions of the ways in
which they are perceived as "acting White" and/or "acting Black." These
perceptions come from White peers, Black peers, and students themselves
as they reflect on their own position in their school and larger community
of origin. Carter (2012) and Mickelson and Velasco (2006) argue that the
ways in which "acting White" is perceived and discussed varies in regard
to student biographies; how, and the degree to which, students internalize
deficit theories about their racial group; and the school's structure, culture,
and practices. Such notions of "acting Black" and "acting White" must be
understood, they suggest, as arising in particularly located environments,
but all must be understood to arise in relation to deep structurally rooted
racism and linked assumptions as to what it means to be "Black" and
"White." Bottom line here is that students live in a social context wherein

systemic racism is woven into the very fabric of its institutions. In such context, there is always someone who is scrutinizing their "choices" and what these "choices" say about their loyalty to or affinity with their racial group, both to those within and outside of their racial group (see Carter 2012). Recall, for example, Steven's explicit comment that he is seen as "the un-Black Black"—a designation that is both put upon him by Whites and that he now claims as his own. Low-income Black students in elite schools are seen as not "acting Black" enough for some and "too Black" for others, but all such designations, whether from without or within any given community, must be understood as forged in relation to particular and narrow constructions of what it means to be Black in the United States. Black students are under constant scrutiny with regard to their own located racial identity as linked to the felt and performative aspects of race.

Reflective of such constant scrutiny, Jennifer states that she is not feared by White students at Bradford because they perceive her as "not really Black," as she "acts more White than Black." Jennifer notes that Black peers outside of Bradford also state that she now "acts and talks more like a White person," due to her extended time in private schools. To be clear, it is not that people do not know that Jennifer is racially Black; rather, she is viewed by her Black peers outside of Bradford as "White" because of her mannerisms, speech, and way of conducting herself. This gets to the heart of the performative aspects of race, a point that Christina takes up when she comments on other non-White students in her class at Matthews:

> There is this girl who is South American, like from Chile or Colombia, I can't remember. Everyone says that she is White because she has White parents. So even though she is not White in terms of ethnicity or race, people see her as White because she was adopted by rich White people who live in the suburbs.

As a person of color brought up by White parents in a predominantly White, affluent community, this student is not seen as *really* Latina or South American. This extends to children of "flexible immigrants" of color, particularly those who are racially marked as Black. When discussing her racial identity, for example, Helene Dickinson openly states that she is conflicted, as, unlike her West Indian immigrant parents, she was born in the United States, but doesn't identify with American Blacks "in a cultural sense, 'cause I don't identify with that culture as I do the typical White culture of America."[19]

Relatedly, both Anna and Breanna point to a Black student at Bradford who, they note, has only White friends. When asked about this student's background, Anna states:

ANNA: Well, she doesn't sit with the Black students during lunch; she just sits with the White students. . . . She hangs out with White students pretty much all of the time. I know this because there are only 30-something girls in the class, and only a couple are Black. So she'd be hanging out with the people I hang out with if she wasn't hanging out with White girls.

HEATHER: Why do you think that is? How well do you know her?

ANNA: I don't know her really well, but Marissa [a Black student not in the research study] does, and says that her family moved out of the city to the suburbs when she was really young. So, I think she went to elementary school in the suburbs, not the city like we did.

Once again, "suburbs" and "city" are code for White and affluent, and Black and working-class/poor, respectively, just as White and Black are classed in previous narratives. Having grown up in a presumably White suburb, the student that Anna speaks of is seen to *perform* Whiteness, both with respect to her mannerisms and the fact that she has an entirely White peer group. Thus, she is "ideologically Whitened" by her family's class background and residence in a suburban (White) neighborhood. Mark similarly elaborates upon such performance as he reflects upon his freshman year in the upper school. After being one of only three low-income Black students in the entire Matthews middle school, Mark expresses concern when an enlarged group of low-income Black students are poised to join him in his upper school class:

MARK: To tell you the truth, I wasn't affiliated with any Black students [in the middle school]. I was kind of scared [when more Blacks entered his class in the upper school] 'cause I spent all that time trying to adjust [to a White environment, and then], trying to adjust back. I don't know, *I just thought of it as two different worlds for some reason.* I don't know, which is, I'm ashamed, 'cause, you know, I really wouldn't think that way. I guess that I was scared of being criticized for, you know, being White or whatever. . . .

HEATHER: Hanging out with the White kids?

MARK: Yeah, being different, or whatever. Then sophomore year that all changed when I joined [a junior fraternity of Black male public school youth], and I kind of saw it as like a reintroducing myself to that "world," the "Black world." And

then, sometime along the way, I just realized that this is stupid. Just hang out with
whoever you want to hang out with, and don't have any anxiety about it. . . .

Importantly, understandings of what it means to "act White" and "act
Black" within elite private schools are tied to behaviors, mannerisms, and
peer groups, but not academic achievement, as *all students* in this environment are seriously engaged in academics.[20] These narratives affirm notions
of color-blind racism, as to "act Black" often means to personify narrow,
culturally deficient notions of Blackness, just as "ideological blackening"
is viewed as "Americanizing" in a "bad" way (Lee 2005) with regard to
the immigrant Hmong students in Lee's research. Under such formulation, Blacks are framed, both by themselves and others, as "choosing" to
perform race in a particular manner, thereby bringing themselves closer
into line with White culture by individually "choosing" to do so, or not.
Importantly, this is not a "choice" that is foisted upon dominant Whites,
and there is no discussion and/or surveillance of the extent to which one
performs Whiteness. As such, this is a burden that is carried by Blacks in a
historically apartheid society with its associated institutional and cultural
racism.[21]

Given these historical and current circumstances, as well as student narratives of naturalizing segregation and wading through insidious assumptions and stereotypes, it is certainly possible that the low-income Black
student participants have, to varying degrees, internalized color-blind
racism (Bonilla-Silva 2006). The data indicate that students' attempts to
represent themselves and their race in positive ways means distancing
themselves from certain forms of Blackness—forms that are clearly linked
to color-blind racism, namely cultural racism as per Bonilla-Silva's (2006)
important formulation. Students such as Steven, Mark, Jennifer, and
Sarah explicitly address this phenomenon—how they seek to represent
their race positively and the ways in which this is tied to "acting White"
and/or not "acting too Black." While this internalization may very well
influence many Blacks (and other people of color) in the United States
given historically apartheid structures, it is certainly possible that the
overwhelming Whiteness and affluence of the elite private school sector
heightens and works to intensify such internalization among this particular group of students. Through this lens, it is arguably the case that Black
students' perpetuation of culturally racist ideas about "other" Blacks is a
manifestation of their own internalized color-blind racism (Bonilla-Silva
2006) as produced in this context.

As noted earlier, Mickelson and Velasco (2006) and Carter (2012) demonstrate that *how* "acting White" and "acting Black" is perceived and discussed varies in relation to students' biographies; how, and the degree to which, students internalize deficit theories about their racial group; and the school's structures, culture, and practices. In the case of the private secondary school, such understandings are forged in a context of within and out-of-school segregation wherein deep stereotypes and differential positions in the opportunity structure of the school play a powerful role in shaping students' lives with regard to whom they hang out with, how they are perceived, how they perceive themselves, and how they perceive others (Whites and Blacks). These identities shape and are shaped by both their neighborhood and within-school peer groups, as well as opportunities to interact with other young people across race and class backgrounds. Rather than reflective of simple "choice," the various stances that students take are intimately connected to both their class backgrounds and their academic lives and identities within their schools.

In the particular case at hand, such stances are also linked to position within the school's structure of opportunities. Although virtually all low-income elite private school Black students are charged with "acting White" within the context of their predominantly Black neighborhood, fine gradations are in evidence with regard to who is seen to be "acting White" within the school itself, what it means, and when one does it. Born of a larger apartheid and racist historical context (Carter 2012), this set of discursive constructions (which changes over time and varies by social context) instantiates, whether intentionally or not, a narrow and stereotypical notion of what it means to be "really" Black in America, suggesting at the same time that one can always "choose" to "perform" differently. For these students, then, their racial identity and allegiance is always under surveillance. Although "acting White" and "acting Black" have different meanings depending on context, the potential and actual discursive charge remains steady, rendering position within the elite private sector discursively difficult both within and outside of the school boundaries.

The extent to which and ways in which low-income Black students grapple with the felt effects of their "outsider within" status as they move into and through postsecondary institutions and beyond is a topic for further consideration. Certainly the "trade-off" parents and students mention is significant, but the low-income Black students under consideration here also demonstrably achieve their stated goal of entering a "good" college.

The question may be asked, how does the predominantly white student and parent population make sense of this population of low-income Black students? This is a difficult question to answer with the data at hand, as we did not specifically probe this issue. With respect to Matthews, however, the fact that we focused on the top 20% of the class means that the predominantly but not entirely White population had little contact with low-income Black students, with the exception of Steven. Although some students exhibit sustained contact with students across the track structure, particularly via participation in sports, their own located position in the opportunity structure of the school largely sets the stage for school-based interactions.[22] Additionally the "multicultural lunch table" means that low-income students of color largely eat lunch together, with more privileged students across race/ethnicity constructing different kinds of friendship groups and associated lunch tables. Although students spend a great deal of time studying together during school hours and before sports/drama practices and so forth, such groupings are largely devoted to accomplishing schoolwork, and students who share classes tend to work together as they have the same assignments, leaving students in the bottom tracks with virtually no contact with those in the AP/Honors track, and vice versa.

While select activities, such as advisee groups that meet several times a week with a given assigned faculty member, cut across the track structure, such cross-cutting activities and spaces *punctuate* rather than fundamentally define students' lives in school. By and large, then, students spend a great deal of time with those who are similarly placed in the school opportunity structure, a phenomenon not unlike what we saw in Cannondale in chapter 3. In the case of the private school under consideration here, this means that the top 20% of the class have little sustained contact with the group of low-income Black students, even in a relatively small private school.

Highly privileged parents, especially those whose children are at the top of the academic hierarchy, are even more disconnected from the population of low-income Black students than their children, exhibiting virtually no contact with them. Privileged parents tend to know students who are placed at the same level in the opportunity structure as their own children, as these are the students with whom their children spend the most amount of time (see chapter 4), and who are visiting and applying to the same kinds of colleges. In the race for postsecondary admissions, which defines so much of the life of privileged parents and children in this school,

low-income Black students and their parents are not on the radar screen—
it is those who sit at the same place in the opportunity structure as their
children do who draw their sustained attention. These tend to be, for
structurally induced reasons, their children's closest friends. They are also
the ones who parents hear about when one or another student gains acceptance to a highly competitive college.

The extent to which this renders race relevant or irrelevant with respect
to class security, insecurity, and/or anxieties is complicated, as it is *only* the
group of low-income Black students who are largely off the radar screen
of the privileged parental population as they and their children go through
the arduous postsecondary admissions process detailed in chapter 4. With
respect to the intensification of admissions to highly valued postsecondary destinations, privileged parents are well aware that their children are
competing with highly qualified students of color from a range of national/
ethnic/racial backgrounds, and that privileged students and parents who
share class background are engaging the college admissions process in
the same way and to the same extent, thereby finding class-linked ground
through which to experience the grueling process as a collective practice.[23]
At a very real level, then, class works to create a sense that "we are all in
this together"; and although the process is certainly competitive in that
individuals script themselves as competing with and against one another
for particularly located destinations, the process is collectively engaged
and shared, thereby creating deep class bonds across race and ethnicity
(Ball 2003). Although class security can no longer be assumed, the "race"
for highly valued postsecondary destinations now includes highly capable
"runners" from a wide range of race and ethnic backgrounds, and everyone knows it.[24]

In sharp contrast, and as we see in chapter 5, low-income Black students and their parents go through the process entirely differently, thereby
finding little ground on which to forge the kind of class bonds across fundamental race/ethnic difference that get forged among those who share
class background to begin with. Interesting enough, in spite of the intensified fortification of *felt* class bonds among those with existing class
privilege as they go through the college admissions process, the population of low-income Black students does exceedingly well with respect to
college matriculations. The extent to which low-income Black students
internalize such shared class status as a result of participation in the college admissions process—what one focal student calls a "marathon"—is,
however, clearly questionable.

In the next section, we map the college matriculation patterns of the three groups of students in this volume. Significantly, despite their marked isolation in elite private schools and felt peer racism, many of these low-income Black students are positioned by virtue of entrance to particularly located postsecondary destinations to become a part of the new upper middle class of the twenty-first century. The extent to which this happens for any particular individual is not known, of course, but all students in this volume, including low-income Black students, are poised to take the next step in this direction.

Matriculation Patterns across Race and Class Groups

We now turn to a targeted focus on college matriculation patterns *across* the three groups of focal students in private and public privileged school sectors, carefully exploring the ways in which lived-out class and race *matter* for experiences and matriculation outcomes. Institutional sectors under consideration here (elite private and affluent public) draw predominantly from a socioeconomically privileged population, comprised largely of White students and parents as well as the children of "flexible immigrants" (both of color and White). Although children of "flexible immigrants" exhibit greater representation in the sample private versus public schools in this geographic location, such children are often heavily represented in privileged suburban publics in large US cities. The seeming "effects" of class and race on college matriculation patterns are rather complex, but the mark of class and race can be seen across the sample populations.

As expected, students apply to a range of colleges, with an eye toward attending the "best" possible postsecondary destination. Students at the top of the opportunity structure at both Cannondale and Matthews apply to almost entirely privates ranked as "Most Competitive," "Highly Competitive+" and "Highly Competitive" (Barron's 2009), including but not limited to Brown, Columbia, Cornell, Dartmouth, Georgetown, Harvard, Johns Hopkins University, Massachusetts Institute of Technology, Northwestern, New York University, Princeton, Stanford, University of Chicago, University of Pennsylvania, University of Rochester, University of Southern California, and Yale. Low-income Black students in the NAIS sector similarly apply to a range of largely privates, generally ranked as "Highly Competitive+," "Highly Competitive," and "Very Competitive," including but not limited to Alleghany, Drexel, Fordham, Sarah Lawrence, and Syracuse.

What is most striking in the application data across groups of sample focal students is the degree to which students apply to and ultimately matriculate at the privates. Relatively few students, in fact, apply to public institutions, although occasionally students apply to one or more of the top "flagship" state universities (or a highly reputable state institution that is not classified as a Research I). This is certainly the case for the "flagship" state university in the geographic region in which we conducted our research, where a number of students apply to (and are accepted into) the Honors program, in particular, which offers full tuition and living expenses. In more cases than not, however, although top-ranked students obtain entrance to the highly coveted Honor's program, they choose to attend school elsewhere, and matriculation outcomes reveal almost entirely private college attendance.

With regard to application and matriculation patterns, the fact that our sample of students across race, class, and sector of secondary school drives almost entirely toward entrance to private postsecondary destinations is noteworthy. As we argue in chapters 3 and 4, privileged students and parents linked to the top of the opportunity structure at both Cannondale and Matthews are positioning for the most valued postsecondary destinations in the nation. More specifically, and in looking carefully at application and matriculation outcomes, they are predominantly positioning for those institutions that are now ranked "Most Competitive" and "Highly Competitive+" as per Barron's *Profiles of American Colleges*. Low-income Black students at Matthews and Bradford are similarly positioning for top privates, both because this is normative practice within these schools and because scholarships are available at a number of well-ranked private colleges to support low-income students of color.

The main point, however, is that this entire population of students is driving toward a particularly located sector of private colleges, with scant attention paid to even the flagship publics in the admissions process. This is partially understandable when we look at the distribution of publics versus privates in the "Most Competitive," "Highly Competitive+," and "Highly Competitive" Barron's categories. Table 1 reports these data for the 2009 and 2013 Barron's *Profiles*.

As Table 1 shows, the vast majority of top-ranked institutions, and particularly those categorized as "Most Competitive," are private. In point of fact, less than 9% of institutions ranked as "Most Competitive" in 2009

TABLE 1 **Percentage of Public vs. Private Postsecondary Institutions Designated as "Most Competitive" and "Highly Competitive," 2009 and 2013**

Barron's Rating	2009			2013		
	Total	Public	Private	Total	Public	Private
MC	100.0%	8.5%	91.5%	100.0%	10.1%	89.9%
	(82)	(7)	(75)	(89)	(9)	(80)
HC:	100.0%	28.4%	71.6%	100.0%	30.3%	69.7%
	(109)	(31)	(78)	(109)	(33)	(76)
HC+	100.0%	22.9%	77.1%	100.0%	23.1%	76.9%
	(35)	(8)	(27)	(39)	(9)	(30)
HC	100.0%	31.1%	68.9%	100.0%	34.3%	65.7%
	(74)	(23)	(51)	(70)	(24)	(46)

Source: Barron's Profiles of American Colleges, 2009 & 2013 (New York: College Division of Barron's Education Services).

are public, with close to 92% comprised of private institutions. By 2013, two additional "Most Competitive" level schools are public, bringing the percentage of "Most Competitive" institutions that are private down to 90%.[25] Such ranking systems now boldly inform parents and students that the most valued postsecondary destinations in the country comprise a narrow band of almost entirely private institutions that now go well beyond the historic Ivies, Stanford, and MIT. In this context, it is understandable why parents and students, who are steadily striving for "distinction" and class advantage via the postsecondary admissions process, head almost entirely toward a narrow band of private colleges. In this sense, then, such ranking schemata now markedly drive postsecondary application patterns in the United States. This is particularly the case for the sector of secondary schools and attending populations that we explore in this volume.

In fairness to Barrons's, this is most certainly not the intent, and this is in fact a competitiveness index rather than any kind of reputational ranking system. However, the fact that it is readily available (online and in print) at a time when parents and students are looking toward creating "distinction" in increasingly uncertain economic times renders such ranking systems very powerful with regard to shaping the structure of desires as linked to postsecondary admissions. In fact, only a tiny proportion of focal students apply to public colleges.

With regard to where students ultimately matriculate, students at the top of the opportunity structure at Matthews tend to matriculate at somewhat more highly ranked institutions than those at Cannondale, although Cannondale students similarly matriculate at outstanding and highly competitive schools and, for the year under investigation, are accepted at all but the very apex of US institutions (Ivies, MIT, Stanford). Table 2 reports matriculation outcomes by school sector and focal student population served.

As we see in Table 2, focal students in the top 20% of the Matthews class matriculate in entirely top private schools (with only one student matriculating at a school ranked below "Highly Competitive+"), comprised of Amherst College, Bard College, Brandeis, California Institute of Technology, Harvard (2), Johns Hopkins (2), Lake Forest College, New York University, Princeton (2), and Tufts.[26] Those at the top of the Cannondale academic hierarchy similarly matriculate at top privates (with only two students matriculating at schools ranked below "Highly Competitive+"), comprised of Emory University, Hobart and William Smith, Johns Hopkins University, New York University, Niagara University, Northwestern, University of Richmond, and University of Rochester. Only one student in this group matriculates at a flagship public—University of Illinois (Urbana-Champaign). Low-income Black students matriculate at Butler University, Case Western Reserve, Howard, Skidmore, St. Joseph's University (Pennsylvania), St. Xavier (Illinois), State University of New York at New Paltz, University of Pennsylvania, University of Pittsburgh, University of Tennessee (Knoxville), University of Central Florida, and Villanova.[27]

Tables 3 and 4 report the proportion of students within each school/focal student population to matriculate at particularly located postsecondary destinations. Importantly, only one is public at Cannondale; and none are public among top-ranked students at Matthews. Three of the low-income Black students at the two private secondary schools matriculate at publics. Data are reported in two ways: Table 3 reports data by school sector and student population served as per the Barron's *Profiles of American Colleges* (2009). Table 4 provides data by school sector and student population served as per the Barron's *Profiles of American Colleges* (2009), with Ivies, MIT, and Stanford pulled out of the "Most Competitive" category and reported separately as IMS (Ivies, MIT, and Stanford). This mirrors the reporting process noted in chapter 4 with regard to top private day and boarding secondary schools in the United States, where Ivies, MIT, and Stanford are widely considered the iconic apex institutions.

TABLE 2 **Focal Students by Sector of Secondary School and College Matriculations**

Matthews (Top 20%)

Students	Attending	Barron's Rating
Brandon Cowan	Bard College	HC+
Nicole Davison	Johns Hopkins University	MC
Helene Dickinson	Harvard University	MC
Ryan Dougherty	Princeton University	MC
Briana Kenney	Brandeis University	MC
Stephanie Larkin	Tufts University	MC
Joe Marino	California Institute of Technology	MC
Chelsea Norwood	Amherst College	MC
Ethan Sanderson	Princeton University	MC
Jason Sheffield	Johns Hopkins University	MC
Samantha Singh	Harvard University	MC
Matt Tomlinson	Lake Forest College	VC+
Lexi Willard	New York University (NYU)	MC

Cannondale (Top 10%)

Students	Attending	Barron's Rating
Melanie Gruzina	University of Richmond	MC
Karina Hoxha	Niagara University	C
Jacob Jacinovic	University of Rochester	MC
Michael Penn	New York University (NYU)	MC
Chloe Rogers	Hobart and William Smith	VC
Nicholas Stowe	Northwestern University	MC
Marley Swanson	University of Illinois (Urbana-Champaign)	HC+
Kelly Tran	Johns Hopkins University	MC
Brad Whitcombe	Emory University	MC

Matthews/Bradford (Black Low-Income)

Students	Attending	Barron's Rating
Breanna Daniels	University of Central Florida	VC+
Christina Gibbons	St. Xavier (Illinois)	C
Mark Jackson	Howard University	C
Steven Jones	University of Pennsylvania	MC
Leila Martin	Villanova University	MC
Anna Nalin	SUNY New Paltz	VC
Sarah Sanchez	University of Tennessee (Knoxville)	VC+
Angela Simmons	Skidmore College	HC+
Marie Thompson	St. Joseph's University (Pennsylvania)	VC
Lucy Vargas	University of Pittsburgh	HC
Nathan Vasquez	Case Western Reserve University	MC
Jennifer Williams	Butler University	VC+

TABLE 3 **Secondary School and Focal Student Population Served by Barron's Selectivity Index of Entering Colleges, 2010**

	C	C+	VC	VC+	HC	HC+	MC
Matthews							
(Top 20%)	0.0%	0.0%	0.0%	7.7%	0.0%	7.7%	84.6%
Cannondale							
(Top 10%)	11.1%	0.0%	11.1%	0.0%	0.0%	11.1%	66.7%
Matthews/Bradford							
(Black Low-Income)	16.7%	0.0%	16.7%	25.0%	8.3%	8.3%	25.0%

TABLE 4 **Secondary School and Focal Student Population Served by Barron's Selectivity Index of Entering Colleges with Ivies, MIT, and Stanford (IMS) Pulled Out, 2010**

	C	C+	VC	VC+	HC	HC+	MC	IMS
Matthews								
(Top 20%)	0.0%	0.0%	0.0%	7.7%	0.0%	7.7%	53.8%	30.8%
Cannondale								
(Top 10%)	11.1%	0.0%	11.1%	0.0%	0.0%	11.1%	66.7%	0.0%
Matthews/Bradford								
(Black Low-Income)	16.7%	0.0%	16.7%	25.0%	8.3%	8.3%	16.7%	8.3%

As evident in Table 3, among all focal students at the top of the academic hierarchy at Matthews, 85% matriculate at a "Most Competitive" institution, with two individuals matriculating at a "Highly Competitive+" and "Very Competitive+," respectively.[28] This compares with 67% who matriculate at a "Most Competitive" institution at Cannondale, and 11% who matriculate at a "Highly Competitive+" and "Very Competitive" institution respectively at this same school. With regard to low-income Black students at the two NAIS institutions, 25% matriculate at a "Most Competitive" institution (this represents one student, Steven, who figures prominently in chapters 5 and 6), 8% at a "Highly Competitive+," 8% at a "Highly Competitive," 25% at a "Very Competitive+," and 17% at a "Very Competitive," with 17% matriculating at an institution ranked as "Competitive." Looking across the three populations, 100% of top-ranked Matthews Academy focal students matriculate at a postsecondary private; 89% of top-ranked Cannondale students similarly matriculate; and 67% of low-income self-identified Black students in the secondary privates matriculate at a private postsecondary destination.

Looking specifically at matriculation to the apex institutions (Ivies, MIT, and Stanford) in Table 4, 31% of top Matthews Academy students matriculate at these schools in 2010, whereas no students who otherwise fall into the "Most Competitive" category from Cannondale enter these institutions. One student from the low-income Black Matthews/Bradford group matriculates at an apex institution (Steven).

Data in tables 2, 3, and 4 must be interpreted cautiously, however, given that the absolute number of focal students is very small. As such, a change in admission for one or two individuals in any given year may drastically change percentage admission patterns to postsecondary destinations. In this regard, matriculation data from all Matthews's students over a five-year period are illuminating in that they provide an overall reference point wherein matriculation patterns of focal students can be understood. Matthews is the only school for which we were able to obtain comparable five-year data.

Among total matriculations over a five-year period (2007–11), Tables 5 and 6 make clear that although an average of 32% of students across Matthews Academy matriculates at "Most Competitive" institutions, 6% of all Matthews students across the five years matriculate at Ivies, MIT, and Stanford. This suggests that although 31% of the top 20% of Matthews students in the particular year under investigation here matriculate at Ivies, MIT, and Stanford, this cannot be considered a common occurrence. What can be said is that a somewhat higher proportion of top students from Matthews matriculate at institutions ranked as "Most Competitive" than is the case at Cannondale. Additionally, there is evidence to suggest that a higher proportion of students from Matthews versus Cannondale matriculate at Ivies, MIT, and Stanford in particular years, and a somewhat higher proportion of students from Matthews versus Cannondale matriculates at these schools over a longer time period.[29]

Low-income Black students in our sample matriculate at institutions more or less on par with those of the overall population of Matthews students. However, for the year under consideration here, low-income Black students matriculate at slightly less competitive institutions than is the case in the larger Matthews population over a five-year time period. Specifically, although 17% of focal Black students matriculate at Competitive institutions in 2010, only 9% of the larger five-year population at Matthews matriculates at this level. The extent to which this is an artifact of the particular year under investigation is not clear, however, and we must interpret these data cautiously.[30] Generally speaking, low-income Black students matriculate at outstanding postsecondary institutions on par with those of the Matthews community as a whole (with the exception of those in the top 20% of the class).

TABLE 5 **Five-Year College Attendance Data (2007–11) by Barron's Selectivity Index: Matthews Academy**

	NR	LC	C	C+	VC	VC+	HC	HC+	MC
2007	5.6%	0.0%	5.6%	3.4%	14.6%	16.9%	14.6%	13.5%	25.8%
2008	3.9%	1.3%	9.1%	5.2%	13.0%	10.4%	20.8%	10.4%	26.0%
2009	3.1%	0.0%	7.3%	1.0%	24.0%	11.5%	13.5%	4.2%	35.4%
2010	2.0%	1.0%	10.0%	2.0%	15.0%	13.0%	10.0%	8.0%	39.0%
2011	3.1%	1.0%	11.2%	3.1%	28.6%	8.2%	6.1%	9.2%	29.6%
2007–11	3.5%	0.7%	8.7%	2.8%	19.3%	12.0%	12.6%	8.9%	31.5%

Note: Total percentages in Years 2008 through 2011 are slightly higher than 100% due to rounding.

TABLE 6 **Five-Year College Attendance Data (2007–11) by Barron's Selectivity Index, with Ivies, MIT, and Stanford (IMS) Pulled Out: Matthews Academy**

	NR	LC	C	C+	VC	VC+	HC	HC+	MC	IMS
2007	5.6%	0.0%	5.6%	3.4%	14.6%	16.9%	14.6%	13.5%	19.1%	6.7%
2008	3.9%	1.3%	9.1%	5.2%	13.0%	10.4%	20.8%	10.4%	22.1%	3.9%
2009	3.1%	0.0%	7.3%	1.0%	24.0%	11.5%	13.5%	4.2%	27.1%	8.3%
2010	2.0%	1.0%	10.0%	2.0%	15.0%	13.0%	10.0%	8.0%	28.0%	11.0%
2011	3.1%	1.0%	11.2%	3.1%	28.6%	8.2%	6.1%	9.2%	28.6%	1.0%
2007–11	3.5%	0.7%	8.7%	2.8%	19.3%	12.0%	12.6%	8.9%	25.2%	6.3%

Note: Total percentages in Years 2008 through 2011 are slightly higher than 100% due to rounding.

Although we cannot be certain of the extent to which school sector *in and of itself* "turbo-charges" (Cookson and Persell 1985) any group of students in the increasingly competitive college admissions process, it is clearly the case that students in the top 10% and 20% of their graduating classes at both Cannondale and Matthews, respectively, garner places in the "Most Competitive" US postsecondary destinations. Interesting too is the degree to which the *most* valued postsecondary destinations are now conceptualized as a *broadened range of private* schools, with markedly little place for flagship publics. As discussed above, the fact that key ranking systems such as Barron's now mark this broadened range of private colleges (beyond the Ivies, MIT, and Stanford) as encompassing the top institutions in the nation serves to heighten interest in this sector of schools among relatively privileged populations—populations that now voraciously seek to mark "distinction" via the postsecondary admissions process.

As Table 7 demonstrates, 72% of the entire Matthews student population matriculates at a private college from 2007–11. Although comparable five-year data for Cannondale are not available, available two-year trend

TABLE 7 **Five-Year (2007–11) Matriculation Data, Matthews Academy: Private, Public, Non-US**

	Private	Public	Non-US
2007	61.8%	32.6%	5.6%
2008	74.0%	24.7%	1.3%
2009	78.1%	18.8%	3.1%
2010	76.2%	22.8%	1.0%
2011	68.0%	29.0%	3.0%
2007–11	71.7%	25.5%	2.8%

data are informative, wherein 53% of Cannondale students who matriculate at a four-year college from the graduating classes of 2008 and 2009 similarly matriculate at a private college. Given that all but one of the Cannondale focal students matriculates at a private college, it is arguably the case that the private-going student population at Cannondale stems largely from the top academic track, as private institutions are now clearly conceptualized as the most highly valued and, as a consequence, where "students like us" go.[31] This is similarly true for Matthews, as the proportion of top-ranked focal students who matriculate at private postsecondary destinations is higher than that of the broader Matthews population.

As argued in chapter 5, low-income Black students initially compare themselves and their educational experiences and outcomes to those of their friends left behind in underresourced, public, inner-city high schools, rather than those who are placed in top tracks at their current schools. While this continues to be the case, these students simultaneously absorb the ranking hierarchies that comprise a continual topic of conversation within privileged secondary schools. Significantly, then, and in spite of the narrated difficulties with respect to the enactment of the college admissions process and the heavily classed/raced terrain in which racial difference manifests itself, this population does exceptionally well in the postsecondary admissions process, matriculating at highly selective and selective four-year privates to only a somewhat lesser extent than all remaining students at Matthews (not including those students at the top of the opportunity structure, i.e., those who comprise the top 20% of the class).

Here we turn to recent work by Hoxby and Avery (2012) to shed light on postsecondary outcomes. As Hoxby and Avery (2012) and others (e.g., Bowen, Chingos, and McPherson 2009) note, the vast majority of high-achieving low-income students do not apply to selective colleges even though they are qualified to do so by virtue of grades, test scores, and the like:

> These (high achieving low-income) students exhibit behavior that is typical of students of their *income* rather than typical of students of their *achievement*. There are however, high-achieving, low-income students who apply in much the same way as their high-income counterparts. These "achievement-typical" students also enroll and persist in college like their high-income counterparts. (p. 29)

Pursuing this point further, they note that income-typical students

> attend school and live in neighborhoods that lack others who have attended or could attend selective colleges. They are insufficiently, geographically concentrated to be reached, cost-effectively, by popular methods of informing students about their college opportunities: visits by admissions staff to high schools, campus visits by students, after school college access programs, contact with teachers who attended selective colleges and the like. (p. 29)

Hoxby and Avery's analysis has deep implications for the low-income Black students under consideration here, all of whom exhibit "achievement-typical" matriculation patterns rather than "income-typical" patterns. Despite their position in the lowest-level classes and felt marginalization throughout secondary school, attendance at Matthews and Bradford enables these students to enter selective and highly selective postsecondary destinations by virtue of being in institutions that are on the radar screen of highly selective postsecondary institutions (in addition, of course, to the imparted knowledge that undergirds such position), a conclusion with which these students wholeheartedly agree. Despite the psychic "trade-off," then, low-income Black students in elite private schools, while no longer turbocharged to the Ivies as they were decades ago, do exceedingly well in the admissions process.

In the final analysis, all students in our tri-school sample accrue great advantage from attendance at privileged secondary schools, whether public or private, and there is some evidence to suggest that *sector of school in and of itself matters* with regard to matriculation patterns, above and beyond test scores, GPA, and the like (Lee and Weis 2012). This is certainly the conclusion of Hoxby and Avery (2012), who note the ways in which particular kinds of institutions work to render high-achieving low-income students "achievement-typical" rather than "income typical" with regard to college matriculation patterns, thereby applying to and gaining acceptance at an array of selective and highly selective colleges that they would never have considered or necessarily even known about had they remained in their "insufficiently, geographically concentrated institutions to be reached, cost-effectively, by popular methods of informing students about their college opportunities" (p. 29).[32]

One additional point needs to be raised with regard to low-income Black students and college matriculation outcomes. At the early stages of the college search process, a notable number of low-income focal Black students expressed interest in attending a college that would provide not only a high-quality education, but also access to significant numbers of people of color, with some expressing potential interest in attending Historically Black Colleges and Universities (HBCU). In spite of this strongly expressed sentiment at the early stages of the college search and application process, however, only two students applied to HBCU, and only one actually enrolled. As the search process intensified, interested students discovered that they would not (or did not, in the case of one student who did apply) receive the kind of financial support that they would or could at a predominantly White institution (PWI).

More important, however, is that several students suggest that HBCU would not provide them with the type of credential or name recognition and access to opportunities that they could find at a (hopefully) diverse PWI. These students maintain that while *they* would value a degree from HBCU, they questioned how such a degree would be valued in society at large and the impact that this would have on their marketability in an increasingly competitive global marketplace. Seeking the type of racial affinity that is arguably available at HBCU, students nevertheless begin to question the ability of such schools to continue to mobilize them academically and socioeconomically in the way that their secondary schools have done. In the final analysis, most students who were initially interested in attending HBCU ultimately questioned the value of the capital that they can gain via these institutions and what they might be able to exchange that capital for in regard to occupations and graduate programs.

Conclusion

Looking across our focal groups, it is clear that all students do very well in the college admissions process. Students at the top of the academic hierarchy in Cannondale and Matthews largely gain admission to "Most

Competitive" institutions, with Matthews students, at least in the year under investigation, matriculating to a greater degree in top institutions like
Ivies, MIT, and Stanford. Low-income Black students do similarly well
with regard to matriculation patterns, with all students gaining entrance to
selective and highly selective four-year institutions. In point of fact, many
obtain entrance to "Highly Competitive" and "Highly Competitive+"
schools, with Steven matriculating at a "Most Competitive" Ivy League
institution.

Also worth noting is that students at the top of the academic hierarchy
at both Cannondale and Matthews matriculate at top *private* institutions.
Entering privates is the norm at Matthews no matter what a student's
standing in relation to the academic hierarchy of the school, where 72%
of students over a five-year time period matriculate at private colleges.
Matriculating at top privates is also the norm for top-ranked students at
Cannondale. In contrast to Matthews, however, a very high proportion of
the remaining four-year college-going population at Cannondale matriculates at public colleges.

In the case of low-income Black students, the decision to attend elite
secondary schools represents a heart wrenching "trade-off" for both students and parents, and it remains unclear whether students will find a *psychological home* as they move into college and beyond. Given that they are
entering postsecondary destinations that largely mirror the sociocultural
habitus of their secondary schools—an environment in which they never
felt comfortable—the extent to which they will continue to feel like "outsiders within" may slow their academic progress. Although many of these
students deal with charges of "acting White" and painful felt separation
from their neighborhood friends and community of origin, they still have
strong and heartfelt support from their parents during their secondary
schooling. Moving away from home to yet another elite environment without parental support on a daily basis may prove challenging. Nevertheless,
not a single student states that they would have done it any differently.[33]

The situation for "flexible immigrants" of color and privileged multigenerational Black students is, as we argue here, markedly different. As
privileged postsecondary institutions seek to diversify their student body
in historically unprecedented fashion, privileged students of color will, by
and large, have no problem finding a "psychological *class* home" in the
most elite and selective postsecondary destinations in the nation, as they
come from similar class backgrounds as the vast majority of students at
these schools. Here again, more highly capitalized Black students can be

expected to have very different experiences than their low-income Black counterparts.

This is not to suggest, however, that such contexts will be devoid of racial micro-aggressions, or that any individual Black student or student or color more broadly will never encounter racism. However, as we note earlier in this chapter, social class dictates, to a notable extent, the salience of race in privileged institutions, thereby making it easier for privileged students of color to transition into elite colleges than is likely to be the case for low-income Black students (as well as other students of color from low-income backgrounds). Thus *race and class, and race/class intersectionality, matter in the United States*—and they matter a lot, despite fantasies associated with notions of a postracial America. Without denying the continued existence of racism and apartheid racial structures in the United States, race and class are considerably more complex than in prior decades. Peering into class and race "productions" in privileged educational secondary schools makes this strikingly clear.

CHAPTER SEVEN

Class, Race, and Postsecondary Destinations in New Global Circumstances

Class Warfare: Class, Race, and College Admissions in Top-Tier Secondary Schools charts the complexity and nature of "class work" in the twenty-first-century United States, offering powerful evidence with respect to the ways in which a particular slice of the broad-based middle class now works to consolidate upper-middle-class privilege for the next generation via access to particularly located postsecondary destinations. As we suggest throughout this volume, although in all likelihood twenty-first-century America will continue to be marked by class and racial apartheid, such apartheid will prevail in complex and newly evolving forms.

In this volume, we explore a specifically located and largely unacknowledged reworking of class as situated in three iconic, affluent public and elite private secondary schools. This purposively selected tri-school student and parent sample enables deep ethnographic focus on actions and activities engaged by differentially located parents, students, counselors, and other school personnel in iconic private and public privileged secondary institutions. While each group independently reveals a great deal about schooling, family practices, and the current college process in the United States, putting these groups in sharp relief, as we do here, starkly portrays the ways in which "class works" and is put to work by varying groups in schools.

Although to most people "class warfare" implies social classes engaged in violent struggle against each other, our use of the term is different and, we argue, more resonant with current realities in the United States.

Rather than focus on classes in violent struggle with and against one another, we focus on tensions *within* a social class as people struggle to maintain and/or gain class advantage for the next generation.[1] A major finding of our research is the intense and targeted "class work" of a now highly insecure broad-based middle class that engages in a very specific form of "class warfare," one in which a segment of the middle class individually and collectively mobilizes and enacts its own located and embodied cultural, social, and economic capital, both to preserve itself in uncertain economic times while attempting to instantiate a distinctly professional and managerial upper middle class through access to particular kinds of postsecondary destinations.

More specifically, privileged parents and students now engage any and all capitals at their disposal as they strive for "distinction" so as to gain entrance to the most highly valued postsecondary destinations in the country. Postsecondary ranking schemata such as Barron's *Profiles of American Colleges* largely drive the perceived relative worth of postsecondary destinations, as they now publicly mark a narrow band of largely private colleges as those most worthy. As such, they increasingly work to drive "consumer choice" among a specifically located fraction of the broad middle class, fingering and instantiating those postsecondary destinations in a now national marketplace that lie at the epicenter of intraclass warfare.

Employing the Weis/Fine theory of method—"critical bifocality" (2012, 2013)—we focus on the mechanisms through which observed, macro-level, globally induced phenomenon are produced at the lived level on a daily basis, whether by explicit design/work, or by virtue of what Bourdieu refers to as " 'habitus'—a system of lasting and transposable dispositions which, integrating past experiences, functions at every moment as a matrix of perceptions, appreciations and actions and makes possible the achievement of infinitely diversified tasks" (Bourdieu and Wacquant 1992, p. 18). As such, we acknowledge the explicit "class work" on the part of a segment of the broad-based middle class involved in maintaining advantage under massively shifting global conditions, and as particularly linked to a now national and increasingly segmented US marketplace (Hoxby 1997) for postsecondary education.

In so arguing, and in contrast to the recent media fray with regard to "helicopter parents," we do not presume that relatively "rich" people have a "culture of anxiety," but rather interrogate the underlying structural conditions that help to produce these expressed panics, paying close attention to the explicit linkages between collected ethnographic action and narratives and what is happening in broad context. These data, then, as well as our ensuing on-the-ground analysis within each of our ethnographic chapters, must be understood as linked to larger social structural arrangements as they simultaneously refract back on such arrangements, thereby *creating,* in part, *future* class structure and relative position of individuals and groups.

Data from this research additionally forecast the increasing contradiction between individual and collective struggles related to the broader middle class. Affluent parents, schools, and students are now positioning for a more highly segmented postsecondary sector, one in which the number of available spaces at the "Most Competitive" colleges and universities—and most specifically the Ivies—remain relatively constant in relation to increased numbers of applicants who both wish to gain admittance to such institutions and are able to "see themselves there." Thus stark contradictions emerge with regard to working on behalf of the class (e.g., working for the secondary school as a whole so as to make all students more competitive for admission) and working for one's children, so as to make them more competitive in relation to other potential applicants.

Given the stakes, and the now conceptualized absolute *centrality* of attendance at particularly located colleges on the part of privileged parents and students such as those who comprise the focus of chapters 3 and 4, it is arguably the case that the middle class increasingly turns upon *itself*, thereby self-fracturing as a *broad-based middle class*, while moving to consolidate individually located position for the next generation, and specifically their own children. We argue that as this segment of the broad middle class now consciously exploits any and all opportunities to position their children for advantage via access to particularly located postsecondary destinations, they effectively constrict access for the rest of the middle classes, thereby cutting themselves off from any kind of larger class base.[2] This is particularly clear in chapters 3 and 4, where largely but not entirely White and privileged parents engage all available capitals at their disposal—social, cultural and economic—so as to consolidate advantage for their sons and daughters.

This struggle plays itself out most fervently over access to "Most Competitive" and "Highly Competitive+" (Barron's *Profiles of American Colleges* 2009, 2013; see chapter 6) private postsecondary institutions in a context in which the postsecondary sector itself is becoming increasingly stratified, with the perceived stakes for admission ever higher. As we argue in chapters 1 and 4, as postsecondary education becomes more widely available, qualitative differences in access to particularly located colleges become an important way of marking "distinction." In line with notions of "effectively maintained inequality" (Lucas 2001), advantage is increasingly marked by the competitiveness index of school to which one gains entrance, rather than by any kind of generalized notion of a "college education," or a four-year versus two-year degree. Such attempts to stake out "distinction" take a specifically located class form as parents position their children for postsecondary entrance via the following: (1) early "concerted cultivation" (Lareau 2003) of their children; (2) specifically located and linked schooling experiences in elementary, middle, and secondary school; and (3) the postsecondary admissions process itself, wherein individual families engage all available capitals to position their children for advantage via entrance to particularly located schools. The latter point is most highly evident among privileged parents at the elite privates. Importantly, such "class warfare" is engaged at an individual family level, although certainly facilitated by the collectively shared college going habitus of secondary schools attended.

As we suggest in chapter 6, although families engage the college admissions process at an individual family level, the process itself, in contradictory fashion, partially works to cement a new form of collective consciousness ("We are all in this together"), as particularly located students and parents now engage an increasingly arduous rite of passage as a class-linked collective. What is largely individualistically driven action on the part of families who work to position their *own* children for class advantage, simultaneously works to consolidate a shared sense of positionality among privileged students and parents who go through the college admissions process in particular kinds of ways. As we suggest in chapters 5 and 6, although low-income Black students who attend elite private secondary schools are poised to be part of the new upper middle class by virtue of "achievement-typical" college matriculation patterns, there is little evidence of *felt* class connection to their highly privileged counterparts.

While the largely individualistic tendencies that explicitly drive the form of class positioning highlighted here may have always been a hallmark of the broader middle class (Reay et al. 2011), we suggest both that the middle class itself was *highly dependent* upon collective class work (Ball, 2003), whether acknowledged or not *and, more important,* that the economy was robust enough to provide "good jobs" for the next generation across difference within this broadly construed class sector. In a substantially altered economic context, this is no longer the case (Brown,

Lauder, and Ashton 2011), and, as a consequence, the professional and managerial upper middle class mobilizes all potential class resources as it attempts to secure advantage for their own children.

The particular form that such class mobilization takes has consequences for future class structure and the ability of the middle class, in the long run, to mobilize *as a class*, rather than a group of atomized individuals. In this sense, the broader collective is fractured as privileged parents voraciously move, as we see in chapter 3 and, more vividly, in chapter 4, to mobilize on behalf of their *own* children. Both Lareau (2003) and Brantlinger (2003) forecast this set of events, but, as we argue here, it is the college applications and admissions process that now constitutes the key site for the battle over class advantage. Put another way, the now nationally located battle over admissions to particularly located postsecondary destinations—specifically, "Most Competitive" and "Highly Competitive+" private institutions—comprises a critical battle site in this new "class war."[3]

As we argue throughout this volume, such "class work" is visibly and most intensely engaged by a particular segment of the middle class as its seeks to markedly pull away from the rest of the middle group, a group that it sees as steadily losing economic ground and from which it is now consciously seeking to distance through attendance at specifically located postsecondary institutions. This is happening at one and the same time as a new and more complex status hierarchy is being instantiated within the postsecondary sector itself, a status hierarchy that is simultaneously being produced and "locked in" by the actions and activities of this particular class fraction on a day-to-day basis, thereby further prompting individualistically driven "class action" on the part of privileged parents and schools. At the same time, of course, such voraciously engaged actions and activities effectively constrict access for the rest of the middle class, a group that will find increasingly little ground on which to compete.

This has marked consequences for both future individual class position and the US class structure as a whole, as a particular segment of postsecondary education additionally functions, both intentionally and by virtue of its very existence, to markedly privilege those in attendance. While this has always been the case, of course, and relatively privileged parents have *always* worked on behalf of their children, there is now deepened anxiety *throughout* the class structure with regard to passing on privilege to the next generation. In this context, middle- and upper-middle-class actors, reflective of deepened tensions *within* the broad-based middle class, engage in a very specific form of inter- and intra- "class warfare"—"warfare" that is designed to maintain and/or gain advantage for the next generation.

The scope of this US situated "class warfare" is dialectically linked to a very particular broad context, one that characterizes and envelops our current historic moment. Such historic "moment" is marked by the interconnections between and among the following: (1) the now global knowledge economy, specifically as connected to certain kinds of increasingly valued academic credentialing processes; (2) constriction of available "good jobs" in the United States; and (3) intensified segmentation within the US situated postsecondary sector, wherein struggle for class position is more explicitly waged via struggle over entrance to particular kinds of postsecondary destinations. Although specific colleges—most particularly the Ivies—were always valued by the highly privileged, elite secondary schools more frequently pipelined into Ivy League colleges than is the case today (Cookson and Persell 1985). In point of fact, even top ranked elite secondary day and boarding schools no longer function as a pipeline into Ivies, MIT, and Stanford. This means that the transference of class status via family background can no longer be assumed, thereby introducing great anxiety into even the most privileged populations. This may not, of course, be the case among the top 1%, as their massive capital and wealth transfer seamlessly to the next generation. For everyone else, however, access to postsecondary destinations is increasingly conceptualized as the way to "lock in" future class status.

Point 3 above is further fueled by historically "struggled over" and simultaneously hard-won democratizing impulses within the United States and, specifically, with regard to its most valued postsecondary destinations. Although the United States still has a long way to go with regard to equity and outcomes, the fact is that more people than ever before, across race/ethnicity, national background, class, and gender can now imagine themselves at institutions historically colonized by objectively very rich White people, all of whom were men. This is not to suggest that entrance to such institutions is now widely available across race/ethnicity and class in the United States, as this is most definitely not the case, and there is stark difference between individual and collective logics (Willis 1977) with regard to entrance to educational institutions and class processes more generally. It is, however, to state unequivocally that a far more comprehensive range of parents and children can imagine themselves and/or their children applying to both America's iconic elite and historically White male institutions (largely the Ivies), *and* a broadened range of highly valued destinations now marked as such by widely available ranking schemata, than ever could before.

In the above context, the role of privileged secondary schools, and particularly elite privates that make it possible for low-income students of color to attend these schools, need further consideration, as this additionally constitutes a particular kind of pathway to the new upper middle class. In chapters 5 and 6, we specifically focus on this population of students, all of whom meet our definition of low income and all of whom self-identify as Black. Initially entering privileged secondary schools wanting to attend "good" colleges—defined as undifferentiated four-year schools—students substantially rework their definition of a "good" college during their secondary school years, ultimately taking into account circulating ranking schemata. Like their more privileged counterparts, they apply to and gain entrance to a range of selective and highly selective postsecondary destinations, thereby engaging the college admissions process as "achievement-typical" students rather than "income-typical" students (Hoxby and Avery 2012), a typicality that is linked to entirely different postsecondary entrance patterns.

Unlike their more privileged counterparts, however, they do not have parents who work to position them for this status from the time they are very young. Although this group of students absorbs generalized information about the college process just from being in the school, neither they nor their parents necessarily know how to put this information to use so as to maximize possibilities for postsecondary admission. So too, although one might expect that students rely heavily on their college counselors for advice, they in fact rarely see their counselors, even though they express great respect for them. In this sense, then, low-income Black students enter and engage highly privileged secondary schools in noticeably different ways than do their highly privileged counterparts, who have been prepped for such institutions all their lives. As such, low-income Black students evidence both a notably different pathway to the new upper middle class than that of their privileged counterparts *and* remain largely psychologically and socially distanced from those privileged counterparts with whom they went to school. A prime example of this relates to the intensification of the college admissions process itself. Whatever collectivity is subjectivity forged among privileged students as a result of participation in the intensified admissions process over a close to two-year period does not blanket low-income Black students, either from their own perspective or that of their more privileged counterparts.

This enacted pathway of low-income Black students to highly valued postsecondary destinations takes its toll. Low-income Black students go through four years of highly privileged secondary schools positioned via specific institutional mechanisms and facially neutral policies and practices as "outsiders within," a position they come to subjectively internalize. Additionally, as we see in chapter 6, the ways that racial difference manifests itself in privileged institutions leads to strong feelings that they are seen only in relation to narrow and stereotypical representations of Blackness, and that they must work hard to contest negative assumptions and stereotypes about their race. Given that they are heading toward similarly privileged postsecondary institutions, it is difficult to predict the extent to which these students will find a psychological home in their colleges. As they are no longer minors, it will perhaps be easier to cope with their new environments than was the case in secondary school. On the other hand, the fact that they are heading for geographic locations devoid of strong day-to-day family support may make coping more difficult. The extent to which either scenario will be the case, however, is as yet unknown.

In this regard, it is noteworthy that there is a population of privileged Black students (across generational status in the United States, ethnicity, and nation of origin) who have a psychological edge in privileged institutions as they share class background with the majority of students. As we discuss in chapter 6, class mediates the salience of race, wherein privileged Black students, while perhaps feeling racially isolated at points, are fundamentally rooted and largely comfortable in privileged and heavily raced/classed environments, as they grew up in them. Although privileged colleges seek to diversify their student bodies, with specific attention to *visible minorities*, they are not explicitly seeking *low-income visible minorities*. As a consequence, rendering the educational space more comfortable for a population of low-income Black students is unlikely to be a high priority for a school. Any given individual can find a psychological home over time, of course, and it is arguably the case that this population is psychologically strong given their prior experiences in privileged secondary schools. The opposite possibility is equally likely, however—that they will find it difficult to find a psychological home "away from home," at one and the same time that privileged students across race/ethnicity and nation of origin will have an easier time of it.

The question can be raised, however, to what extent will privileged postsecondary institutions take responsibility for making the space more comfortable for low-income minorities. Here the recent work of Nancy

Leong (2013) is exceptionally provocative. Leong argues that our current focus on affirmative action helps to produce what she calls "racial capitalism"—"the process of deriving social or economic value from racial identity" (p. 2). Although not challenging affirmative action, she notes the extent to which affirmative action tends to be reduced to numerical diversity, with little attempt on the part of predominantly White institutions to value a commensurate diversity of cultures and identities. As she argues: "This instrumental view is antithetical to a view of non-whiteness—and race more generally—as a personal characteristic intrinsically deserving of respect. Worse still, the instrumental view of non-whiteness fails utterly to inspire efforts at genuine racial inclusiveness and cross-racial understanding" (p. 4). Continuing, she states: "The irony, then, is that our legal and social emphasis on diversity—while intended to produce progress toward a racially egalitarian society—has instead created a state of affairs that degrades non-whiteness by commodifying it and that relegates non-white individuals to the status of 'trophies' or 'passive emblems'" (pp. 4–5). Relegating non-White individuals to the status of "trophies" or "passive emblems" does not bode well on the part of privileged colleges to take steps toward full inclusion of low-income minorities in campus life, both academic and social.

Taking Leong's point seriously helps to explain the *relative abandonment in practice* of low-income minorities in privileged educational sites. As argued earlier, facially neutral policies and practices within educational environments contribute to a deepening of linked race/class inequalities, as institutions do little to level the playing field once low-income Black students and other low-income minorities of color are admitted. This affirms Leong's notion of "racial capitalism," as it is the commodification of race that leads to the practice of numerical representation, without consequent attention to facilitating either equal outcomes or respect for a range of cultural identities and practices. This in no way constitutes an anti–affirmative action argument. In contrast, it comprises a stark statement that until privileged educational institutions take more responsibility for the psychological comfort and academic success of low-income minority students, potential and desired outcomes as evidenced by admittance will not be fully realized.

In this broad *field* of action, it is important to recall that privileged parents are simultaneously mobilizing all available class resources so as to situate their children for future advantage. In this regard, they both contest the notion that class is "simply the manner to which one is born" and intentionally work to solidify the border between the middle- and upper-middle professional and managerial classes. In so doing, they attempt to ensure their children's position in what is perceived as a less vulnerable class segment in new economic context. This must be seen as a targeted attempt on the part of those already advantaged both to instantiate future deep difference *within* the middle class and to ensure that their own children fall on the right side of the anticipated and "locked in" divide in a now highly competitive global arena. Importantly, this is taking place commensurate with what we detail above with regard to low-income minority students. Although both groups are driving toward future advantage by virtue of attendance at privileged secondary schools, *they do so in notably different ways and with different metaphoric baggage.*

As the US middle and upper middle class is both rearticulated and simultaneously rearticulates itself in relation to other classes and class fractions, both within the United States and between the United States and nations across the globe (where classes are similarly in flux), the relationship between class and race becomes more complex. In contrast to maintaining White privilege in any kind of streamlined fashion, as the work of Reay et al. (2011) on the White middle class in the United Kingdom suggests, we argue that current upper-middle-class construction in the United States both pierces and *partially* dislodges historically rooted US race/class lines, as privileged secondary and postsecondary sectors now embody somewhat democratizing impulses around race (Bowen and Bok 1998). As we see in chapters 5 and 6, low-income as well as privileged Black students now attend these schools. Such democratizing impulses in both public (Carnoy and Levin 1985) and private education sectors, however, embody deep contradictions. This is particularly the case for low-income multigenerational Black students who are distanced by virtue of such attendance from their historic social and political base, a base with which they would have perhaps remained connected had they not attended elite educational institutions (Jenkins 2011).

Importantly, with regard to race/ethnicity and class in the twenty-first century, this is coupled with the fact that increasing numbers of children of transnational migrants of color who possess "flexible citizenship" (Ong 1999) now attend public and private privileged secondary schools and engage in the culture of explicit and voracious "class work" that becomes normative practice in such institutions. While such "flexible immigrants" of color bring their own educational understandings and expectations to the United States with regard to the work of schooling (Li 2005), they are part and parcel of normative class culture in privileged secondary schools, as they are *fundamentally* "class insiders." Under this formulation, such voracious "class work" cannot *be attributed to, or blamed on*, increasing numbers of "flexible immigrants," a sentiment that is, at times, evidenced in the popular press. As we demonstrate here, comparable struggles are clearly in evidence among a range of school attendees and, in fact, become *normative practice* in privileged educational sites, wherein "flexible immigrants" as well as their privileged multigenerational White, Black, Latino/a and Asian counterparts work to produce the particular shape and form of "class warfare" evidenced in this volume.[4]

Although race and class are now made more complex by virtue of the fact that the new upper middle class will most certainly not be entirely White, such complexity, as we suggest in chapter 6, is tied to the construction of a particular kind of racial "other"–one that simultaneously encourages neoliberal subjectivity across race and class lines, wherein all students are encouraged to believe that they can "construct themselves," their racial identities, and their own futures. While the White working-class fraction has struggled to maintain itself as a class fraction based partially on its own assertion of Whiteness as well as deep gender realignment (Weis 2004), the carving out of a *new* upper middle class works across race/ethnicity in unprecedented fashion. While giving credence to the general theoretical discussions regarding the "anxiety" noted by Reay et al. (2011), around the perceived disintegration of a distinctly White middle-class identity in the United Kingdom, there is, in the United States, a commensurate *piercing* of Whiteness tied to the consolidation of an emerging upper middle class *across* racial/ethnic difference. This is linked, in key ways, to the distinct centrality of a particular sector of postsecondary destinations.

Privileged Educational Sites in a New Context

As noted earlier in this volume, important scholarly work has been done in and on privileged educational sites (Cookson and Persell 1985; Demerath 2011; Gaztambide-Fernández 2009; Howard 2007; Howard and Gaztambide-Fernández 2010; Horvat and Antonio 1999; Khan 2011; Proweller 1998), and Annette Lareau (1989, 2003), in particular, has engaged well-known work on middle-class childrearing patterns in the United States. With great respect for this overall corpus of work, we suggest that individual and collective social practices, as documented ethnographically, can be even more deeply understood and theorized in relation to substantially altered constraints in global economic context and, more specifically, the extent to which and the ways in which such constraints play on national and locally specific levels.

With the exception of McDonough (1997), Horvat and Antonio (1999), and Lareau and Weininger (2010), there has been remarkably little ethnographic attention paid to the *specific* secondary-to-postsecondary linkage. Such existing research was largely conducted prior to the current iteration of globalization and neoliberalism with all attendant-swelling inequalities. Generally speaking, then, this body of otherwise excellent work on privileged settings cannot engage the ways in which entrance to increasingly valued postsecondary destinations in a now national (and increasingly international) marketplace must be theorized as an attempt to "maintain distinction" and mark class boundaries in new context.

Class Warfare specifically theorizes the current actions and activities of parents, students, and schools as targeted "class work," thereby encouraging and enabling us to move beyond the notion of individual parent and student pathology and/or the "overmonitoring" of children as a class-linked form of love. Instead, we point toward an understanding of new and distinctly located class processes that are designed to stake out and preserve privilege in this new context. This is particularly useful in light of the deafening media-driven construct of the "helicopter parent," which, although "practically powerful" in the sense that it appeals broadly and therefore "sells," positions individual parents as largely crazy and individual children as largely unwilling or unable to grow up. Demanding that we reposition parents *as class actors in very specific and constricting environments,* both in a global economic sense and with regard to the postsecondary sector in the United States, we underscore the extent to which parents have been convinced that quality education is now a scarce resource. In so doing, we reposition the work of parents as the targeted "class work" of specifically located actors in a particular time and space rather than individuals who neurotically hover over their children much longer than they should if the next generation is to grow into healthy forms of adulthood.

In the case at hand, what we have come to call "class work," by virtue of our multisited ethnographic investigation, is targeted work that is engaged on a day-to-day and week-by-week basis in elite and affluent classrooms, homes, and schools—work that is specifically engaged by parents, children, and school personnel so that marked "distinction" can to be accomplished. Rather than "class struggle" taking place largely by men in the workplace against a more powerful class, and vice versa, as is arguably the case in an industrially based economy, a great deal of individual and collective "class work/struggle" is, on a daily basis, now located in families and schools, and *within* class groups, with specific attention to the production of the next generation of class subjects, in this case, class subjects of privilege. This has deep implications for scholarly understandings related to gender and ongoing "class warfare." Although it is not our purpose to consider the subject of gender at length, we offer comments related to gender at a later point in the chapter.

Class Warfare additionally focuses on the contradictions and complexities of privileged sites serving as racially and ethnically democratizing territory, no matter what the stated intent. Although penetrating the notion that privileged class actors of the future will be entirely White, our sample population of low-income Black students, in particular, affords a lens through which we gain increased understanding of the complexities of race and class, as well as the newly constructed racial/class subject both within and among White, Black, and transnational communities.

Ironically, perhaps, in light of historically based apartheid and associated racialized constructions in the United States, the most serious piercing of Whiteness as privilege is taking root in the most privileged educational sectors. This is suggestive of a new form of American apartheid, one that certainly embeds blatant and continuing racial inequalities, but one that simultaneously *marks social class divisions* as partially transcending race and ethnicity. Given the struggles of low-income self-identified Black students in contrast to Black students of far more privileged background, we suspect that this group, more than any other, will find it relatively difficult to locate a psychological home in the new upper middle class, irrespective of the fact that they have spent considerable time in highly privileged educational sites. This has a material component as well, as successful members of this group will undoubtedly be called upon to financially support those family members "left behind."

In contrast, we anticipate that those with privilege across race/ethnicity/national origin will find it relatively easy to position, and be positioned for, long-term advantage in comparison to low-income minority students whose class background marks them as "outsiders within" the habitus of privileged educational institutions. While not dismissing the, at times, individually felt "outsider" status of any student of color in a predominantly White institution, and/or individually experienced racially charged microaggressions associated with such status (Solórzano, Ceja, and Yosso 2000;

Solórzano 1998), it is, as we argue in this volume, a particular combination of race and social class that marks a given *group* of students as true "outsiders within" privileged educational institutions.

This has implications for the power and applicability of notions of "effectively maintained" inequality (Lucas 2001) in the twenty-first century, where it is arguably the case that a key marker of twenty-first-century US class structure and associated production of inequalities is that children of privileged families *across* race/ethnicity/national origin will be able to continue to pass on their privilege to the next generation via entrance to particularly located postsecondary institutions. If we are correct in our speculation, the upper middle class in the United States will be increasingly racially and ethnically diverse, populated with children of privileged parents across race and ethnicity, a phenomenon that works both to trouble notions of class and race while leaving intact a set of discursive constructions about "Blacks" that can be expected to tear through both the newly constituted upper middle class as well as communities of color that are increasingly comprised of "those left behind."[5]

The above is tied, of course, to three structural phenomena: (1) the increasing battle over educational credentials in the "global auction"; (2) intensified competition for particular kinds of educational credentials given massification of the postsecondary educational system wherein many more students attend *some* kind of postsecondary institution; and (3) the markedly ramped-up level of intellectual labor now required in upper-middle-class secondary schools, both in an absolute sense and as compared to what is demanded in nonprivileged educational sites. Rather than suggestive of any kind of simplistic individually and psychologically driven postracial America, however, this constitutes a stark statement as to the altered shape and form of class structure, as well as associated future possibilities for class/race struggle in any collective sense. The marking of "distinction" as now located in the production of the upper middle class means that students from low-income Black communities mark "distinction" in a particularly racialized fashion with regard to those left behind, serving, in the final analysis, to fracture formerly collectivized racial communities far more intensively along class lines than ever before. In spite of our argument around the production of a new upper middle class that works across lines of race/ethnicity and national origin, racial apartheid will, unfortunately, simultaneously continue to mark America. Given its evolving complexity as discussed in this volume, conceptualizing a strategy for fundamentally attacking deeply rooted class/race inequalities across the American landscape will, we fear, prove increasingly challenging.

The question must be asked, though, to what extent will a newly constituted upper middle class be able to maintain its anticipated standard of living absent a broader class base? Even the top 1%, which ostensibly is the moneyed upper class, does not maintain and reproduce itself solely as individuals. Although the upper class will undoubtedly continue to be 100% dependent on an upper-middle "brokering class" of lawyers and finance and investment people (a class of salaried workers who are so necessary to the exponential growth of capital that they can perhaps maintain their lucrative positions devoid of an broader class base), it is arguably the case that the overwhelming majority of those poised to comprise the new upper middle class will occupy positions in the "dominated fraction of the dominant class" (Bourdieu 1979)—or, what Chauvel (2010) later calls "the increasingly dominated fraction of the dominant class" (p. 87).[6] As such, they are likely to be brought into the labor force when necessary and released when expendable, rendering the long-term financial health and stability of the new upper middle class highly uncertain. If our prediction is correct, parental and personal investment in their own children at the expense of broader class connections will not necessarily serve the class "winners" well over time.

What we see in the ethnography is the clawing for position via postsecondary entrance patterns, and particularly the most highly valued postsecondary privates. As such, success represents the culmination of a set of *individual* struggles in that individuals who succeed at one level earn the right to proceed to the next round—what James Rosenbaum (1978) refers to as a "tournament model." Under such model, "winning" is never assured, as winners at one stage merely earn the right to proceed to the next, wherein the drive for status represents a continual jockeying for position in relation to one another.

Under such scenario, "winners" can always be knocked off. With no larger class base from which to mount sustained struggle for relative job and career continuation and security, we can expect that individuals will fall by the wayside at every point in the battle for class position. In spite of the fact that Matthews senior Jason Sheffield refers to this as a "marathon," there is no finish line for the millions of "runners" who now participate in this race.

The extent to which "class winners" can sustain themselves as individuals and/or ultimately cohere as a class is unknown at this point. The newly comprised upper middle class could implode from within, given the lack of a broader class base, or be challenged and fractured from outside itself by virtue of organizational capacity among those "left behind" (and perhaps fueled by those "runners" who dropped to the sidelines along the way). As such, the continued nature and scope of *class warfare* along the lines we outline here is highly uncertain.

What is clear, however, is that the "winners" of the tournament model in many ways go it alone, with little enacted sense of a broader class base. Although certainly propped up by their families who help to position them throughout the process, and surrounded by individuals who accompany them on their journey (with a sense of "We are all in this together" as per the college admissions process), in the final analysis, they are devoid of a larger collective that *works for the good of the class rather than the good of any given individual*. Like anything else, of course, this could change with time. As it stands now, however, the new upper middle class of the twenty-first century is likely to be comprised of an enormous number of individual "winners" across race/ethnicity/national origin. These "winners" emerge victorious by virtue of a new *individualistically driven "class war" of position*, under which "winners" emerge at each stage in the process, but substantially devoid of any larger collective that can be mobilized for common purpose.[7]

To be clear, we engage this volume as social analysts. As such, readers should not assume that we condone the shape and form of these new class production processes, although the notable piercing of race and class boundaries and barriers is laudable. The psychic toll of this particular form of "class warfare" is likely to be high, however. We suggest earlier that low-income Black students may have difficulty finding a "home" in their privileged postsecondary schools and in the upper middle class of the future. So, too, although we can expect that privileged students across race and ethnicity will have little difficulty in finding a psychological home in their postsecondary destinations and the new upper middle class more generally, the relentless "war of positioning" in which each individual must prove him- or herself every step of the way will, we suspect, exact different but no less consequential tolls on this population. It will not be psychologically or practically easy for any of these students to keep moving forward so as to engage yet one more round of struggle for position, and this is, we fear, what America of the twenty-first century may look like with respect to this group.

One more point needs to be raised with regard to this particular form of "class warfare." Although privileged parents largely support their children monetarily through their undergraduate years, it remains to be seen what kind of debt students will incur as a result of this sustained and individualistically engaged "war of positioning." Even the most privileged parents may, at some point, insist that their children take out loans to pursue graduate and/or professional school. With the constricted US economy, it is not clear what the return on this investment will ultimately be, and the extent to which even this group of students will be able to pay off their loans is unknown. Although these are the ostensible "winners" in the drive toward class advantage, the road is likely to be bumpy at many points, potentially contributing to the anticipated student loan "debt bubble," even within this highly privileged population.

A Note on Gender

Noticeably apparent in our data is the fact that there is little difference between male and female students in their drive toward "distinction," as all students in our tri-school sample are intently positioning for particular kinds of postsecondary destinations by virtue of their attendance at privileged secondary schools. As we see in chapter 5, low-income Black students enter the privileged secondary school sector with the intent of attending "good" colleges. By this they and their parents mean four-year institutions. Despite considerable struggles within the elite private sector, all low-income Black students in our sample enter highly selective postsecondary destinations, and the vast majority matriculate at "Very Competitive," "Highly Competitive," and "Highly Competitive+" destinations. Those students positioned at the top of the academic hierarchy in their respective public and private secondary institutions matriculate almost entirely at top privates. This is the case for both males and females, across race, ethnicity, and secondary school sector (public versus private).

This raises the question of the extent to which and the ways in which gender intersects with the production and maintenance of the new upper middle class. Goldin (2006, p. 1) argues "women's increased involvement in the economy was the most significant change in labor markets during the past century." Speaking of three evolutionary phases and one revolutionary phase, she states:

> The transition from evolution to revolution was a change from static decision-making, with limited or intermittent horizons, to dynamic decision-making, with long-term horizons. It was a change from agents who work because they

and their families "need the money" to those who are employed, at least in part, because occupation and employment define one's fundamental identity and societal worth. It involved a change from "jobs" to "careers," where the distinction between these two concepts concerns both horizon and human capital investment. (p. 1)[8]

As Goldin (2006, p. 19) states, as we moved into the 1980s and 1990s, "wives were less often secondary workers, the flotsam and jetsam of the labor market," and women's workforce participation was less influenced by the earnings of their husbands.

Our data are resonant with Goldin's important points, although the extent to which young men and women consciously articulate such gender-fueled understandings at this moment in their lives is less than clear. The fact is, however, that young men and women in our tri-school student sample are part of a "quiet revolution" in which there is substantial rearrangement of women's employment, family, and education. As a consequence, both women and men are similarly positioning for class advantage via matriculation at highly selective private postsecondary destinations.

Although gender differences in types of institutions attended have been narrowing for quite some time now, and women graduate with higher degrees at all levels, it is nevertheless striking that there is not a hint of gender imbalance in the collected data with regard to driving toward particular postsecondary destinations, even with respect to anticipated field of study, where young men and women express similar interests in the arts, social sciences, humanities, STEM fields, and so forth. The extent to which they will be able to access and actualize such professional desires is not known, but at this moment in their lives, they are driving toward comparable goals.

The ultimate shape and form of gender relations as linked to the new upper middle class is not yet known, and it is additionally not clear what professional and managerial fields women and men will find themselves in and how this will serve to impact domestic and/or professional/managerial life. In other words, like class and its links to race and ethnicity, particularly with regard to low-income Black students, the relationship between gender and lived-out professional and managerial outcomes remains unclear. What we do know, though, is that young men and women in privileged secondary schools are positioning in the same ways and to the same extent with regard to access to particularly located postsecondary destinations.

Based on data presented in chapters 3 and 4, we additionally know that privileged parents engage in considerable "class work" to enable this to happen, and the extent and direction of such "class work" is not dependent on the gender of their children. What the future will hold in this regard is unknown, of course, as men and women of the new upper middle class will grow into adulthood and attempt to meet the challenges of actualizing their class status while contemplating their own likely desires for family life. In this regard, and as we argue in chapter 4 in particular, it is women's labor that largely works to position children for the new upper middle class. Mothers are the ones who predominantly set, maintain, and monitor the larger two-year agenda with regard to the increasingly complex and demanding postsecondary admissions process in the United States, with all attendant deadlines, applications, essays, visits to schools, and so forth. It is, therefore, largely but not entirely "mother labor" that substantially enables and props up this set of lived-out class processes and the "class warfare" that we detail in this volume.

At the moment, a notable proportion of these women balance significant professional and/or managerial careers as they simultaneously engage highly intensified "class work" on behalf of the next generation. In this sense, this entire process is "gender engaged," with the ultimate outcome that their sons and daughters are comparably positioned for future class privilege.[9] The extent to which such gendered enactments around raising the next generation and/or gender trade-offs as we move further into the twenty-first century will mark future family life is unclear at this moment. We do know, however, that women's family-sited labor (in concert with men's and women's income-producing labor) substantially works to position *both* sons and daughters for comparable access to highly desired postsecondary destinations and beyond.

Additionally unclear is the extent to which men and women, as they move forward in their educational lives and careers, will be able to actualize professional and managerial status to the same extent. In particular, we do not know whether the ubiquitous "glass ceiling" will continue to define women's professional and managerial lives, and/or decisions will be made by both men and women within families (of whatever form) to curtail professional and managerial life so as to raise the next generation. Also unknown is the extent to which dual-income upper-middle-class life will be wholly dependent on the availability and purchase of external services such as individuals to help raise children, clean the home, prepare meals, and so forth. If such group is less available in the future, men and women of the upper middle class will have an increasingly difficult time "having it all."

At the moment, however, young men and women in privileged secondary schools, both private and public, are being positioned for and simultaneously position themselves for a new upper middle class via access to particularly located postsecondary destinations. Importantly, they are doing so under the assumption that they have equal rights and responsibilities to engage and be part of this professional and managerial class fraction via access to postsecondary destinations *and* linked professional and/or managerial future careers. They are the beneficiaries of the "quiet revolution" detailed by Goldin (2006), whether consciously aware of this or not.

Final Thoughts on Class and US Colleges and Universities

We suggest in this volume that individuals who are positioning and being positioned for what we call a "new" upper middle class are instantiating, through their own actions and activities, a sector of particular private colleges and universities as *the* sector that will position for future class advantage—a slice of the larger postsecondary arena that now sits, we argue, at the very epicenter of a new form of "class warfare," wherein struggle is waged over admittance to what are considered the "Most Competitive" and "Highly Competitive+" private institutions, in particular. Although individuals still maintain strong desires to enter the most elite of this sector—Ivy (where the US elite historically had an admissions "lock"), MIT, and Stanford, increasing numbers of applicants to these schools mean both that these institutions have become more competitive by virtue of a higher rejection rate and that the children of multigenerational legacy families do not necessarily gain admission.

In light of this, the next sector down—in this case, a *broadened* range of private institutions deemed "Most Competitive" and "Highly Competitive+," in particular, are similarly struggled over at the point of college admissions, wherein parents bring to bear all class resources in an attempt to position their children for this sector of schools if Ivies, MIT, and Stanford prove to be out of reach. In so doing, they stretch and simultaneously instantiate the "Most Competitive" and "Highly Competitive+" *privates* as *the schools—in addition to Ivies, MIT, and Stanford*—to attend, thereby rendering these schools more highly competitive in the ubiquitous ranking systems (as they now reject more students given increasing applicants) while at the same time largely populating them with particular kinds of classed subjects. The extent to which this happens has deep implications for many now highly prestigious publics, as even highly prestigious publics become *relatively* marginalized in the race for college admissions among a particular group of students and parents.[10] As discussed in chapter 6, Barron's and other ranking schemata encourage the instantiation of this broader range of almost entirely private schools as *the* schools most worthy of attendance within this particular class fraction.

We see this not only through the ethnographic data but also with regard to Lee and Weis's (2012) work based on National Center for Education Statistics (NCES) longitudinal databases (NELS and ELS). Evidence suggests that students who attend privileged public and private secondary schools garner more places in a now broadened range of elite and quasi-elite private colleges, a sector comprised of institutions, among others, such as Boston College, Bowdoin, Carnegie Mellon, Middlebury, Swarthmore, Tufts, University of Chicago, University of Rochester, Wesleyan, and Williams, a sector of schools that is increasingly difficult to get into at one and the same time as the sector itself becomes more prestigious. This relationship holds even when relevant background characteristics and "merit factors" are held constant in the analysis.

Additionally, and as previously noted, research by Stephan, Rosenbaum, and Person (2009) concludes that *where* one goes to postsecondary school predicts persistence and graduation rates above and beyond the entering characteristics of admitted students. As they state, "academic preparation is an important mechanism of stratification at college entry, but even comparable students (similar on many characteristics, including preparation) have different degree completion chances at different types of colleges" (p. 14). Selectivity of institution *in and of itself matters*, then, with regard to outcomes, as more selective postsecondary institutions exhibit much higher persistence and graduation rates than less selective institutions.

Beyond higher rates of persistence and graduation, we also know that more highly selective institutions are better resourced than less selective institutions and confer on their graduates both special entrée to the best graduate and professional programs in the country (Eide, Brewer, and Ehrenberg 1998) and well-documented labor market advantages (Bowen and Bok 1998; Rumberger and Thomas 1993; Thomas 2000; Thomas and Zhang 2005). Again, this relationship holds even when characteristics of entering students are held constant in the analysis.

Important recent work on research universities by Leslie, Slaughter, Taylor, and Zhang (2012) suggests that institutional and research expenditures vary in key ways by private versus public institutions, and that private research universities are now rising head and shoulders above even the state flagship universities in terms of expenditures with regard to the pursuit of so-called merit aid and research. As they note, while research publics deploy an increasing proportion of their revenue in the functional category of instruction, private universities "evidence a somewhat different pattern, with revenues generally expended in the pursuit of merit aid and research" (p. 614). As they state, "this suggests that private universities strategically deploy revenues from a wide variety of sources to secure particular students and to conduct research activities" (p. 614)—goals more in line with the iconic US research university. This offers further evidence of increasing stratification in the postsecondary sector, in this case linked to public versus private research institutions.

On the whole, then, evidence suggests that, controlling for incoming characteristics of students, the more selective the institution, the more short- and long-term advantages accrue to the attending population. The intensification of such inequalities is clearly evident and, barring major upheaval in the postsecondary sector, will likely persist. In the long run, this will work to further advantage those already advantaged by virtue of entrance to more highly selective institutions, in terms of graduation rates, opportunities for postgraduate programs, occupational destinations, and income. Importantly, although we know that the flagship publics increasingly draw upon a more highly selective and privileged population than was the case in past decades (Bowen, Chingos, and McPherson 2009)—a turn of events that is in contradistinction with the original intent of these schools (Thomas and Bell 2008)—a particular high-end slice of the middle class is seeking further "distinction" by matriculating at "Most Competitive" and "Highly Competitive+" privates, thereby instantiating *this* group of students as the ones who will be best poised to actualize professional and managerial upper-middle-class status.

Conclusion

Focusing on the remaking of the American White working class, Weis (2004, p. 2) argues as follows:

> Based on a form of what I call ethnographic longitudinality, *Class Reunion* is
> the 2004 story of the individuals who first appeared in *Working Class Without*

Work (Weis 1990). More than just a story of thirty-one individuals whom I re-interviewed in 2000–2001, however, *Class Reunion* is an exploration, empirically and longitudinally, of the re-making of the American White working class in the latter quarter of the twentieth century. Arguing that we cannot write off the working class simply because white men no longer have access to well-paying laboring jobs in the primary labor marker (Edwards 1979), jobs that spawned a distinctive place for labor in the capital-labor accord (Hunter 1978; Apple 2001), I track and theorize the re-making of this group as a distinct class fraction, both discursively and behaviorally inside radical, globally–based economic restructuring (Reich 1991, 2001; Rogers and Teixeira 2000; McCall 2001).

Class Warfare similarly focuses on the production of what we see as a new class fraction and, by extension, twenty-first-century social and economic structure and linked opportunities. Unlike *Class Reunion*, however, where Weis chronicles the remaking of the White working-class fraction in the United States in the latter quarter of the twentieth century by virtue of data gathered over a 15-year time period, *Class Warfare* looks forward, speculating on the implications of our findings for future class structure and associated individual and group positionality. The groups we ethnographically and/or analytically explore here—privileged Whites, privileged multigenerational Blacks, children of "flexible immigrants" of color, and low-income self-identified Black students, all of whom attend privileged public and private secondary schools—jockey for position between and among themselves as they drive toward "distinction" by virtue of desired and enacted entrance to a particular slice of US colleges and universities.

Despite all being in privileged secondary schools, however, such students continue to be differentially positioned within their schools by virtue of prior academic preparation; institutional mechanisms that work to separate students; and facially neutral policies and practices that, in the long run, intensify linked race/class inequalities rather than interrupt them. This works to create an environment in which racial and class difference take on particularly located meanings, thereby establishing a context within which different populations of students move through and experience privileged institutions in markedly different ways.

For low-income Black students, although opportunities are *substantially* opened by virtue of attendance at privileged schools, such attendance comes with its own set of personal "trade-offs." Privileged White students and privileged Black students within their schools, whether of multigenerational status or the children of "flexible immigrants," are uniformly "at home" in privileged institutions by virtue of their class background. As such, they do not generally experience the isolation and loneliness associated with the structurally induced position of "outsider within"—a set of experiences that may have long-term psychological consequences for low-income Black students, in particular. Having said this, privileged students across race/ethnicity are themselves not without baggage as they move into the postsecondary sector. Given the stunning success of those who sit at the top of the academic hierarchy within their respective privileged public and private secondary schools, we can expect that these students will continue to be held to exceptionally high academic standards, both by themselves and by others. Given that the stress associated with this sustained level of pressure can be palpable, we can only hope that they, like our population of low-income Black students, will be able to cope with whatever comes their way.

In spite of the pressure these students are under in new global and national circumstances, they exude excitement with regard to their own future prospects in college and beyond. The fact that privileged secondary schools catapult students into this arena is notable. Each and every one of them is highly educated by virtue of their attendance at such schools. As such, they have all the tools necessary to unpack any and all drivers that work to create the conditions that underlie their own lives and those of their families. Postsecondary institutions are known to encourage strongly informed critical reflection based on intense interaction with scholarly text. It is with this thought that we close *Class Warfare*.

Details and Reflections on Theory and Methods

As Paul Willis stated some ten years ago, "Class needs ethnography to show its long reach into the fine details of human destiny and ethnography needs 'class' to draw out its full analytic and historical powers and potentials" (Willis 2004, back cover of Weis, *Class Reunion: The Remaking of the American White Working Class*). Employing what Weis and Fine (2012) call "critical bifocality"—a theory of method that documents at once the linkages and capillaries of structural arrangements and the discursive and lived-out practices by which individuals make sense of their circumstances (Weis and Fine 2012, 2013)—*Class Warfare* connects the story of students, parents, and school personnel to broad social and economic arrangements through specific focus on the secondary to post-secondary linking process.

Access to particularly located postsecondary institutions has become a space of intensified struggle, particularly for more socially and economically privileged groups, who are poised to take advantage of their position to maximize opportunity for their offspring (Lareau 2000). Such struggle is linked to the now globalized knowledge economy, in which competition for jobs has increased while economic security, particularly for the middle and upper middle class, has become less stable (Brown, Lauder, and Ashton 2011; Reay 2011; Ehrenreich 1990; Harvey 2005; Reich 2008). Given massification and accompanying intensified stratification of the postsecondary sector in the United States, middle- and upper middle-class parents/families work to maximize their advantage via access to particularly located postsecondary destinations (Gamoran 2008; Lucas 2001; Raftery and Hout 1993), a topic that we take up at great length in this volume.

We draw upon data from three ethnographic studies of relatively elite coeducational secondary schools and one relatively elite single-sex secondary school (elite is defined as high ranking with regard to the educational sector of the nation) located in tier-2, "nonglobal" cities in the northeastern United States. As detailed in chapter 1, *Class Warfare* takes up this theoretically located "class" project via multiyear ethnographic research with three distinct groups of students in three upper-middle-class secondary schools, as follows: (1) a representative sample of largely, but not entirely, White students who fall, by virtue of class rank, in the top 10% of their secondary school graduating class in a highly affluent suburban public high school; (2) a representative sample of largely, but not entirely, highly affluent White students and the children of "flexible immigrants" of color who fall, by virtue of class rank, in the top 20% of their graduating class at an NAIS (National Association of Independent Schools) private coeducational day school; and (3) a representative sample of low-income self-defined Black students in two NAIS day schools (one coeducational, one single-sex female) who, with two exceptions, attended predominantly Black and Latino poorly resourced inner-city public and Catholic elementary and middle schools and are almost entirely placed at the bottom of the opportunity structure of their respective secondary schools.

This purposively selected tri-school student sample enables deep ethnographic focus on actions and activities engaged by differentially located parents, students, and school personnel across class and race/ethnicity in both iconic private and public privileged secondary institutions. While each group independently reveals a great deal about schooling, family practices, and the college process, putting these groups in sharp relief, as we do here, starkly portrays the ways in which "class works" and is put to work by varying groups in schools.

We focus our investigation on the graduating class of 2010 (to protect the anonymity of participants, we mask the actual year of graduation), and each researcher was deeply immersed within her respective research site for one full year, with limited additional engagement before or after this year. Two of the projects began as dissertations—Kristin Cipollone conducted her dissertation research at Cannondale, the suburban public high school in our purposively selected school sample, and Heather Jenkins conducted her dissertation research among low-income self-identified Black students at two NAIS private institutions—Matthews Academy and Bradford Academy. Lois Weis similarly engaged research at Matthews Academy, but focused her attention on the top 20% of the graduating class.

Although the three ethnographies were, at a practical ethnographic level, conducted separately, we designed the tri-school research in such a way as to hold critical aspects of the research process constant across site, a topic that will be further discussed at a later point in this epilogue. The three investigators engaged their research largely in tandem, discussing findings at various points throughout the data-gathering process and sharing tentative conclusions. Although major aspects of the tri-school study were jointly conceptualized, ethnographic details do differ to some extent. In all three studies, we collected far more data on a range of topics than appear in this volume. Data from teachers, for example, do not appear here, but will be the subject of future articles.

In each site, a list of students who met the criteria for inclusion in the respective school samples was drawn up in consultation with the lead counselor. From this initial list, focal students were selected largely randomly, although occasionally the counselors suggested that we approach particular students whose individual experiences they believed would be relevant to our study. Students were, by and large, happy to be included in the study, as were parents (who had to approve student participation as per Institutional Review Board [IRB] requirements). In the case of low-income Black students at Bradford and Matthews, all students who met the relevant criteria were asked to participate, as there are relatively few low-income Black students at these schools. There were two such students at Bradford who did not end up in the final sample. One of the two declined, but did not provide a reason; the other agreed, but Heather was unable to obtain parental consent, despite repeated attempts to do so. Among the top-ranked students at Matthews whose parents were initially approached, one parent at Matthews declined to have his child participate, as the father was concerned that the student was just "too stressed" and "this would be just another thing he would have to do." In another case, the child did not show up for any of the interviews, and the counselor advised us not to pursue the student further.

All potential participants were contacted via letter sent to their homes, and, as per IRB requirements, parents were fully informed as to the purpose of the investigation and the fact that the school supported the research. In the same envelope, two consent forms were included so that parents could themselves consent to be interviewed as well as consenting to allow their children to participate. Upon receiving parental consent forms, children were approached directly, whereupon the project was explained to them as per IRB requirements and they were handed consent forms that they were asked to fill out. All students who were approached in this manner agreed to be part of the study and filled out the forms. All had, in fact, heard about the study from their parents and, with the exception of the one student noted above, were happy to participate.

In the case of Cannondale, the process was somewhat different. With the help of the school counseling office (who identified the top 10% of the senior class) and in compliance with IRB standards, Kristin sought to recruit 12 students for this project. The counseling department divides its caseload by students' last names (alphabetically), and each counselor reached out to his or her students in the top 10%, beginning with those who were most highly ranked. Each counselor selected the most highly ranked male and female students (again, always in the top 10%) and met with them to explain the project and encourage their participation. Students were given informational materials, including a letter explaining the project (and their expected commitment—approximately three hours over the course of the year) and consent and assent forms for their review. Students were instructed to go home and speak with their parents about participation.

After this initial counselor meeting, Kristin held a brief meeting for selected students to explain the project and answer any questions they might have prior to making a decision to participate. This brief meeting was held in the counseling office immediately after school. The numbers one- and two-ranked students, both males, agreed to participate immediately. Securing additional students, however, was more difficult. Several students, namely girls, told Kristin that they were too busy this year to take time to participate in this study. Between sports, clubs, rigorous course schedules, and applying to college, they felt that they were too stressed already to take on this additional task. After approximately one month of outreach, ten students agreed to participate, including five male and five female students. Prior to his first interview, one student dropped out of the study. A close family member passed away, and the student said he needed to withdraw.

In each of the sites, we conducted a set of interviews over time with the students, focusing on their early thoughts with respect to the college process, their initial list of possible schools and how they came up with it, the applications they ultimately submitted, their final decision-making process in light of the schools that they were accepted at, and their final college "choice." We probed specifically for the nature of their interaction with the college counselors as well as any others who may have helped them through the year and a half process. We also conducted numerous hours of participant observations and document analysis, both of which will be discussed in greater detail below.

Data Collection by Site

Cannondale, Kristin

At Cannondale, 37 total participants were interviewed and participated in three focus group sessions. Study participants include students (9 in the top 10% of the class), parents (11), school counselors (8), counseling support staff (2), eleventh- and twelfth-grade core subject teachers (5), and administrators (2). All participants were interviewed between one and three times. In addition to interviews, over 200 hours were spent in the field observing classes, counselor sessions, college-related presentations, course advisement, parent information meetings, SAT test administration, and many other less-formal occurrences (e.g., spending time in the College Center while students researched schools). Rigorous field notes were kept to document these observations. Informal observational field notes were also written after interviews.

School documents were drawn upon to contextualize the study and provide background information as needed. As Bogdan and Biklen (2007, p. 137) argue, organizational documents often "[represent] the biases of the promoters and, when written for external consumption, [present] an unrealistically glowing picture of how the organization functions." It is precisely for this reason that many of these documents came to be so useful in this research. Such documents both speak to the underlying culture of the school and community and provide explicit examples of how the college application process is carried out. Examples of the documents collected include course offering guides, student transcripts, teacher assignments, school profiles, and college-related handouts. Kristin also drew information from the school website and the "Record," a school-created database that tracks student college acceptance outcomes.

Matthews, Lois

Data collection among the top 20% of the class at Matthews was engaged largely similarly to that in Cannondale. A total of 38 individuals were interviewed, including students (13 in the top 20% of the class), head of the upper school, head of college counseling (1 of 2 counselors in the school), parents (18), and teachers of core junior and senior-year subjects (5). Participants were interviewed between one and three times, as relevant. Additionally, a total of 100 hours were spent in the field observing classes, college-related presentations, parent information meetings, and other less-formal interactions such as time spent in the senior lounge as students engaged the college process, and so forth. As with Cannondale, relevant school documents were collected and rigorous field notes were kept to document both formal and informal participant observation sessions.

Matthews and Bradford, Heather

A total of 9 low-income Black students were interviewed at Matthews (5) and Bradford (4). All of these students self-identified as African American, African (in one case), or bi/multiracial, with their identity solidly as Black students. Of these 9 students, 4 had parents who agreed to participate in the research. In addition, the lead college counselors from each site (2) were asked for their participation after permission was granted by the schools' administrators. Both of the counselors identified as White and middle class.

Semi-structured interviews and follow-up interviews were conducted with the student and parent participants. All participants were asked questions about experiences related to their racial and class identities, their processes of entering their secondary schools, experiences within their secondary schools, and their thoughts about college and the college application and admissions process. Follow-up interviews were based on the information gathered during the initial interviews, with the aim of chronicling the college process for the students. Lastly, semi-structured initial interviews with the college counselors were conducted to obtain background information on the counselors' education and professional training, information on the way each school structures its college counseling program, and data regarding the student research participants. Similar data from college counselors were gathered by Lois and Kristin in their respective sites. Heather visited each of her school sites weekly for purposes of participant observation. In line with practices engaged by Kristin and Lois, school documents were analyzed to get a general sense of each site's organizational habitus, as this is critical to understanding students' and parents' narrations of the secondary school experiences.

Although all three investigators intended to interview parents of student participants, this proved to be challenging in the case of our low-income Black sample. As a result, we have less rich data from these parents than those in the other two groups. Heather made numerous attempts to seek participation among those parents who gave their children permission to participate in the study. She sent letters (two per parent) detailing the need for parental perspectives regarding the college process and followed up with numerous phone calls, wherein messages were left on voicemail, urging parents to meet face to face to hear more about the study wherein any outstanding questions could be addressed. Despite Heather's best efforts, only four low-income Black parents agreed to participate.

Heather's experience with parents is markedly different than that of either Kristin or Lois, who worked with students who were at the top of their respective classes, most of whom were highly privileged. In this latter case, both parents at times desired to be interviewed together, as both were heavily invested in the college applications process and wished to be part of the conversation. This is particularly the case among privileged parents at Matthews, as we suggest in chapter 4.

It is worth speculating why low-income Black parents were reluctant to participate. This cannot be readily attributed to the time of interview, as Heather was more than willing to work around parent schedules, a point that was communicated from the outset. More likely is that this group of parents may have felt uncomfortable given the class difference between themselves and the researcher, and evidence suggests that this might have been the case. As Heather's research was comprised of data from several schools other than Matthews and Bradford, a conversation with a parent from the larger sample (schools/students not discussed in this volume) is relevant. At the end of Heather's 3.5 hour interview with this parent, she and her entire family hugged Heather goodbye, and the mother admitted that she did not want to participate, even though she readily consented for her son to be part of the study. She stated that she was "worried" about having Heather in her home—what Heather might think of their home, what judgments Heather might make about them as people and as parents. She confessed her fear that Heather may "look down on" her and her husband, as they are far less educated than the researcher. It is likely that other low-income Black parents harbored similar concerns, worrying about our judgment of their class circumstances. Additionally, it is certainly possible that these parents, who receive significant financial support from these schools, may have been concerned about communicating anything negative in that they feared that such sentiments would be relayed to school personnel. Although we stated in our letters that this would not be the case, concerns may have lingered. As a result of difficulties associated with interviewing this population of parents, their voices are heard in this volume to a lesser extent than those of privileged Matthews and Cannondale parents. This does not, however, interrupt our fundamental argument with regard to this group around the college admissions process, as we know from the narrated experiences of their children that we are interpreting this accurately.

Data Analysis and Interpretation

Upon completing data collection, careful attention was paid to the two overarching principles that underlie Standards for Reporting on Empirical Social Science Research published by the American Educational Research Association (2006): sufficiency of warrants and transparency of reporting. Taking these broad principles seriously, the following conventions were followed. Upon completing all individual interviews and classroom observations, data (full transcripts) were fully de-identified, transcribed, punctuated for readability, and input into Hyper Research, a computer based analytic program for qualitative data. Employing traditional qualitative analysis techniques (Bogdan and Biklen 2007; Bogdan and Taylor 1975; Weis and Fine 2000), we read though at least one-quarter of all transcripts and established categories for coding—descriptive labels through which data could be segmented and readied for analysis. The number of initial coding categories is not relevant here, as once full scale coding begins, categories that are not supported by the data at hand, either as clear examples of trends or supporting divergence from such trends, fall away at the analysis stage.

Upon establishing working coding categories, three individuals coded the qualitative data, marking segments in the database that reflect the category under consideration. Inter-rater reliability coefficients of at least 0.80 were established. If such inter-rater reliability coefficients were not reached, the code was not judged to describe the data segment at hand. Each code was assigned a shorter code in the larger qualitative data set so that the process was less cumbersome. The three researchers then coded the data, using the established classificatory coding system and marking, as appropriate, on hard copy by bracketing relevant data segments. Data segments were double and triple coded (in other words, segments or parts of segments might be coded as reflective of two or more coding categories simultaneously). After coding on hard copy, all transcripts were coded on screen. The analysis package acts as a clean filing system only, as the three researchers accomplish all conceptual and theoretical work. Data segments were printed out and placed in appropriately labeled manila file folders by code and by relevant demographic group (male versus female, racial group, and so forth). We continued to read all full transcripts as well as decontextualized folders of coded data, ultimately intellectually weighing data under each code and constructing arguments. Once initial classifications and pattern descriptions were developed, the three researchers reviewed the available data to locate all relevant instances that support the claims as well as search for evidence that is disconfirming of such claims (Fine and Weis 1998; Weis and Fine 2000; AERA 2006).

We subsequently looked at how Bradford, Matthews, and Cannondale students talk about their academic work in relation to classroom observation notes in their schools, and their schools' documents on academics and course placement. After this process was completed for all three sites, data were analyzed comparatively across the three research sites. Data were then considered through the lens of the theoretical framework (taking an intersectional approach) and interpreted in relation to existing scholarly literature as we simultaneously broke new theoretical and empirical ground by virtue of the evidence at hand. We began, for example, to interpret the data in regard to what it told us about an individual's social and cultural capital and habitus in relation to the habitus of a given research site, and how these findings spoke back to scholarly literature on secondary level opportunity structures, postsecondary admissions and access, and the role that class and race play in structuring educational opportunity. Specifically with regard to the populations under study, we further considered and reflected upon specific economic and social drivers as they impact the student research participants' opportunities and their own and their parents' perspectives about those opportunities. It is in this massively altered context that families in first wave-industrialized nations seek to instantiate opportunities for their children at one and the same time as such within-nation opportunities are objectively increasingly scarce (Brown, Lauder, and Ashton 2011), the seriousness of which cannot be overlooked when thinking through our data.

Researchers' Biographies and Positionalities

All three researchers have relationships with their primary research sites—not only the institutions themselves, but also various people within these institutions. The importance of these relationships cannot be overlooked, as they are inextricably tied to the data collection and analysis process, not to mention the processes of gaining access to this range of privileged schools. As such, it is important that we detail these relationships and how they enabled relatively uninhibited access to the sites, the participants, and organizational documents. That being said, this discussion will be loose and will intentionally obfuscate some of the details to protect the anonymity of the research sites and participants, as their privacy is of the upmost importance. Throughout this volume, we have taken great care to alter specific language that appears on school websites as well as identifying characteristics of individuals and schools.

Lois has personal relationships with a number of families, teachers, and administrators in her primary research site. These relationships enabled her to gain access to the site, as she is perceived as someone who could be trusted to study the school in great detail. Lois shares the same general race and class background as the vast majority of families and school personnel, although Lois is White and Jewish, and there are relatively low numbers of Jewish families in this school. These biographical factors worked to create a sense of commonality and familiarity that enabled her to build easy relationships with her participants. When asking questions that call for participants to address complex and, at times, uncomfortable issues, parental participants, in particular, felt a sense of affinity with her as they correctly sensed that she could identify with their situation. Lois had full access to the school, the students, and their families, as the school fully supported this research.

Although Lois has personal connections to this school such that she is perceived to have both an insider *and* outsider eye, her access was additionally facilitated by the fact that school personnel feel strongly that they offer students an outstanding education. Cookson and Persell (1985) express similar sentiments with regard to their own access to a range of elite US boarding schools. These schools are very proud of the education that they impart to their students and are often willing to share their pride with outsiders, including researchers (Cookson and Persell 1985; Gaztambide-Fernández 2009). Although Lois shares class background with many in the institution, she easily retains her analyst's outsider eye given her vast ethnographic experiences in a range of communities of varying class and race/ethnicity.

Knowing people who are part of a given education system allows one to use these relationships to help open doors and gain access to institutions, such as schools, that do not generally allow *just anyone* to probe what they do and how they do it. Kristin drew upon a relationship with a close friend and colleague to facilitate access to Cannondale. This colleague sent an e-mail on Kristin's behalf to the superintendent, who subsequently referred her to the lead counselor at the high school, after which she was provided complete access to the institution.[1] Similar to Lois, as a White researcher of solidly middle- and upper-middle-class background, Kristin shares biographical similarities with the students that she studied. Also like them, she graduated at the top of her class in high school and sought to gain entrance (and ultimately did) to a "Most Competitive" private (Barron's 2009) postsecondary institution. At times Kristin pondered her similarities to her participants, questioning whether these similarities hindered her ability to be an effective analyst. To address this, Kristin shared the de-identified data with two of her colleagues. While both female, they had very different experiences from each other and from Kristin—experiences growing up, attending high school, and transitioning to college. Talking through the data during the coding process and discussing some of her initial thinking about possible themes proved to be incredibly helpful. Their insights helped to create necessary distance between the data and Kristin so that she could begin to see and hear her participants' words and actions with fresh eyes.

Heather has been providing professional development workshops on race, class, and gender in a number of private middle and secondary schools over the past six years. She has well-developed personal connections with the Head of School, faculty, and staff members at numerous private institutions, and she was welcomed as a researcher by all relevant gatekeepers. In addition, she is a graduate of a private secondary school similar to Matthews and Bradford.

Heather's Black-White biracial identity and solidly middle-class upbringing position her differently than her student and parent participants. Having grown up within a predominantly White middle-class environment as a result of her mother's biography and social networks, she entered elite private schooling with more valued (by the school) social and cultural capital than did her low-income students. Additionally, most likely because of her biracial identity and White middle-class upbringing, as a student she was often told that she was "not really Black" or "not like *other* Black people." This experience sets Heather apart from most of her low-income participants, as most are viewed, first and foremost, as Black within their school communities. Similarly, most of the student participants report having predominantly Black peer groups at the time of data collection and for the better part of their lives.

Although many of Heather's experiences are quite different from those of her participants, as a person of color, she could often relate personally and academically to their experiences, concerns, and frustrations, a point that was commented upon by both students and parents. Although there were a few instances where Heather could not personally relate to circumstances described by one of the participants, there were far more instances where she was able to readily relate to students' and parents' experiences. In looking over her transcripts, phrases such as such as "you know how it is," "you know what it's like," and "I mean, I don't have to tell you" routinely pepper the conversations. Such phrases clearly suggest that it was not only Heather's sense that she and her student and parent participants shared similar experiences; it was their sense as well.

Although all three of us worked hard to bracket our assumptions and biographies, no researcher enters a site devoid of preconceptions, and we recognize the complexities of our own raced, classed, gendered, and schooled standpoints. As a consequence, we continued to reflect upon our felt understandings and assumptions throughout the research and writing process. Most notably, we consciously built mechanisms of reflexivity into our daily lives and researcher selves. We maintain that our biographies and connections to the research sites, and the time spent reflecting upon these biographies and linked experiences enabled us to build strong and sincere relationships with our research participants across class, ethnicity, gender, and level of education. In short, while our biographies serve as a primary lens through which we view our research sites and participants, and they certainly facilitated access to these sites, we maintain that these unique lenses encourage us to think deeply and analytically about what we see and hear. Our insistence on continued reflexivity kept us tuned into our participants and research sites and the multiple ongoing relationships, of which "our selves" were at the center, at all times. We do not claim to have captured every potentially observable phenomenon, nor do we claim to have fully analyzed every possible statement or question. However, we do suggest that through our diligence in regard to our methodology, we have captured the essence of the participants and the research sites in relation to the research questions posed.

Our biographies surfaced in particularly powerful and sometimes uncomfortable ways as we engaged the collective writing process, at times bumping up against one another as we theorized the production of the upper middle class and the role of parents, students, and school personnel across sites and populations in this set of processes. What we did not anticipate when we began the writing process is that putting the three groups in sharp relief, as we do here, means that we unintentionally, at times, appeared to be making statements, issuing judgments, and coming to unwarranted conclusions about each group/site in relation to the others. We quickly found ourselves in the murky territory of being quite protective of our populations as well as our own sense of how the world "works" and "should work."

Kristin, for example, justifiably wanted to make sure that the Cannondale parents were not seen to do "less" of a certain kind of "class work" with respect to their children than privileged parents at Matthews, as *all* parents in the three school sites do a great deal for their children. Kristin pushed hard on this point, and we collectively came to understand that particularly located schools, in this case, privileged publics versus privileged privates (in tier-2 cities), develop "normative cultures and practices" around parental "class work." In this regard, we agreed that what we saw in Matthews versus Cannondale among similarly privileged parents and comparably located students at the top of the opportunity structure reflects the ways in which certain kinds of "normative practices" develop in particular sites. This understanding both pressed and enabled us to theorize the implications of such school-based normative practices and what they might mean for future possibilities and class positionalities.

Heather was justifiably concerned that the experiences of her low-income Black parents and students with respect to elite private schools would be appropriately understood and theorized. She pushed hard on Kristin and Lois to make it clear that while these students were coming in with great academic disadvantage relative to their more privileged peers by virtue of their prior education in inner-city schools that serve almost entirely Black and Latino populations, private schools have a *responsibility* to make sure that these students are more than just tokens in an elite sector diversity initiative. Our thinking with respect to facially neutral policies and practices and the implications of such policies and practices for those who come in differentially positioned than the majority of students stems from Heather's pushing.

Lois's biography is wholly laced with experiences in public schools and universities (including teaching at the University at Buffalo), whereas Kristin and Heather have attended and taught in both public and private schools. In this regard, the staunch assertion of the *primacy* of highly selective *private* postsecondary destinations as a way of creating "distinction" stunned Lois, prompting extensive conversations among Lois, Kristin, and Heather about the widespread restructuring of postsecondary aspirations in the United States and Lois's felt depreciation of flagship publics in the drive for "distinction." Our point here is that putting our data in sharp relief across site and population prompted critical points of tension—ones that we would not necessarily have anticipated. It is the analytic "working across" that produced some of our most important theoretical work. While each of us entered this project with largely shared strong feelings about historic and current racial and class injustices in the United States, we came to understand that we all have something that we wish to protect. It is our *own intellectual and personal intersectionality during the writing process* that most prominently created the "intellectual rub" from which we collectively produced this volume—a volume that each of us is very proud of.

Using Ethnography to Study Class

At the beginning of this epilogue, we reference Paul Willis's (2004) incisive statement that "class needs ethnography to show its long reach into the fine details of human destiny and . . . ethnography needs 'class' to draw out its full analytic and historical powers and potentials" (Weis 2004, back cover). Willis reminds us that class is complex, situational, and contextual. As such, studying class—how it works in various geographical regions, how it affects different people's opportunities, how it is defined and/or discussed over time, and so forth—requires the kind of analysis that can come only from a deep ethnographic approach. Throughout the writing of this volume, we took Willis's statement, along with those of other scholars who study class (e.g., Bourdieu 1984; Lareau 2003; Reay et al. 2011; Weis 2004) very seriously, and placed tremendous responsibility on ourselves to investigate the production and lived-out components of class as deeply and comprehensively as possible. This section will highlight a few illustrative examples supporting the notion that class needs ethnography and vice versa.

At the same time that we ascertained the class locations of our research participants through measures such as school tuition (in regard to the elite private schools) and financial aid received, and geographic location and property values of their communities, we also asked the participants questions that enabled them to locate themselves (and, by extension, others). Most participants did this by using various markers of class—tangibles such as neighborhoods and vehicles, and intangibles such as values and sensibilities—and by comparing themselves to others who are both similar to and different from them. Recall that Steven talked about shying away from having friends from Matthews over to his house because he could not provide appropriate "accommodations," all of which centered on the classed differences between Steven, a low-income Black student, and his largely White affluent peers. Likewise, recall that Cannondale students talked about the reality that not everyone can buy into Cannondale, meaning that some are shut out of opportunities within the community by virtue of not being able to purchase a home within the school catchment area. Without an ethnographic approach, data such as these, along with countless other examples, would not have been collected or subsequently analyzed in a way that allows us to ponder what these statements actually mean to the students, what they tell us about Matthews's and Cannondale's cultures, and what they tell us about the "way class works" inside Matthews, Cannondale, and US society more broadly.

Although secondary analyses of large-scale databases and/or survey research more broadly certainly have their place and are critically important with regard to the linkages between and among class, race, academic achievement, academic attainment, occupational status, and so forth, such data do not allow us to peer beneath the surface to understand *the ways in which* such interconnections are produced on the ground by parents, students, teachers, and others on a day-to-day and year-by-year basis. Additionally, they do not facilitate our understanding with regard to *how* individuals and groups conceptualize the reasons for such empirically located difference. In this sense, then, although we fully support outstanding quantitative work and draw upon it in this volume, as relevant, the role of ethnography in understanding both the nature of class/race productions, as well as the mechanisms and reasons behind them, cannot be underestimated.

As Weis and Fine (2004) point out, it is *relatively* easy to produce a descriptive ethnography. While we learn a great deal from such descriptive ethnographies with respect to any given group at any moment in time, it is by employing important analytical constructs like class that ethnography becomes inextricably tied to larger conversations about the production and/or reproduction of social structure—conversations that are going on all over the world (Weis and Dolby 2012). Without engaging such broader analytical constructs, ethnographies are less likely to go beyond themselves so as to engage a broad-based scholarly community in a set of important questions and debates.

The above illustrates the importance of an ethnographic approach when studying something as multifaceted and multidimensional as class. As noted earlier, ethnography helps us understand the lived-out and produced linkages between the lives of individuals and collectivities, and broader social structures. When we talked with adults at Matthews, Bradford, and Cannondale, for example, about their perspectives with regard to the ways in which and extent to which the college admissions process changed over the past decade, becoming increasingly competitive (e.g., how and why younger students and their parents increasingly seek meetings with college counselors; changes in course offerings, particularly in science and math), such conversations not only tell us about changes happening within these particular schools, but also how these changes are linked to the intensified stratification in postsecondary education, increased credentialing in US society and globally, and the global knowledge economy more broadly. Willis's trenchant statement—that "class needs ethnography to show its long reach into the fine details of human destiny and . . . ethnography needs 'class' to draw out its full analytic and historical powers and potentials"—remains highly salient.

Conclusion

Weis and Dolby (2012) argue that a range of economic and culturally linked drivers, including but not limited to massive global economic realignment, the accompanying instantiation of the global knowledge economy, and the movement of peoples, as refugees or immigrants, across national borders, including those who possess "flexible citizenship" (Ong 1999), fundamentally alters class cultural productions in nations across the globe. The nature of such class cultural forms and the factors that serve to produce such new forms can be empirically captured and understood *only* by virtue of an ethnographic method that, at its inception, takes as foundational the massively altered broad-based social and economic context within which such productions now take shape. We must, then, analytically begin with large context and work our way down to the ways in which people produce and live out their lives in newly forged institutional and social circumstances (Weis and Fine 2012, 2013).

This set of above detailed economic and social drivers, coupled with the economic crash of 2008, renders the economic future of the next generation in first-wave industrialized nations highly uncertain. It is in this context that families in these nations seek to instantiate opportunities for their children at one and the same time as such opportunities are objectively increasingly scarce (Brown, Lauder, and Ashton 2011). Those who are highly educated, and those who are not, now live and work inside a globally driven knowledge economy that alters the fulcrum of educational experiences, processes, and social and economic outcomes, whether students and families articulate it or not. The stark fact is that global realignment coupled with the movement of peoples is creating new "winners" and "losers" across the globe. This is accompanied by deepening inequalities both within and between nations (Chauvel 2010; Gilbert 2003; Piketty and Saez 2003, 2006, 2012; Saez 2013; Sherman and Aron-Dine 2007), a situation that establishes an entirely new context within which class cultural productions take place all over the world.

Weis and Fine's (2012, 2013) *critical bifocality* deliberately interrogates the circuits of structures, histories, and lives, encouraging research designs that trace how such widening inequality gaps penetrate lives and communities across and within nations; how the neoliberal realignment of opportunities and resources exacerbates race and class stratification as well as other nodes of difference, as relevant, in varying nations; how the accumulation of privilege is implicated in contexts of deepening poverty; and how those who benefit and those who lose make very different sense of our contemporary economic and political circumstances. This set of broad-based concerns is global and circuited, enabling and encouraging a range of studies across local, national, and international contexts.

We end this set of reflections, and the volume more broadly, with a call for further research that employs *critical bifocaliy*, a framework and set of lenses that enables us, in this volume, to more fully understand both the production of new class cultural forms and the ways in which those who are connected to privileged secondary schools (across class and race/

ethnicity) work, in a highly on-the-ground fashion, to shape opportunities for their own children. Here we focus on one slice of such new class/race productions in very specific circumstances—those tied to global economic realignment and the intensification of stratification within the US post-secondary sector. The method, however, can be usefully employed in a wide range of national contexts, as we collectively work to understand the rearticulation of social structures in massively shifting times.

Notes

Chapter One

1. Kumon, a program that was developed in Japan, is designed to increase students' math and reading scores. It is generally considered to be a "drill and skill" kind of program. For more information, see http://www.kumon.com.

2. Astin and Oseguera (2002) argue that one should be cautious when using intuitional completion rates, as entering student-level factors can mostly explain why selective institutions have higher completion rates. Research by Bowen, Chingos, and McPherson (2009) and Stephan, Rosenbaum, and Person (2009) strongly suggests that institutional selectivity matters with regard to short- and long-term outcomes, even when controlling for entering characteristics of students.

3. Ehrenreich (1990) discusses how the middle class (particularly the "professional middle class") is an anxious class that is worried about losing its class position and advantage. She states: "Yet the professional middle class is still only a *middle class*, located well below the ultimate elite of wealth and power. Its only 'capital' is knowledge and skill, or at least the credentials imputing skill and knowledge. And unlike real capital, these cannot be hoarded against hard times, preserved beyond the lifetime of an individual, or of course, bequeathed" (p. 15). She goes on to assert that "the 'capital' belonging to the middle class is far more evanescent than wealth, and must be renewed in each individual through fresh effort and commitment" (p. 15). In this way, class position is not guaranteed; it must be "won," which leads to a fear that the successive generation may lose its position, or "fall."

4. Our thanks to Richard Arum for pointing out that this study represents an inversion of Mitchell Stevens's work.

5. We use the phrase "sector of school" to describe the location of particular types of schools within available comparable level options in the United States. The US system of education is marked both by its local control and by its varying sectors—public versus private, suburban versus urban versus rural, test-in entrance as often linked to highly selective "star" urban publics versus nonselective urban

publics, diocesan Catholics versus independent privates, and so forth. In the case at hand, we consider a third-ring suburban public secondary school—defined as high socioeconomic status and low minority (see Lee and Weis 2012), and two National Association of Independent Schools (NAIS) as exemplifying varying sector.

6. This historic moment is additionally marked by neoliberal discourses, practices, and policies that characterize the current political economy. Although it is not our intent in this volume to fully unpack the effects of this set of discourses and practices, we later touch upon the extent to which the "class work" of this group reflects a neoliberal subjectivity that now saturates the consciousness of this group.

7. We are not unaware of criticisms with regard to institutional ranking systems. However, the fact is that they are now driving numerous aspects of student decision-making processes with regard to the college admissions process in the United States. We rely specifically on Barron's Competitiveness Index ratings throughout this volume, and provide detail with regard to this ranking system in chapter 6.

8. Throughout this volume we employ the language of "high school" and "secondary school." When referring to the affluent public school, Cannondale, we use the term "high school," as this term is historically used to describe this set of public schools in the United States. Private schools, in contrast, tend to employ the term "secondary school" when referring to comparable institutions. In this volume, we use the term "high school" when referring to Cannondale and "secondary school" when referring to Matthews Academy and Bradford Academy. When referring more broadly to schools that offer grades 9 through 12, we use "secondary school."

9. We focused upon the top 10% at the affluent public high school because the senior class was rather large (approximately 600 students) as compared with the private schools, whose senior class was dramatically smaller.

10. We use the term "self-identify" as students are asked to identify their race on their admissions applications to Matthews and Bradford. The schools then categorize students based upon how they self-identify. Only students who chose to identify as "Black" were included in this study. After this point, however, we refer to these students as "low-income Black students."

11. Although one of our NAIS schools is single sex and the other coeducational, we do not take up the specifically gendered implications of attendance at one site versus the other. Although we address the question of gender and class in the final chapter, we do not focus on the lived experiences and/or consequences of a single-sex versus coeducational institution.

12. For purposes of this study, low-income self-identified Black students meet definitional income criteria through eligibility for City Prep, a program largely funded by the Jamison Foundation that provides full four-year scholarships for "economically disadvantaged" youth of color who enter private NAIS or Catholic secondary schools in the geographic area. When this program was founded in 1989, the income threshold was $30,000 (adjusted gross income). The threshold

has increased steadily since that time, now standing at $60,000. City Prep and the Jamison Foundation represent pseudonyms to protect anonymity of participants. The income definition employed here is somewhat higher than that of Hoxby and Avery (2012), who categorize low-income students as being in the bottom quartile of the 2008 income distribution among families who had a child in their senior year of high school. "Low-income Black students" in our study are those students who meet the above-noted income specifications and additionally self-identify as Black on relevant school forms and in our interviews.

13. The specific academic year has been altered so as to further maintain anonymity of participants. Full ethnographic research was engaged in each site during the last two years of secondary school (grades 11 and 12 in the United States), when preparation for postsecondary admissions is in full swing. Data are comprised as follows: (1) participant observation in academic classes and sessions/meetings specifically tied to the postsecondary admissions process; (2) interviews with focal students in the top 20 percent of the elite private secondary school and the top 10 percent of the third-ring suburban public school; and (3) formal in-depth interviews with targeted teachers of these students, school counselors, parents, and administrators. The sample at the public school was limited to the top 10% because of the large class size (over 600 students in the grade).

14. All data were coded and analyzed in accordance with guidelines released by the American Educational Research Association (2006). These guidelines do not prescribe specific and detailed movement with regard to coding procedures or structure of argument. Details of coding and so forth are reported in the epilogue.

15. According to NAIS, the median tuition for its member day schools in 2008–9 was $17,441. Tuition in the particular school under investigation here ran $18,250 for the 2008–9 school year, slightly above the median figure cited by NAIS. Tuition for boarding schools was approximately $37,017. Out of 28,384 private (not public) schools in the United States, about 1,050 are NAIS. Average tuition for other private schools is substantially less, with day schools running about $10,841 and boarding schools approximately $23,448. See http://www.greatschools.org/find-a -school/defining-your-ideal/59-private-vs-public-schools.gs.

16. As stated earlier, in accordance with normative public and private school practice in the United States, we employ the term "secondary school" when discussing the private school and "high school" when referring to the public school.

17. Further altering broad context is the fact that a form of financialization now sits at the center of our increasingly globalized and knowledge-based economy, with substantial implications for class processes in nations across the globe. As Kenway and Fahey note (2010):

> Ultimately another manifestation of the capitalist accumulation
> process emerged in the form of "financialization" with the USA
> as epicentre, but which swiftly spread around the world. Foster

> and Magdoff (2009: 45) call this the "monopoly capital" phase of
> capitalism. This involved Money-to-Money (M-M) rather than
> Money-Commodities—Money (M-C-M) in Marx's terms. The
> "new outlets for surplus were in the finance, insurance and real
> estate (FIRE) sector," mainly though not exclusively, in the form
> of financial speculation in securities, real estate and commodities
> markets rather than investment in capital goods (Foster and Mag-
> doff 2009: 67). Financialization involves a situation where "the tra-
> ditional role of finance as a helpful servant to production has been
> stood on its head, with finance now dominating over production."
> (Foster and Magdoff 2009, p. 100, as quoted in Kenway and Fahey
> 2010, pp. 719–20)

Such financialization has critically important implications for class production
worldwide, as it fundamentally rearranges the kind and amount of paid labor that
people have access to in varying nations, and the linkages between educational
credentialing and class cultural productions.

18. Such movement is clearly fueled by larger processes of financialization and
the global economy more generally. However, financialization and accompanying
economic drivers cannot fully explain all forms of movement, as the worldwide
movement of peoples is linked to an array of social and political phenomena, including current and/or anticipated political and social persecution.

19. The concept of "flexible citizenship" is developed by Ong (1999), who states
"in the era of globalization, individuals as well as governments develop a flexible notion of citizenship and sovereignty as strategies to accumulate capital and
power." She continues: " 'Flexible citizenship' refers to the cultural logics of capitalist accumulation, travel, and displacement that induce subjects to respond fluidly
and opportunistically to changing political-economic conditions. In their quest to
accumulate capital and social prestige in the global arena, subjects emphasize, and
are regulated by, practices favoring flexibility, mobility, and repositioning in relation to markets, governments—and cultural regimes. These logics and practices
are produced within particular structures of meaning about family, gender, nationality, class mobility, and social power' " (p. 6). In this volume, we refer to the children of those with "flexible citizenship" as the children of "flexible immigrants." In
practice, "flexible immigrants" are highly educated and bring particular kinds of
academic, social, and economic capital to nations like the United States. Many such
individuals attended undergraduate or more likely graduate and/or professional
school in the United States. A high proportion of such individuals would be seen as
"non-White" in the United States and come from a wide range of nations.

20. An important exception is elite privates such as Harvard, Yale, and Princeton that have sizable enough endowments to enable full support of low-income majority and minority candidates who otherwise meet all standards for admission.

21. An important caveat here is that contrary information exists with regard

to STEM (Science, Technology, Engineering, Mathematics) majors, where, as Arcidiacono (2004) suggests, majoring in STEM fields of study predicts short- and long-term outcomes of interest to a greater extent than does institutional selectivity. Economists report that differences in returns to majors are much larger than differences in returns to college quality, suggesting that, as James et al. (1989) note, "while sending your child to Harvard appears to be a good investment, sending him to your local state university to major in Engineering, to take lots of math, and preferably to attain a high GPA, is an even better private investment" (p. 252, as cited in Arcidiacono 2004, p. 343).

Chapter Two

1. Data in this section, unless noted otherwise, come from field notes from informal conversations with staff, observations, and from school documents (electronic and paper). As discussed in the epilogue, identifying language and details have been altered in this volume to protect the anonymity of institutions and research participants.

2. ASVAB stands for Armed Services Vocational Aptitude Battery. "The ASVAB is a timed multi-aptitude test, which is given at over 14,000 schools and Military Entrance Processing Stations (MEPS) nationwide and is developed and maintained by the Department of Defense" (http://www.military.com/ASVAB).

3. For a variety of reasons to be articulated throughout this volume, the fact that these data were collected in tier-2 cities as opposed to a global city such as New York City is relevant. For example, there is both less intensity with regard to admissions to NAIS privates in tier-2 cities, and tier-2 cities are not centers of massive capital and wealth. Additionally, our points about immigrants of color are relevant here, as we might expect greater interaction between and among families based on country of origin irrespective of social class in tier-2 cities than would likely be the case in a much larger city, which exhibits greater concentrations of people from any given nation. In the cities under consideration here, there is relatively greater familiarity across social class lines within any given originating nationality than there might be in a larger context, a phenomenon linked, at least partially, to geographic spatial location. This fact has important implications for the extent to which families can imagine themselves and their children at particular kinds of high schools and postsecondary destinations.

4. Cannondale High, like all other identifying information, is a pseudonym.

5. In line with empirically driven recent research by Lee and Weis (2012), a third-ring suburb is one that is high socioeconomic status and low minority. Cannondale meets this criterion for inclusion in this category.

6. According to the US Census Bureau, there are 367 metropolitan areas in the United States, and 51 of these have populations exceeding 1 million. These cities are considered "large." The Riverside metropolitan area can be classified as such.

7. Again, all course information provided in this section is from the 2009–10 academic year unless noted otherwise.

8. Students must achieve a score of at least 3 to obtain AP course credit (although an AP course will, if a student has taken it, appear as such on a student transcript, they do not receive formal AP course credit for scores lower than 3). Scores of 4 and 5 are generally considered "distinction" in the sense that they signal excellence to college admissions committees.

9. The IB program is a rigorous course of study focused on the development of critical thinking and analytical and research skills. It was brought to the district for a number of reasons, one being raising the academic profile of the school and making students more competitive in the college process (conversation with IB director, July 2009). For a complete overview of the program, see http://www.ibo.org/.

10. We are aware, of course, of potential felt marginalization among students who are not Christian given that this ostensibly public space resembles a church. However, the student body is, in fact, quite diverse racially, ethnically, and religiously, and there is no evidence to suggest religious marginalization in the school. Increasingly students of varying faiths are entering the institution. Although we recognize the symbolic power embedded within particular kinds of spaces with regard to felt marginalization, it is not our intent to explore these issues here.

11. We emphasize the word "dominant" here because despite being a comprehensive high school serving students with an array of needs and aspirations, Cannondale embraces a college culture that emphasizes matriculation at selective, four-year institutions. This college culture very much mirrors the desires and expectations of the students in the top 10% of the class. While proportionately a small number of the student body, this group wields a great deal of influence in establishing college expectations, and much of the college advising caters to this predisposition of college matriculation.

12. The Common Application, or "Common App" as it is most often referred to, is a generalized college application form that can be filled out once and then submitted to several colleges (https://www.commonapp.org/CommonApp/Default.aspx). The Common Application is a not-for-profit organization that aims to streamline the college application process by providing a standardized form for incoming students. Only colleges and universities using a holistic admissions approach are eligible to join. In many instances, colleges and universities will require supplemental forms to be completed in addition to what is required by the Common App. These forms often times ask students to compose additional essays. Harvard, for example, asks students to complete two "optional" essays on their supplemental application. The types of schools that students in this study apply to often require completion of supplemental materials.

Chapter Three

1. This chapter is based upon Kristin's dissertation research (Cipollone 2012).

2. These constraints will be discussed in further detail later in the chapter. Here we wish to acknowledge some of the factors that limit both the presence and impact

of students not in the top 10%: hidden prerequisites (e.g., one needs to have been accelerated in math by eighth grade to have access to AP calculus senior year), and the fact that many in the top 10% move together through all of their classes so that the presence of a couple of students here or there who are not in the top 10% does not pierce the group identity of the more highly ranked group.

3. It is the case that many parents, including those without children in the top 10% of the class, opt to settle in Cannondale because of the reputation of the schools. Real estate agents actively promote this reputation, as do school personnel. While participant observations were conducted at various events in which students and parents in the remaining 90% of the class attended, the positioning practices of families with students not found in the top 10% of the class are largely beyond the scope of this study.

4. According to the 2010 Census Bureau report on *Income, Poverty, and Health Insurance Coverage in the United States: 2010*, households in the lowest quintile had incomes of $20,000 or less. Those in the second quintile had incomes of $20,001 to $38,043; those in the third quintile had incomes of $38,044 to $61,735; and those in the fourth quintile had incomes of $61,736 to $100,065. Households in the highest quintile had incomes of $100,066 or more.

5. Housing prices, income, and cost of living are all tied to geography.

6. Andelina Hoxha and Sandra Whitcombe were the two who did not mention the schools as their reason for settling in Cannondale. Andelina and her family settled here immediately upon arrival to the United States, as they had family already residing here. Kristin failed to ask Sandra why they opted to move here. Both women, however, indicated that they have been happy with the school district.

7. Expectations (perhaps misplaced) and entitlement regarding college admissions certainly are present outside the top 10%. Counselors and counseling staff relayed one particular story of a young woman applying to 16 colleges at the direction of a private counselor, many of which ultimately rejected her. According to the counselors, she and her parents were unhappy with the college suggestions made by the counselor and sought out the assistance of a private counselor who they believed would help her access the types of colleges she *deserved*. Stories such as this, shared anecdotally, hint at how some students outside the top 10% interact with the college admissions process. However, sustained study of this group falls outside the scope of this research.

8. It is unclear what motivates Robert Parker's disdain, or perhaps resentment, in this example. At the time of this study, as the lead union representative, he was embroiled in district politics. Two points of concern that he shared with Kristin were grade inflation and parental pressure regarding access to higher-level courses like the APs. Perhaps his comment about "ticky-tacky neighborhoods" can be partially explained by his frustrations with parental pressures on his job, perhaps speaking to the existence of high expectations and entitlement beyond the top 10%.

9. Again, this is not to point a finger at parents and argue that if they only did more, the outcomes for their children would be different. While parents' childrearing

techniques may vary, parents' actions are informed and shaped by their social and geographic location, making childrearing a class process rather than an individual project.

10. A common critique of Lareau (2003) is that she classifies families as "middle class" that would more frequently be referred to as "upper middle class."

11. Karina Hoxha and Chloe Rogers were the only two students not placed in this program. While it is impossible at this point to know why Chloe was not in this program or whether her mother attempted (unsuccessfully) to get her placed in it, it is possible to speculate that Karina was not included in this program because she did not arrive to this country until she was nine years old. As an ESL student, new to the district and to the United States as a whole, it makes sense that she would not have been part of the "gifted and talented" program.

12. Placement in the top 10% is a point of distinction, not only in the school itself, but also at the point of college admissions. Savvy parents and students, cognizant of this, would commonly ask counselors which was the better scenario: take the easier class (and presumably get a higher grade that would subsequently give a student a boost in terms of rank) or the more difficult one (and potentially sacrifice the grade). The answer given most frequently: you need both. There were certainly some students in the top 10% of the class who were not found in the top-track classes, but more often than not, students who found themselves in the top 10% were generally the students who could "do both."

13. This number fluctuates from year to year, generally hovering between 66% and 70%. We cite the 2010 data here, as these data are reflective of the class of 2010 from which study participants were drawn.

14. It's important to note that approximately one-quarter of graduating seniors who are college bound at Cannondale do choose to attend community college. Community colleges can offer excellent transition opportunities to students, particularly Riverside Community College, which is known for its successful 2+2 program, while allowing students the benefits of small class sizes and affordability. Focal students, however, script themselves as so incredibly different from students who attend community college (who are in other academic tracks and have little contact with focal students, at least during school hours), further differentiating themselves from the reality of the more broad attendance patterns in this affluent public

15. State classes are classes that require a state exam at their conclusion and are considered to be quite basic at a school such as Cannondale. Students need to pass a certain number of state-level classes and exams to graduate. Many students, such as those in this study, begin taking state-level tests in eighth grade and by tenth grade have more than exceeded the required amount. Also, many of the Honors-level classes conclude with the state test.

16. See the discussion previously in this chapter that addresses the fact that while some state students are found in AP and IB classes, their presence is limited

to small numbers that do not affect the overall culture of the AP/IB track—the culture to which the focal students subscribe.

17. Both Khan (2011) and Gaztambide-Fernández (2009) note that despite the fact elite private schools confer advantage and distinction across students, it is not uniform and there are differences and hierarchies here, too. This is further explored in chapter 4.

18. The concept of *leading from behind* is one that has gained popularity (or notoriety, depending upon one's political persuasion) early in 2011 as a term that described the Obama administration's approach to dealing with Libya.

19. In so stating, and as noted earlier, we do not mean to imply that parents whose children are not in the top 10% do not similarly engage in "up-front class work" such as purchasing homes in this particular school district and so forth. It is most certainly the case that a high proportion of parents associated with this school district similarly attempt to position their children for future advantage via the purchase of homes in this district, in particular. Our focus on the top 10% of the class is not meant to deny the hard work of many other students and parents associated with this school, but rather to focus our attention on the extent to which and the ways in which parents and students at the top of the class position for future positionality and, most particularly, the college admissions process in increasingly competitive times.

Chapter Four

1. Roksa and Potter (2011) make the provocative argument that parents' ability to transfer advantage is at least partially affected by their childhood social class background, not just their current class status. They examine four groups: middle-class parents who grew up middle class (stable middle), upwardly mobile middle class (new middle), downwardly mobile working class (new working class), and working-class parents who grew up working class (stable working class). What emerges from their data is a complex and interesting picture of how social mobility affects different groups. It appears that the upwardly mobile "new middle-class" mothers are able to adopt class practices (childrearing and expectations) that more closely approximate "stable middle-class" families and to close the academic gap so that both groups perform similarly. Downwardly mobile "new working-class" mothers, however, are not able to retain the advantages inherent to their class origin, and while their children seem to perform better academically than children from "stable working-class" homes, there is little difference in educational expectations and childrearing practices between the two groups.

2. In referencing the most highly valued postsecondary institutions in the United States, we draw upon Barron's selectivity index (*Profiles of American Colleges* 2009, 2013), focusing specifically on what are defined as "Highly Competitive+" and "Most Competitive" institutions. Both state/public institutions and private

institutions fall into both competitiveness categories, although, as we clearly demonstrate in chapter 6, proportionally few public institutions are ranked "Highly Competitive+" and even fewer are ranked "Most Competitive."

3. Important work has been done in both the United Kingdom (Reay et al. 2011) and United States (Horvat and Cucchiara 2009) on privileged parents who, for expressed reasons of social justice, send their children to educational institutions with students of a broad range of SES backgrounds. This is relatively unusual, however, and evidence suggests SES/race/ethnic convergence in friendship groupings within the school when parents make such well-intentioned decisions. This is particularly borne out in the work of Horvat and Cucchiara (2009).

4. Engaging participant observation in African American and White working-class and poor families versus middle- and upper-middle-class families of comparable race, Lareau targets the myriad ways that parental social class impacts life experiences, leading her to conclude that "key elements of family life cohere to form a cultural logic of child rearing" (2008, p. 117). Specifically, she states that middle-class parents work to "develop" the talents of their children in a concerted fashion through organized activities controlled and directed by their mothers and fathers. Unlike children in more privileged families who have a "steady diet of adult organized activities, the working class and poor children have more control over the character of their leisure activities" (2003, p. 5), playing with children of friends and relatives on their streets of residence rather than engaging heavily in parentally programmed options, thereby facilitating what Lareau calls "the accomplishment of natural growth" (2003, p. 5). By Lareau's own admission, she focuses solely on early childrearing practices rather than on the ways in which later institutionally linked factors, particularly those embedded in schools, work to additionally maintain class priviledge or the lack thereof.

Lareau and Weininger's (2010) follow-up research with the same individuals similarly reveals only a partial story, as their design cannot take into account the ways in which school sector itself is linked to the production of privilege. Our data, in contrast, suggest that a range of institutionally linked factors work to produce the new "upper middle class" via elite secondary schools that both draw upon and augment parental control of children when they are in elementary school.

5. At both Cannondale and Matthews Academy, families and children are additionally comparably *highly privileged* in relation to the larger metropolitan context in which they are located. So, too, they are comparably *less privileged* in relation to comparably located families in cities (such as New York City) of far greater concentrations of capital and wealth. Cannondale and Matthews residents and school children, then, are *relatively and objectively both more and less privileged* in the same kinds of ways, depending on the reference point; the most meaningful difference between the two populations lies with the schools their children attend, a point that has critical implications for the nature of class positioning and likely future relative class location in new national and global context. In similar fashion,

although gaining entrance into particularly located private nursery, elementary, and secondary schools in wealthier cities has become hypercompetitive, this is not the case in cities of far less concentration of wealth, where far fewer people can afford the price of attendance. For this reason, competition for entrance into private institutions in the geographic area under consideration is not particularly intense. Rather than turn large numbers of prospective applicants away by virtue of a rigorous admissions process as is the case in New York City, for example, private schools in tier-2 cities work hard to *entice* residents to send their children to their respective institutions. For this reason, students at both elite private and public schools are largely similar with regard to academic ability, particularly in the top academic tracks, which is the focus of this study.

6. There are, of course, some quite wealthy families in the private sector, but such "trust fund" children are few and far between. The extent to which there are families of deeply rooted multigenerational privilege in the two sectors, along the lines of Roksa and Potter's (2011) argument, is additionally not known. However, the clear majority of students in this particularly located sector of private day schools are not from families of multigenerational deep privilege, a point that is regularly commented upon by long-term administrators, counselors, and teachers at these schools.

7. In point of fact, many private schools, including the two NAIS institutions under consideration here, do not take children who do not meet minimum academic entrance criteria. Therefore the nature of grouping takes on a fundamentally different shape and form than curricula in "gifted and talented" programs. In so arguing, we do not mean to suggest that there is no curricular tracking in private schools, as this is not the case. However, programmatic tracking at the elementary level such as that embedded in the "gifted and talented" notion is not common. Although pretracking begins in middle school, such placements tend to be more fluid than those embedded in public schools and do not map neatly onto secondary course placements, where greater shift in track placements are possible in the privates. Having said this, it is important to point out that not all private schools establish minimum academic entrance criteria, and some schools prioritize non-academic admissions criteria reflective of different values. In this case, entrance criteria would differ.

8. In so arguing, we emphatically do not mean to suggest that comparable "up-front" class work does not characterize private school parents. Indeed, such work clearly characterizes this group, as the extent to which privileged parents attempt to enroll even their unborn children in particular nursery schools in New York City makes clear. Our point here is that such work dramatically intensifies within this parental group, as children approach the postsecondary admissions process.

9. Ability grouping at the elementary level is markedly different from *formal* curricular tracking, which generally begins in grade 8 or 9. Given sequenced curricula, it is difficult to "jump tracks" at the secondary school level, rendering initial track placement of consequence over the course of the secondary school career.

Ability grouping and particularly tracking has been the subject of much scholarly writing. See Kelly (2008) for a recent summary of this work. It is the case, however, that pretracking often begins in grade 6 (in many Catholic schools, in particular), especially in mathematics, where students are tracked in a "soft" way into accelerated and regular math. The content of these courses can differ greatly, with consequences for future track placement unless a given child can make up notable curricular ground. The point, however, is that there are no *formal structures or designations* that map neatly onto secondary track placements, and ability grouping is relatively fluid in the early grades in particular, as it is generally understood that cognitive strength emerges at different ages.

10. The extent to which "class positioning" involves selecting a sequence of institutions will differ by school location. In New York City, for example, there are a number of high-profile K–12 institutions, in which case our point could be somewhat less relevant in this context. Even in this case, however, some movement between and among schools can be expected in our now highly marketized and consumerist climate.

11. In decades past, attendance at particular private schools was generally linked to lineage or family/community tradition, and children were not expected to have any say in this process. Although this is still the case to some extent, the broadened range of people who access private schools, as well as the generally more consumerist culture in the United States, means that school selection processes increasingly take place within an educational marketplace, wherein value, mission, and "fit" are assessed at every turn. In this new context, parents accessing the private school sector increasingly enter the market as a consumer and make choices on this basis.

12. It is additionally the case that not all children at the top of the academic hierarchy in these schools are White, as the children of multigenerational privileged Black and Latino/a parents as well as the children of "flexible immigrants" attend these schools and often achieve rank at the top of the class, thereby falling into the group that comprises the focus of this chapter. Although we do not take up this point in chapter 4, we devote chapter 6 to serious examination of race, class, and "flexible immigrants" of color with regard to the production of the new upper middle class. Although Helene, who is introduced in chapter 6, falls within the focal group discussed in this chapter by virtue of her rank in the top 20% of the class, we focus on her situation as the daughter of "flexible immigrants" from Jamaica in chapter 6.

13. It must be pointed out, however, that the college counseling office at Matthews is still woefully understaffed compared to comparable offices at more prestigious private day and boarding school that have substantially larger endowments than Matthews.

14. There are stunning differences in endowment levels within this sector of schools. Endowment at boarding schools Phillips Andover and St. Paul's is $683 mil-

lion and $346 million respectively; at day schools Trinity and Matthews, endowments sit at $40 million and $26 million respectively. Brearley, an all-female school, has an endowment of $106 million as compared to the endowment of Bradford Academy (one of the schools in chapter 5), where the endowment sits at approximately $10 million. See Laneri (2010) for further information on endowments.

15. This empirical question cannot be addressed here. The veteran Director of College Counseling at Matthews, however, is clear that this is the case—in other words, that it is increasingly difficult to get into the most valued postsecondary destinations if one is approaching the marketplace from a tier-2 city rather than from institutions that are wealthier and draw from wealthier tier-1 clients to begin with.

16. We do not mean to imply that the most highly valued postsecondary destinations are not comprised largely of students of high social class background, but rather that elite private schools no longer have a stranglehold on admissions, as colleges now work to somewhat diversify their entering classes.

17. Social class, for example, is a field, and there are assumed to be particular practices associated with one's location within the field. For example, if one is upper middle class, there are particular expectations about how one might engage childrearing, practices that are informed by *habitus* and the *field*. Dimitriadis and Kamberelis (2006, p. 67) explain that "practices involve conscious, intentional actions and unconscious, unintentional action. Social actors develop a certain 'feel for the game' of any field, which enables them to act more or less automatically."

18. It is not uncommon for this group of children to apply to between 9 and 16 postsecondary institutions. Students at Cannondale generally applied to less; 6 schools was the average.

19. As noted in chapter 2, at Cannondale, all students meet individually with their counselor for a "junior review" in which they discuss coursework for the upcoming year as well as postsecondary plans. The counseling department orchestrates several group meetings about college, but there is no requirement that students and parents together meet with counselors individually (although many students, particularly those in the top 10%, do meet with their counselors regularly). During students' senior year, counselors will schedule a "senior review" to check in with students and assess what type of assistance is needed in planning for postsecondary life.

One set of parents notably did not follow the pattern of micromanagement that is so highly prevalent at Matthews, as detailed at length in this chapter. However, by the parents' own admission, their son was "very focused through the whole process and he knew he was doing the right subjects; he worked really hard." Additionally, he had a sister who went through the process only two years earlier and had already seen a large number of colleges. As the father also noted, "to be modest about it, we knew that they'd [son and daughter] get into some decent schools. Had there been some doubt, we may have gotten more involved." In fact, his son (and earlier, his daughter) gained admission at a range of Ivies and apex colleges. The parents attributed their own relative lack of involvement to "personality."

20. All postsecondary institution names have been changed and have been substituted with equally ranked schools in the relevant public or private category as per Barron's (2009). Relevant personal details of the parents and students have also been altered so as to protect the anonymity of project participants.

21. It is additionally important to point out that Matt is a hockey player and his father heard a rumor that "Harvard is looking for hockey players." Dave Henderson, in a separate interview, did not confirm that he told Ron Tomlinson that this is the case. It is the true, however, that an "athletic hook" could be helpful in gaining admission to particular institutions, but this is only the case if skill and talent levels are judged to be sufficiently high and the coach strongly supports the applicant as a member of his or her team, in which case the student would go through a separate admissions process and come in as an athletic recruit. The fact that Dave Henderson denies that he suggested to Matt that he might get in as an athletic recruit suggests that Ron Tomlinson may have constructed this possibility out of something he heard elsewhere. During the interview, Ron Tomlinson tried to enlist Lois to speak to his son about the importance of applying to the Ivies, particularly Harvard. He complained that Dave Henderson would not take on this role.

22. Within Matthews, the all-consuming nature of the postsecondary admissions process means that at any given moment, all available out-of-classroom space—including the college counseling office, junior and senior lounges, study halls, lunch tables, hallways, and so forth—is filled with students talking about homework; studying for tests; drilling one another on practice SAT, ACT and/or SAT Subject Tests; discussing college essays; dissecting the process in general; and so forth. Whatever else might be going on in their lives, these students are highly interconnected, both at school and at home, as they position for the "top."

23. The issue of field of study is important here. In the United States, students are not generally admitted into particular fields of study at the undergraduate level. Only schools of engineering consistently admit students to the major at the point of admissions, in which case number and type of STEM courses at the secondary level becomes critical with regard to the admissions process. Generally speaking, students apply and are admitted to institutions rather than majors. In the vast majority of cases, students declare majors at the end of sophomore year, a practice that markedly differentiates the United States from numerous other nations. In spite of this, students are beginning to double up on math and science so as to mark themselves with "distinction" in an increasingly competitive process, and there is some evidence to suggest that high-level math and science courses act as gatekeepers to top schools (Grodsky and Riegle-Crumb 2010).

24. Parent Lisa Norwood shared with Lois that in the thick of college admissions, her daughter and her closest friends got together for a house party (movies, food, etc.) designed to take their mind off the admissions process. They spent the

whole evening dissecting and rehashing the process. Lisa Norwood tried to step in and redirect the conversation, pointing out that this was supposed to be fun rather than stressful, but to no avail.

25. A field is defined primarily in terms of the kinds of practices that are common within it and the kinds of capital that may accrue to the individuals who engage in those practices, and secondarily as the kinds of social relations that develop as people work to acquire and maintain the kinds of capital with the most purchase in the field. The boundaries of any specific field with respect to the stakes, and the kinds of individuals drawn into its domain of practice, are not fixed but fluid because fields develop and are maintained by the practices that occur within them. (Dimitriadis and Kamberelis 2006, p. 67). In this sense, the postsecondary education sector is a field (with many subfields), and students engage particular actions (practice) within the field, which are partially informed by habitus as well as by conscious strategy (which, ultimately, is also shaped by habitus and capital). Practice, in other words, can be thought of in terms of agency, yet this agency is deeply tied to the larger dynamics of one's social field and, consequently, by habitus. Habitus shapes practice (agency), yet it is undoubtedly shaped by the larger social structure (or field). Fields are dynamic, too, and because the field can change or shift, or perhaps have different iterations based upon context, the actions one takes (those informed by habitus) may result in different outcomes, or perhaps, even look different. It is important to note that Bourdieu uses the term "strategy" to mean action (practice) that is informed by one's habitus. In a sense, one is playing by the rules of the game, and one's actions (what is viable, what is not) are more or less shaped by habitus and all it entails. Bourdieu understands all action to be informed by logic; the logic undergirding one's habitus (Bourdieu and Wacquant 1992, pp. 128–29). This definition differs somewhat from more traditional interpretations of strategy, which often imply conscious and careful planning and action, and what we see parents and students at Matthews engaging (and Cannondale folks as well) is a combination of both types of strategy.

26. This is a widely agreed-upon point, for which there are two main explanations. (1) Early applicants tend, on average, to comprise a particular group of students, and dossiers tend to be relatively stronger overall than those garnered in the regular admissions cycle. (2) Equally important is that Early Admissions, in most cases, is binding—in other words, if one is admitted under an Early Admissions cycle, the student must attend the institution. As student yield (proportion of students who are offered admission who actually attend any given school) is a factor in many ranking systems, colleges are incentivized to fill as much of their entering class as practical via Early Admissions, so long as they do not compromise other ranking system indicators such as SAT scores. Early Action, in contrast, is not binding; however, students who apply under this program often end up attending one of the schools that offer acceptance, similarly contributing to the yield. Some top institutions have exhibited concern over the potential for early applications

processes to differentially benefit students from higher SES backgrounds. For this reason, Princeton, Harvard, and University of Virginia shut down their early admissions cycles in 2006, in the hopes of spurring similar actions among a broader range of top schools. This did not happen, and all three colleges reinstituted an Early Action cycle in 2011. While perhaps not a yield issue in this particular case, it is arguably the case that when the concept did not spread to other top institutions, Harvard, Princeton, and UVA did not want to lose a portion of their peak applicant pool that could be admitted via early admissions elsewhere. For further information, see *Inside Higher Education*, February 25, 2011. For a general discussion of Early Admission practices and outcomes, see Avery and Levin (2010) and Chapman and Dickert-Conlin (2012). For a discussion of the psychological effects of Early Admission practices, see Schneider (2009).

27. Harvard, Yale, and Princeton inevitably fall into this latter category for even the most stellar of students, as, in Dave Henderson's words, one needs a "hook" to gain admission to these schools (Soares 2007; Stevens 2007; interviews with college counselor at Matthews). As acceptance rates now hover around 9 %, admittance is not guaranteed, no matter how stellar the applicant. Also, we should note here that Cannondale students engage a much similar strategy involving reaches, probables (good fits), and safeties (although some students, such as Brad from chapter 3, choose not to adhere fully to this).

28. The case of the European parents as well as the parents of other "flexible immigrants" in the focal group sample is noteworthy. Two points are relevant here: (1) The vast majority of postsecondary entrance processes worldwide do not rely on the preparation of a dossier that includes extracurriculars to mark "distinction," but rather a set of examinations that enable entrance. This encourages a very different kind of positioning work than occurs in the United States. (2) It is arguably the case that as students in many nations, particularly Europe, apply to a field of study rather than the broader university, the kinds of extracurriculars as a way of marking "distinction" in evidence in the United States become irrelevant in other nations. Top universities outside the United States, for example, are not interested in the fact that one is a highly trained vocalist unless one applies to study music.

29. Once students receive letters from all institutions, generally around April 1 of their senior year, a great deal of work goes into thinking through which schools should remain on their list—in other words, which schools should they visit again, generally staying overnight on campus. Interviews suggest that parents are engaged in this crucial set of "live cuts" every step of the way.

30. Lucas's (2001) concept of *effectively maintained inequality* (EMI) is instrumental to understanding the heightened competition around the college application process. Lucas argues that at levels of universality (increased access of a college education, for example), "competition will occur around the type of education attained" (p. 1652). In other words, increased access does not lead to democra-

tization, or, stated in the terms of EMI, universality does not erase stratification, as those who are well positioned will continue to seek out *qualitative* differences that will be advantageous "and use their advantages to secure quantitatively similar but qualitatively better education" (p. 1652).

31. This point holds for all school sites in this study. In only one case at each school under consideration is the father the primary driver of the process. In one case, the father is divorced and is the primary caregiver, with the mother wholly uninvolved in the college process. In the other two cases, one father is retired and the mother continues to hold professional positions, and in the other, while both parents are immigrants with professional jobs, the father's job is more high status and he therefore felt the need to drive the process.

32. Ken Sanderson clearly states that these are the roles in his household. We have no reason to lodge any kind of critique at fathers' role in this process. Figuring out how to cover the costs of soaring postsecondary attendance is, in fact, increasingly difficult. Our point here is that the "class work" remains highly gendered, with mothers engaging the majority of the planning and execution of actions and activities that are seen to be increasingly necessary to maintain advantage for the next generation. Ron Tomlinson, of course, is an exception here, as he took an incredibly active role in his son's college process.

Chapter Five

1. Data reported in this chapter are drawn from Heather's dissertation (Jenkins 2011).

2. Since 2010, City Prep has made significant changes to its Primary, Secondary, and Postsecondary Prep programs. The organization has retained an outside consultant to assist with program and student outcomes evaluation, and an academic director to create research-based curricula throughout all of the programs. Importantly, the Postsecondary Prep Director is now full time and is in the process of creating a comprehensive college counseling program that serves grades 9 through 12, with one-on-one advisement beginning during the spring of junior year.

3. The concept of a "good" college is highly contextual. It is important to remind the reader that these self-identified, lower-income Black participants compare themselves to those they left behind in their public schools and neighborhoods, and not their more privileged peers at Matthews and Bradford. As such, "good" schools come to mean better than the schools they imagine they would have applied to had they not entered elite private secondary schools. While they acknowledge, of course, that schools like Harvard and Cornell are "good" schools, when they invoke this term, they mean schools that grant four-year degrees with at least a modest level of competitiveness (e.g., those ranked as "Very Competitive" and "Competitive," not only those ranked as "Most Competitive" and "Highly Competitive+"). As we suggest in this chapter, the conception of what comprises

a "good" college perceptively shifts as this group of students engages the college process in this sector of secondary schools.

4. With respect to Breanna's expressed goal to go to one of the HBCU like Fisk "because they have a nice accounting program," one might question where Breanna locates her future self in the structure of opportunities with respect to this particular field. Although there are certainly demanding and exceptionally interesting accounting jobs, we might ask about the extent to which Breanna understands the larger structure within which such varying possibilities lie. In this regard, her own class background may limit her sense of possibilities with respect this occupation, a sense that could, of course, be challenged at a more selective college. Our thanks to Elizabeth Branch Dyson for drawing our attention to this issue.

5. Matthews and Bradford, for example, have recently started holding meetings with parents of freshman and sophomores at the explicit request of privileged parents who want to begin the process earlier than junior year. College counselors do not approve of this move, but feel pressured to enact it. Such early meetings are conceived by the schools as working to calm the parents down, a move that has scant chance of success in this sector.

6. The linked class and race assumptions embedded in this statement are palpable. Low-income Black students in the elite private schools rarely have parents who attempt to make it "their process," much less grandparents.

7. Thanks to Nelson Rivera who made this point in a series of class discussions.

8. Several all-class meetings are held on the college process over the course of junior and senior year. In addition, students are reminded to make appointments with their counselors, meet deadlines, and so forth, in advisee meetings, generally held weekly. Advisee groups are a ubiquitous part of the private school landscape, with a faculty or staff member generally in charge of a small group of students who they often see through their entire high school careers.

9. Lareau's (2003) work is useful here as she maintains that low-income parents, across race, do not display or teach their children the same level of entitlement evidenced in the parental work of middle- and upper-middle-class parents. Rather, low-income parents engage in parental processes of "natural growth" (Lareau 2003). Thus, it stands to reason that low-income Black parents, as race and class "outsiders within" the elite private school habitus, would leave the education of their children firmly in the hands of the professional educators without intervention. Further, our data also indicate the these parents and students believe that simply being part of these schools points one toward "good" four-year colleges and do not fully understand the type and quantity of work to be done during the college process.

10. Although Breanna falls back on the expressed notion that others in the school hire private college counselors, this is in fact very rare in this context. This is not to deny her point that there is an assumption of wealth and class/race privilege in these schools, but rather to indicate that the hiring of private counselors is not routinely engaged as the within-school college counseling is almost always seen as

sufficient. Private college counselors are far more likely to be engaged in the affluent public sector where, as noted in chapter 2, college counseling is one among many tasks of counselors in public high schools.

11. Although fee waivers for SATs, ACTs, and application costs are available through the school, students must be bold enough to approach the counseling office for such waivers. They are, at times, reluctant to do so as this further marks them as "outsiders within." Unfortunately, neither City Prep nor others related to the college process are currently filling this gap.

12. In spite of the fact that Breanna notes that several students at Bradford hired private college counselors, we saw no evidence of focal students engaging this activity at either Cannondale or Matthews (Cannondale counselors share a couple of examples of nonfocal students who they believe employed private counselors). This is not to say that this does not occur, simply that it is not, at this moment in time, normative practice in this sector of schools.

13. A very small number of Matthews students engage a "postgraduate year." The option is always there, however, and counselors are willing to provide information on such programs, as relevant and desired.

14. Although such on-site visits do not extensively factor into admissions decisions, some admissions offices at private liberal arts institutions, in particular, take note of such visits (and often accompanying interviews) in their decision-making process.

Chapter Six

1. In discussing policies and practices around course assignment, course availability, college counseling, and so forth, we are referring to "soft" policies and associated practices that emerge within the school itself rather than broader policies that are driven by external entities/agencies such as those associated with the state and/or federal government (including the courts). Our point here is that we are not referring to macro-level policies, but rather school-based policies that are under the control of the institution. Such policies lead to particular kinds of practices, and it is this level of policy and practice that comprise our focus in chapters 5 and 6.

2. While race may very well be a salient factor for some students at Cannondale (given the small percentage of students of color in this predominantly White space), data reveal that race did not emerge as a key structuring factor in focal students' experiences. Had the sample of students been different (say, for instance, had we sought out students of color who participate in the Urban-Suburban exchange program), findings regarding race would most likely be different. Cannondale, to be certain, is entrenched in Whiteness and "White Privilege"; however, the rich data regarding race, detailed by the self-identified low-income Black students at Matthews and Bradford, did not emerge given Cannondale's largely White (with the exception of Kelly Tran) sample. This is not surprising given that Whiteness often functions as an "absent present" (Frankenburg 1993).

3. Henry Louis Gates and Lani Guinier draw attention to this point. As Sara Rimer and Karon W. Arenson (2004) report in a *New York Times* article, "while about 8 percent, or about 530, of Harvard's undergraduates were black, Lani Grunier, a Harvard law professor, and Henry Louis Gates Jr., the Chairman of Harvard's African and African-American studies department, pointed out that the majority of them—perhaps as many as two-thirds—were West Indian and African immigrants or their children, or to a lesser extent, children of biracial couples. They said that only about a third of the students were from families in which all four grandparents were born in this country, descendants of slaves. Many argue that it was students like these, disadvantaged by the legacy of Jim Crow laws, segregation and decades of racism, poverty and inferior schools, who were intended as principal beneficiaries of affirmative action in university admissions."

4. Thanks to the anonymous reviewers for offering this analogy.

5. There has been some writing on the experience of working-class Whites in elite private schools, but the fact that they are racial insiders makes their experiences and feelings of isolation less apparent than that of low-income Black students. See Reichert (2000).

6. Although not discussing the elite private school sector, Beverly Tatum's (1997) work is highly illuminating in this regard.

7. Black masculinity has been the subject of much excellent scholarly writing. See, e.g., McCarthy et al. (2005), Blount and Cunningham (1996), and Belton (1996).

8. A clear exception to this would be some schools in California where the dominant population is one or another Asian group. In general though, the dominant population in privileged schools is likely to be White.

9. Although Kelly Tran is the only student of color in the top track at Cannondale, her experiences and those of her parents are similar to those of a range of "flexible immigrants" at our two private schools. By this we mean that neither she nor her parents occupy the status of "outsider within" that almost entirely characterizes the low-income Black population we discuss in chapter 5.

10. Issues around race and class exclusion are exceptionally complex, and we do not mean to imply that some privileged students of color do not feel like outsiders within privileged institutions. We also do not mean to suggest that privileged students of color are never in contexts wherein they are both class and race insiders, as this is not necessarily the case. Asian students on the West Coast, for example, are often dominant in privileged schools, and there are larger populations of privileged Black students in some cities than in the city under investigation here. This is complex territory, and we do not mean to simplify it. Nevertheless, there are notable differences between the experiences of low-income Black students in elite schools and Black students of highly privileged background.

11. Again, this is not to dismiss the potential felt position of racial outsider

among students of color who come from families more closely aligned with the habitus of the school. However, it is to state clearly that such privileged families of color do not frame choosing strong academics versus racial/ethnic diversity to be a point of discussion or consideration.

12. In so arguing, we are not unaware that many privileged African Americans, in particular, attend churches that are located in the city core, and that they have family members who are not as affluent as they are—family members with whom they maintain close connections. Having said this, multigenerational Black families of privilege do not conceive of sending their children to underresourced predominantly Black and Latino schools as a viable option.

13. Although we focus here on children who would be marked as racially Black inside the elite school context but whose class background differs from that of low-income Black students, it is worth noting that Kelly Tran would undoubtedly be similarly marked as ideologically or symbolically White in the context of Cannondale. However, the situation in Cannondale with respect to race/ethnicity differs from that of Matthews/Bradford, as Cannondale evidences markedly little presence of race/ethnic diversity, and Kelly Tran is the only focal student of color in the top 10% of the Cannondale class. In this context, she, like those privileged students of color in the elite private school sector, would no doubt be marked as symbolically White. The nature of such symbolic marking is, however, likely to be different from that which characterizes the Matthews context. Such symbolic Whitening, then, would evidence itself similar to such Whitening noted by Stacey Lee (2005) with respect to the high performing East Asians, in particular, in the "good" school in which she gathered her data, where the Hmong were ideologically Blackened in contrast to the East Asians. This suggests that the process of symbolic Whitening is dependent not only on the particular racial/ethnic group in evidence, but on the on-site context in which such symbolic Whitening unfolds and in relation to the available presence, or not, of an "other" of color against whom such marking takes shape and form. This is not to deny the larger discursive and material context within which all on-site marking occurs, but rather, to note the importance of *both* particular and broad context. Weis (1990, 2004) addresses this issue with respect to "othering" in Freeway, taking particular note of Whites, African Americans, and later, Yemenites

14. The ideological Blackening of the Hmong in the US imagination is clearly evident in popular culture. In the 2008 film *Gran Torino*, the Clint Eastwood character lives in a community populated by a clearly ideologically Blackened group of Hmong youth.

15. According to Eduardo Bonilla-Silva (2006), the racial ideology of the Jim Crow era characterized by overt, intentional racism and legal segregation has been replaced by "a powerful ideology . . . to defend the contemporary racial order: the ideology of color-blind racism" (p. 25). Bonilla-Silva (2003) asserts that color-blind racism, a subtle, insidious form of racism, has four main tenets: abstract liberalism,

naturalization, cultural racism, and minimization of racism. During Bonilla-Silva's (2003) discussion of the naturalization frame of color-blind racism, he drew attention to how Whites naturalize the enduring presence of racial segregation. Discussions of "reverse racism" among Whites are an example of both the abstract liberalism and minimization frames of color-blind racism (Bonilla-Silva 2003). Cultural racism is often associated with deficit-orientated ideas about Blacks, sometimes in regard to academic capabilities (noted throughout this chapter), as byproduct of the deficiencies within "Black culture" (Bonilla-Silva 2003). These frames of color-blind racism, which are present in various social interactions and social and cultural contexts, allow racism to thrive "under the radar," so to speak, of often well-intentioned Whites who do not perceive themselves to be perpetuating racism. Bonilla-Silva (2003) emphasizes that the prevalence of color-blind racism in US society ensures its presence in US intuitions, such as schools. Just as Jim Crow racism permeated all parts of the US social structure, so too does color-blind racism in the post–civil rights era.

16. As this is not our central research question, we do not have comparable data from White and highly privileged students. We are quite certain, however, that White students would elaborate similar explanations for why racially segregated peer groups define their school, and that they similarly would conceptualize their largely privileged Black peers who are in their classes as "not really Black."

17. Our observations indicate that students at this table appear to be Black or Latino, and only two White students (based on appearance) were recorded as dining at the table during any of the extensive observation sessions at Matthews.

18. Steven, however, characterizes himself as "the un-Black Black," thereby removing himself from the battle over racial representations.

19. For Helene, growing up in a predominantly White affluent suburb and attending predominantly White affluent schools since the age of three, White culture and upper middle-class culture are interconnected. This is not unlike the sentiments expressed by low-income Black focal students. Helene expresses a strong desire to connect with Blacks of similar class background when she goes off to Harvard in the fall.

20. Importantly, this is notably different than what is reported in Ogbu (2008) and Fordham and Ogbu (1986). "Acting White" in these instances equates Whiteness with academic achievement. We disagree with this association and found no evidence that it existed at Matthews or Bradford. All students in the study strove for academic excellence.

21. This is not to say that this kind of racial surveillance does not characterize other racial/ethnic minorities, Latinos in particular where there is some evidence that similar formulations exist (Foley 2010a). Our focus, however, is low-income Black students in the elite private secondary school sector, and we do not consider other minorities.

22. Holland's (2012) research in an affluent, majority White, public high school

suggests that sports enables Black and Latino males to gain social status vis-à-vis their peers in ways that Black and Latina females do not. We see no evidence of this phenomenon in the secondary day private school under investigation here. This suggests that sports may not serve a comparable function in the two sectors.

23. The point about experiences and class solidification across race/ethnicity must perhaps be tempered with respect to the particular geographic location in which these schools sit. Although privileged students of color do not by any means define the population at elite secondary schools in this location, there are enough such students in this community so as to make their presence in no way unique. This certainly would be the case on both coasts in the United States as well as many large cities in a range of geographic areas of the country. However, anecdotal evidence suggests that privileged children of color in geographic locations where they would be considered more "unique" may work to isolate them (and their families) in a way that is not the case in the communities under consideration here. Although we would argue that our analysis works for much of the United States, it may not work for communities in which privileged people of color have little to no presence.

24. This is not to suggest that this is a seamless process in which no skirmishes take place with respect to which students obtain entrance to particularly valued postsecondary destinations, most notably the Ivies. With prevalent misunderstandings as to the meaning of "affirmative action" at colleges and universities, there are certainly charges leveled at students of color that they were accepted at a given institution "because they are Black"; "because they are Hispanic"; or because a class of colleges is "looking for students of color" (thereby explaining why any given individual whose parents were born in Turkey, India, or China gained admission to a highly valued postsecondary destination). Although such accusations are at times hurled over the course of senior year when accept/reject/wait-list letters begin to come out, this does not fundamentally challenge our larger point as to the collectively shared and highly classed nature of the intense college admission process, one that works to solidify class *across* race/ethnic difference as students transition into the postsecondary sector. Such *class solidification* among the next generation simultaneously and additionally marks low-income Black students who have attended elite private secondary school as inextricably and fundamentally class/race outsiders.

25. As noted in the text itself, the number of "Most Competitive" schools increased by seven between 2009 and 2013, and two of the new "Most Competitive"-level schools are public, bringing the percentage of "Most Competitive" public institutions up to 10% from 8.5%. The number of schools in the broad category of "Highly Competitive" remained the same between 2009 and 2013, though there were some changes in the schools making up the broad "Highly Competitive" category. (This category is additionally split into two subcategories: "Highly Competitive+" and "Highly Competitive.") Overall, the number of "Highly Competitive"

public schools increased by two in total, one additional public school in both the sub-"Highly Competitive" and "Highly Competitive+" categories. In 2009 and 2013 public institutions accounted for about 23% of "Highly Competitive+" schools and 31% and 34%, respectively, of the subcategory "Highly Competitive."

26. All colleges are de-identified, with comparable substitutions made on the basis of the Barron's competitive index and private/public categorizations. Barron's competitive scale ratings for American colleges (*Profiles of American Colleges* 2009) are based entirely on student competitiveness. Barron's determines student competitiveness based on a combination of the following factors: high school rank, grade point average, median SAT and ACT scores, and percentage of applicants admitted by the institution.

27. Although classified as a "state-related" institution, University of Pittsburgh is a private college, used here to represent the private college at which the student actually matriculated.

28. It must be pointed out here that the individual who matriculated at the "Highly Competitive+" institution obtained entrance to several "Most Competitive" institutions, but had personal and family reasons for matriculating here instead.

29. This finding is in line with findings reported in Lee and Weis (2012), as based on NELS and ELS data over time. For Matthews matriculation data 2007–2011: The category "Not Ranked" (NR) covers colleges and universities attended by Mathews graduates that are not included in Barron's *Profiles of American Colleges* 2009. The NR category includes eight postsecondary institutions. Seven of these schools are outside of the United States (five in Canada, one in the United Kingdom, and one in Ireland), and one is within the United States but not described by Barron's.

30. It is also the case that some of these students are Bradford rather than Matthews attendees. Although Bradford also has a stellar placement record, it is not quite as distinguished as that of Matthews, perhaps due to the relative size of the schools. Given the lack of five-year Bradford data, we cannot test this more carefully. Again, however, given our small focal group sample size, we must be careful not to overinterpret these numbers as they could radically change year to year. In general, low-income Black students matriculate at institutions that are largely on par with the overall matriculation pattern at Matthews. They do not, however, matriculate in large numbers at "Most Competitive" institutions, as they are not in the top academic track.

31. The situation at Cannondale with regard to college matriculations is considerably more complex than at Matthews. Significantly, however, this is not the case at the top of the academic hierarchy. At Cannondale, a proportion of students matriculate at the local two-year college (whether for reasons of job linkage, cost, size of classes, etc.), which is not the case at Matthews, where virtually *all* students attend the four-year sector. Too, and as noted here, a higher proportion of Cannon-

dale four-year attendees matriculate at public institutions than is the case for Matthews. In spite of these clear differences in overall school sending patterns, at the top levels of the two schools, students largely apply to and are accepted at "Most Competitive" and "Highly Competitive+" private institutions. This gives credence to Attewell's (2001) point that in affluent suburban high schools, the "winners take all." Top-ranked students at Cannondale reap the benefits of their position in the opportunity structure at their particular brand of privileged secondary school to almost the same extent as do top students at Matthews. The overall postsecondary attendance benefits *beneath* this top sector differ markedly, however, where linkages to the most highly valued postsecondary destinations are more widespread in the independent private than the affluent public. The extent to which *where* postsecondary destination patterns break by position in the opportunity structure in these two types of privileged institutions, and particularly in the large suburban affluent publics, can profitably be the subject of future research, as we do not address this question here.

32. Although we cannot estimate with any degree of certainty the extent to which students would gain entrance to comparatively located postsecondary destinations had they attended other secondary schools, our conclusion parallels that of Lee and Weis (2012), who argue that sector of institution attended asserts an independent effect on entrance patterns to postsecondary institutions.

33. This finding parallels that of Horvat and Antonio (1999), who argue that Black students incur considerable emotional costs while attending elite private secondary schools, but the benefits, in the end, are deemed worth the costs.

Chapter Seven

1. Our sincere thanks to an anonymous reviewer for the *British Journal of Sociology of Education* for pointing this out to Lois and Kristin.

2. The intensified mobilization of a segment of the middle class has clear implications for low-income and working-class students, where the possibility of entrance to highly selective postsecondary institutions can be expected to go down except in cases such as our low-income self-identified Black students who attend affluent and elite secondary schools. We can also expect this exceptionality to hold for "star" urban publics (such as certain magnet schools), where recent data suggest that low-income students are able to position for such institutions given the apparent power of this sector. See Lee and Weis (2012).

3. It must be clear here, however, that this research was not carried out in a state like California, where flagship publics are perhaps still far more popular among those parents and students who are linked to privileged public and private secondary schools than is the case under consideration here. However, three points must be made. One is that only a relatively small number of flagship public institutions fall within the "Most Competitive" and "Highly Competitive +"

categories. Second, analysis of nationally derived NELS and ELS data confirm that students at NAIS and third-ring suburban public secondary schools are proportionally matriculating at "Most Competitive" and "Highly Competitive+" *privates* to a far greater extent than students from any other secondary school sector in the nation. This affirms the widespread desirability and draw of "Most Competitive" and "Highly Competitive+" privates among this particular group across the United States (Lee and Weis, 2012), thereby affirming our finding that the "prize" within this particular class segment is now widely understood to be particularly located private colleges. Third, although the elite in the United States have always sent their children to private colleges, with their keen eye on the Ivies in particular, and elite private secondary schools historically offered a pathway to such institutions (e.g., Cookson and Persell 1985; Karabel 2005), this is now a much more broad-based phenomena, wherein a wider base of students both apply to and matriculate at a substantially enlarged range of top-ranked private colleges. In this sense, it is arguably the case that the top privates represent the "prize" for those seeking to instantiate themselves in what we suggest is a newly articulating upper middle class of the twenty-first century—an upper middle class that shares historic roots with the broad-based middle class in the United States rather than the moneyed elite of America, but from which it is attempting to distance itself by virtue of matriculation at top private postsecondary destinations.

4. The work of Guofang Li (2005) suggests that the movement of peoples across national borders, including those who possess "flexible citizenship" by virtue of possession of high-status knowledge, bring new demands to, among others, US and Canadian school systems. By way of example, upper-middle-class Hong Kong Chinese parents in Vancouver have little use for what they see as the "soft" curriculum associated with North American schooling. Given class-linked cultural and economic capital, such privileged world citizens are demanding more strongly framed knowledge and less of the "fluff" that they associate with Western and particularly North American schooling, even though they currently reside in Canada. This scene is being played out in schools up and down the Pacific North American coast, where a new form of "White flight" is taking place as White parents are removing their children from schools heavily populated by Asians. As our data suggest, however, although perhaps engaged differently, the struggle for class advantage cannot be attributed to "flexible immigrants," as such struggle is now normative practice within a segment of the broad middle class as it seeks to instantiate advantage for the next generation.

5. Our evidence additionally suggests that the low-income Black students in our sample already find it difficult to sustain enrollment at their highly selective private colleges. In contrast, our samples of privileged students across race and ethnicity have all maintained continuous enrollment in comparable postsecondary institutions. As numbers are small in our sample, we must interpret this cautiously. Nevertheless, all low-income Black students had a mix of full and partial scholarships to attend highly selective private colleges, but a number returned to Blair

before the end of their second year. This is not the case for other students in our sample. Although there could be many reasons for this, our point is that these students find it more difficult than privileged students across race/ethnicity to maximize advantage via their college of choice. Additionally, unlike the case for privileged students across race/ethnicity, those who return to Blair shift to community college or a four-year comprehensive college.

6. As used by Bourdieu and Chauvel, "the dominated fraction of the dominant class" refers to those who hold an "ambiguous social position of symbolic superiority but lack economic resources, assets and wealth, which are the sole source of real domination" (Chauvel 2010, p. 87). A key example Bourdieu uses is intellectuals, as intellectuals have amassed and possess a great fortune of other forms of capital—symbolic, social, and cultural—as well as corresponding privileges, but, lacking great economic capital, they are dominated by those with vast amounts of wealth. Given massive alterations in the global economy and the fact that Bourdieu's and Chauvel's work was done in France, the applicability of this concept in new global circumstances, and to the United States in particular, needs further thought. We introduce the concept to suggest that a number of those who will comprise the new upper middle class by virtue of the pathway outlined in this volume may be usefully understood as positioned in the "dominated fraction of the dominant class," a position that has implications for the overall financial viability of this group. Our thanks to Loïc Wacquant who engaged in extensive e-mail conversation with Lois Weis with respect to this concept. See also Wacquant (1993). Our thanks, as well, to Cameron McCarthy who suggested this line of thought to Lois.

7. The capacity of technology and particularly social media to instantaneously encourage and ultimately produce such a larger class base is currently unknown. If "runners" become disenchanted as they wage these highly intensified and individualistically driven struggles for advantage, it is arguably the case that this generation and the next could quickly cohere as a class and/or class fraction, thereby challenging current arrangements.

8. As Goldin (2006, p. 1) notes, "The distinction used here between 'job' and 'career' concerns the degree to which the individual believes she will be in the labor force for a sufficient time to engage in substantial human capital investment both in formal schooling and on-the-job training. Those whose participation will be intermittent will take positions that involve less depreciation during work absences, whereas those with a long time horizon of employment will take positions that require more formal education, involve more internal promotion, and have a greater loss from out-of work spells."

9. Although this could be so engaged with a singular eye toward the "marriage market" in particularly located colleges, we quite frankly heard not a word about this, from mothers, fathers, and/or children, and, at this point in children's lives, men and women are working hard to equally position their sons and daughters for class advantage via access to particularly located and exceptionally difficult-to-gain-entrance-to postsecondary destinations.

10. There are, however, as noted earlier, a slice of flagship publics that remain highly desired among this group, although not nearly to the extent of the highly coveted privates. Such schools include but are not limited to UC Berkeley, UCLA, University of Michigan, and University of North Carolina, Chapel Hill.

Epilogue

1. As Cipollone and Stich (2010) note, gaining access is not a one-time endeavor but rather a process, and a great deal of care must be paid to maintaining access and relationships. It is important to note this here as Kristin almost had her access revoked because the superintendent, who had advised her to run all research decisions by the lead counselor, was upset when the counselor directed her to speak with board members and told her that he was going to cancel the research. After some negotiating and explaining by the lead counselor and Kristin, she was able to continue without input from the board of education.

References

Allatt, P. (1993) Becoming privileged: The role of family processes. In I. Bates and G. Riseborough (Eds.), *Youth and inequality* (pp. 139–59). Buckingham: Open University.

Altbach, P. G., Reisberg, L., and Rumbley, L. E. (2009). Trends in global higher education: Tracking an academic revolution. A report prepared for the UNESCO 2009 World Conference on Higher Education. Paris: UNESCO.

American Educational Research Association (AERA). (2006). Standards for reporting on empirical social science research in AERA publications. *Educational Researcher, 35*(6), 33–40.

Andre-Bechely, L. (2005). Public school choice at the intersection of voluntary integration and not so good neighborhood schools: Lessons from parents' experiences. *Educational Administration Quarterly, 41*(2), 267–305.

Anyon, J. (1980). Social class and the hidden curriculum of work. *Journal of Education, 162*(1), 67–92.

———. (1997). *Ghetto schooling: A political economy of urban educational reform.* New York: Teachers College Press.

———. (2014). *Radical possibilities: Public policy, urban education, and a new social movement* (2nd ed.). New York: Routledge.

Apple, M. (2010). Global crisis, social justice and education: An introduction. In M. Apple (Ed.), *Global crises, social justice and education* (pp. 1–24). New York: Routledge.

Arcidiacono, P. (2004). Ability sorting and the returns to college major. *Journal of Econometrics, 121*(1–2), 343–75.

Aron-Dine, A., Shapiro, I., and Center on Budget and Policy Priorities. (2006). *In first half of 2006, wages and salaries captured smallest share of income on record: Share of income going to corporate profits at highest level since 1950.* Washington, DC: Center on Budget and Policy Priorities.

Arrington, E. G., Hall, D. M., and Stevenson, H. C. (2003). The success of African American students in independent schools. *Independent School Magazine, 62,* 10–21.

Arum, R., Gamoran, A., and Shavit, Y. (2007). More inclusion than diversion: Expansion, differentiation, and market structure in higher education. In Y. Shavit, R. Arum, and A. Gamoran (Eds.), *Stratification in higher education: A comparative study* (pp. 1–35). Stanford: Stanford University Press.

Astin, A. W., and Oseguera, L. (2002). *Degree attainment rates at American colleges and universities*. Los Angeles: Higher Education Research Institute, UCLA.

Attewell, P. (2001, October). The winner-take-all high school: Organizational adaptations to educational stratification. *Sociology of Education, 74*, 267–95.

Avery, C., Fairbanks, A., and Zeckhauser, R. (2003). *The early admissions game: Joining the elite*. Cambridge, MA: Harvard University Press.

Avery, C., and Kane, T. (2004) Student perceptions of college opportunities: The Boston COACH program. In C. Hoxby (Ed.), *College decisions: The new economics of choosing, attending, and completing college* (pp. 355–94). Chicago: University of Chicago Press.

Avery, C., and Levin, J. (2010). Early admissions at selective colleges. *American Economic Review, 100*(5), 2125–56.

Ayalon, H., and Shavit, Y. (2004). Educational reforms and inequalities in Israel: The MMI hypothesis revisited. *Sociology of Education 77*(2), 103–20.

Bailey, M. J., Dynarski, S. M., and National Bureau of Economic Research. (2011). *Gains and gaps: Changing inequality in U.S. college entry and completion*. Cambridge, MA: National Bureau of Economic Research.

Ball, S. (2003). *Class strategies and education markets: The middle classes and social advantage*. London: Routledge Falmer.

Ball, S., and Vincent, C. (2006). *Childcare, choice and class practices: Middle class parents and their children*. New York: Routledge.

Barron's (2009). *Profiles of American colleges* (28th ed.). New York: College Division of Barron's Educational Series, Inc.

———. (2013). *Profiles of American colleges* (30th ed.). New York: College Division of Barron's Educational Series, Inc.

Bell, D. (2004). *Silent covenants:* Brown v. Board of Education *and the unfulfilled hopes for racial reform*. New York: Oxford University Press.

Belton, D. (1996). *Speak my name: Black men on masculinity and the American dream*. Boston: Beacon Press.

Bishop, B. (2008). *The big sort: Why the clustering of like-minded America is tearing us apart*. Boston: Houghton Mifflin.

Bloom, J. (2005). Hallowing the promise of higher education: Inside the political economy of access to college. In L. Weis and M. Fine (Eds.), *Beyond silenced voices: Class, race, and gender in United States schools* (Rev. ed., pp. 63–81). Albany: SUNY Press.

Blount, M., and Cunningham, G. (1996). *Representing black men*. New York: Routledge.

Bogdan, R. C., and Biklen, S. (2007). *Qualitative research for education: An introduction to theories and methods* (5th ed.). Boston: Allyn and Bacon.

Bogdan, R., and Taylor, S. (1975). *Introduction to qualitative research methods: A phenomenological approach to the social sciences*. New York: John Wiley and Sons.

Bonilla-Silva, E. (2006). *Racism without racists: Color-blind racism and the persistence of racial inequality of the United States*. New York: Rowman and Littlefield.

Bourdieu, P. (1979). *La Distinction: Critique sociale du jugement*. Paris: Editions de Minuit.

———. (1984) *Distinction: A social critique of the judgement of taste*. Cambridge, MA: Harvard University Press.

Bourdieu, P., and Wacquant, L. J. D. (1992). *An invitation to reflexive sociology*. Chicago: University of Chicago Press.

Bowen, W., and Bok, D. (1998). *The shape of the river: Long-term consequences of considering race in college and university admissions*. Princeton: Princeton University Press.

Bowen, W. G., Chingos, M. M., and McPherson, M. S. (2009). *Crossing the finish line: Completing college at America's public universities*. Princeton: Princeton University Press.

Bowen, W. G., Kurzweil, M. A., and Tobin, E. M. (2005). *Equity and excellence in American higher education*. Charlottesville: University of Virginia Press.

Bowles, S., and Gintis, H. (1976). *Schooling in capitalist America*. New York: Basic Books.

Brantlinger, E. (2003). *Dividing classes: How the middle class negotiates and rationalizes school advantage*. New York: Routledge Falmer.

Brint, S., and Karabel, J. (1989). *The diverted dream: Community colleges and the promise of educational opportunity in America, 1900–1985*. New York: Oxford University Press.

Brown, P., Lauder, H., and Ashton, D. (2011). *The global auction: The promise of education, jobs, and income*. New York: Oxford University Press.

Brown, P., and Tannock, S. (2009). Education, meritocracy, and the global war for talent. *Journal of Education Policy, 24*(4), 377–94.

Campbell, J. R., Hombo, C. M., and Mazzeo, J. (2000). *NAEP 1999 trends in academic progress: Three decades of student performance*. Washington, DC: US Department of Education.

Carnevale, A. (2012, July 2). The great sorting. *The Chronicle of Higher Education*. Retrieved from http://chronicle.com/article/The-Great-Sorting/132635/.

Carnoy, M., and Levin, H. (1985). *Schooling and work in the democratic state*. Stanford: Stanford University Press.

Carter, P. L. (2012). *Stubborn roots: Race, culture, and inequality in U.S. and South African schools*. New York: Oxford University Press.

Chapman, G., and Dickert-Conlin, S. (2012). Applying Early Decision: Student and college incentives and outcomes. *Economics of Education Review, 31*, 749–63.

Chauvel, L. (2010). The increasingly dominated fraction of the dominant class: French sociologists facing the challenges of precarity and middle class destabilization. In Michael Burawoy, Mau-kuei Chang, and Michelle Fei-yu Hsieh (Eds.);

Abigail Andrews, Emine Fidan Elcioglu, and Laura K. Nelson (Associate Eds.), *Facing an unequal world: Challenges for a global sociology* (vol. 3, pp. 87–121). Taipei, Taiwan: Institute of Sociology at Academia Sinica, Council of National Associations of the International Sociological Association, and Academia Sinica.

Cipollone, K. (2012). *Leveraging privilege: The college process and advantage in an affluent public high school.* (Unpublished doctoral dissertation). SUNY at Buffalo, Buffalo, NY.

Cipollone, K., and Stich, A. E. (2012). Researching (in)access: Centering a significant "side" issue. *Ethnography in Education, 7*(1), 21–38.

Clark, B. (1960). The "cooling-out" function in higher education. *The American Journal of Sociology, 65*(6): 569–76.

Cook, P. J., and Frank, R. H. (1993). The growing concentration of top students at elite schools. In C. T. Clotfelter and M. Rotchschild (Eds.), *Studies of supply and demand in higher education* (pp. 121–40). Chicago: University of Chicago Press.

Cookson, P., and Persell, C. (1985). *Preparing for power: America's elite boarding schools.* New York: Basic Books.

———. (1991). Race and class in America's elite preparatory schools: African Americans as "outsiders within." *The Journal of Negro Education, 60,* 219–28.

Crenshaw, K. W. (1991). Mapping the margins: Intersectionality, identity politics, and violence against women of color. *Stanford Law Review, 43*(6), 1241–99.

Delpit, L. (2006). *Other people's children: Cultural conflict in the classroom.* New York: The New Press.

Demerath, P. (2009). *Producing success: The culture of personal advancement in an American high school.* Chicago: University of Chicago Press.

Dimitriadis, G., and Kamberelis, G. (2006). *Theory for education.* New York: Routledge.

Dougherty, K. J., and Kienzl, G. S. (2006). It's not enough to get through the open door: Inequalities by social background in transfer from community colleges to four-year colleges. *Teachers College Record, 108*(3), 452–87.

Ehrenreich, B. (1990). *Fear of falling: The inner life of the middle class.* New York: Harper Collins–First Harper Perennial Edition.

Eide, E., Brewer, D., and Ehrenberg, R. (1998). Does it pay to attend an elite private college? Evidence of the effect of undergraduate college quality on graduate school attendance. *Economics of Education Review, 17,* 371–76.

Ellwood, D., and Kane, T. J. (2000). Who is getting a college education: Family background and the growing gaps in enrollment. In S. Danziger and J. Waldfogel (Eds.), *Securing the future* (pp. 283–324). New York: Russell Sage Foundation.

Espenshade, T. J., and Radford, A. W. (2009). *No longer separate, not yet equal: Race and class in elite college admission and campus life.* Princeton: Princeton University Press.

Feagin, J. (2000). *Racist America: Roots, current realities, and future reparations.* New York: Routledge.

Fine, M. (1991). *Framing dropouts: Notes on the politics of an urban public high school.* Albany: SUNY Press.

Fine, M., and Weis, L. (1998). *The unknown city: The lives of poor and working class young adults.* Boston: Beacon Press.

Fine, M., Weis, L., Powell Pruitt, L., and Burns, A. (2004). *Off white: Readings on power, privilege, and resistance* (2nd ed.). New York: Routledge.

Fine M., Weis, L., Powell, L., and Wong, M. (1997). *Off white: Readings on race, power and society.* New York: Routledge.

Foley, D. E. (2010a). *Learning capitalist culture: Deep in the heart of Tejas.* 2nd ed. Philadelphia: University of Pennsylvania Press.

———. (2010b). The rise of class culture theory in educational anthropology. *Anthropology and Education Quarterly, 41*(3), 215–27.

Fordham, S., and Ogbu J. (1986). Black students' school success: Coping with the "burden of 'acting white.'" *The Urban Review, 18*(3), 176–206.

Frank, R. H., and Cook, P. J. (1995). *The winner-take-all society: How more and more Americans compete for ever fewer and bigger prizes, encouraging economic waste, income inequality, and an impoverished cultural life.* New York: Free Press.

Frankenberg, R. (1993). *White women, race matters: The social construction of whiteness.* Minneapolis: University of Minnesota Press.

Gamoran, A. (2008). Persisting social class inequality in US education. In L. Weis (Ed.), *The way class works: Readings on school, family, and the economy* (pp. 169–79). New York: Routledge.

Gaztambide-Fernández, R. (2009). *The best of the best: Becoming elite at an American boarding school.* Cambridge, MA: Harvard University Press.

Gaztambide-Fernández, R., and DiAquoi, R. (2010). A part and apart: Students of color negotiating boundaries at an elite boarding school. In A. Howard and R. Gaztambide-Fernández (Eds.), *Educating elites: Class privilege and educational advantage* (pp. 55–78). New York: Rowman and Littlefield Education.

Gilbert, D. (2003). *The American class structure in an age of growing inequality.* Belmont, CA: Wadsworth.

Gladieux, L. E. (2002). Federal student aid in historical perspective. In D. E. Heller (Ed.), *Conditions of access: Higher education for lower income students* (pp. 45–58). Westport, CT: Praeger.

Goldin, C. D., and National Bureau of Economic Research. (2006). *The quiet revolution that transformed women's employment, education, and family.* Cambridge, MA: National Bureau of Economic Research.

Grodsky, E., and Riegle-Crumb, C. (2010). Those who choose and those who don't: Social background and college orientation. *The ANNALS of the American Academy of Political and Social Science, 627,* 14–36.

Gumport, P. (2007). *Sociology of higher education: Contributions and their contexts*. Baltimore: Johns Hopkins University Press.

Harvey, D. (2005). *A brief history of neoliberalism*. New York: Oxford University Press.

Hearn, J. C. (1991). Academic and nonacademic influences on the college destinations of 1980 high school graduates. *Sociology of Education, 64, 158–71*.

Heller, D. E. (2001). *The states and public higher education policy: Affordability, access, and accountability*. Baltimore: Johns Hopkins University Press.

———. (2002). *Condition of access: Higher education for low income students*. Westport: American Council on Education and Praeger.

Hill, L. (2008). School strategies and the college-linking process: Reconsidering the effects of high schools on college enrollment. *Sociology of Education, 81*, 53–76.

Hochschild, J., and Scovronick, N. (2003). *The American dream and public schools*. Oxford: Oxford University Press.

Holland, M. (2012). Only here for the day: The social integration of minority students at a majority white high school. *Sociology of Education, 85*(2), 101–20.

Holmes, J. (2002). Buying homes, buying schools: School choice and the social construction of school quality. *Harvard Educational Review, 72*(2), 177–205.

Horvat, E., and Antonio, A. (1999). Hey, those shoes are out of uniform: African American girls in an elite high school and the importance of habitus. *Anthropology and Education Quarterly, 30*(3), 317–42.

Horvat, E., and Cucchiara, M. (2009). Perils and promises: Middle-class parental involvement in urban schools. *American Education Research Journal, 46*(4), 974–1004.

Hossler, D., Schmit, J., and Vesper, N. (1999). *Going to college: How social, economic, and educational factors influence the decisions students make*. Baltimore: John Hopkins University Press.

Hout, M., Raftery, A., and Bell, E. O. (1993). Making the grade: Educational stratification in the United States, 1925–1989. In Y. Shavit and H. P. Blossfeld (Eds.), *Persistent inequality: Changing educational attainment in thirteen countries* (pp. 25–49). Boulder: Westview Press.

Howard, A. (2007). *Learning privilege: Lessons of power and identity in affluent schooling*. New York: Routledge.

Howard, A., and Gaztambide-Fernández, R. (2010). *Educating elites: Class privilege and educational advantage*. Lanham: Rowan and Littlefield.

Hoxby, C. M. (1997, December). *How the changing market structure of U.S. higher education explains college tuition* (Working Paper 6323). Cambridge, MA: National Bureau of Economic Research.

———. (2004). *College choices: The economics of where to go, when to go, and how to pay for it*. Chicago: University of Chicago Press.

Hoxby, C. M., and Avery, C. (2012, December). *The missing "one offs": The hidden supply of high-achieving, low income students* (Working Paper 18586). Cambridge, MA: National Bureau of Economic Research.

Hurtado, S., Inkelas, K. K., Briggs, C., and Rhee, B. (1997). Differences in college access and choice among racial/ethnic groups: Identifying continuing barriers. *Research in Higher Education, 38*(1), 43–75.

James, E., Nabeel, A., Conaty, J., and To, D. (1989). College quality and future earnings: Where should you send your child to college? *American Economic Review, 79,* 247–52.

Jaschik, Scott. (2011, February 25). Surrender to Early Admissions. *Inside Higher Ed.* Retrieved from http://www.insidehighered.com/news/2011/02/25/harvard_and_princeton_restore_early_admissions_option.

Jenkins, H. (2011). *Under the best of circumstances: The constrained opportunities of black students inside elite private secondary schools.* (Unpublished doctoral dissertation). SUNY at Buffalo, Buffalo, NY.

Johnson, B. H. (2011). The great equalizer and the key to the American dream. In Jeanne Ballantine and Joan Spade (Eds.), *Schools and society: A sociological approach to education* (4th ed., pp. 271–82). Thousand Oaks, CA: Pine Forge Press.

Karabel, J. (1972). Community colleges and social stratification. *Harvard Educational Review, 42,* 521–62.

———. (2005). *The chosen: The hidden history of admission and exclusion at Harvard, Yale and Princeton.* Boston: Houghton Mifflin.

Karen, D. (2002). Changes in access to higher education in the United States: 1980–1992. *Sociology of Education, 75*(3), 191–210.

Kaufman, P. (2005). Middle-class social reproduction: The activation and negotiation of structured advantages. *Sociological Forum, 20*(2), 245–70.

Kelly, S. P. (2008). Social class and tracking within schools. In L. Weis (Ed.), *The way class works: Readings on school, family, and the economy* (pp. 210–24). New York: Routledge.

Kenway, J., and Fahey, J. (2010). Is greed still good? Was it ever? Exploring the emoscapes of the global financial crisis. *Journal of Education Policy, 25*(6): 717–27.

Kerckhoff, A. (1993). *Diverging pathways: Social structure and career deflections.* New York: Cambridge University Press.

———. (1995). Institutional arrangements and stratification processes in industrial countries. *Annual Review of Sociology, 21,* 323–47.

———. (2001). Education and social stratification processes in comparative perspective. *Sociology of Education, 4,* 3–18.

Khan, S. R. (2011). *Privilege: The making of an adolescent elite at St. Paul's School.* Princeton: Princeton University Press.

Kingston, P. W., and Lewis, L. S. (Eds.). (1990). *The high-status track: Studies of elite schools and stratification.* Albany: SUNY Press. Knapp, Kelly-Reid and Ginder, 2009

Kivel, P. (2004). *You call this a democracy?* New York: Apex Press.

Knapp, L. G., Kelly-Reid, J. E., and Ginder, S. A. (2009). Enrollment in postsecondary institutions, fall 2007; graduation rates, 2001 & 2004 cohorts, and financial statistics, fiscal year 2007 (NCES 2009-155). Washington, DC: National Center for Education Statistics, Institute of Education Sciences, U.S. Department of Education. Retrieved from http://nces.ed.gov/pubs2009/2009155.pdf.

Kozol, J. (2005). *The shame of a nation: The restoration of apartheid schooling in America.* New York: Crown.

Laneri, R. (2010, April 29). America's best prep schools. *Forbes.* Retrieved from http://www.forbes.com/2010/04/29/best-prep-schools-2010-opinions-private-education.html.

Lareau, A. (1987). Social class differences in family-school relationships: The importance of cultural capital. *Sociology of Education, 60*(2), 73–85.

———. (1989). *Home advantage: Social class and parental intervention in elementary education.* London: Falmer.

———. (2000). *Home advantage: Social class and parental intervention in elementary education* (2nd ed.). Lanham: Rowman and Littlefield.

———. (2003). *Unequal childhoods: Class, race and family life.* Berkeley: University of California Press.

———. (2008). Watching, waiting, and deciding when to intervene: Race, class, and the transmission of advantage. In L. Weis (Ed.), *The way class works: Readings on school, family, and the economy* (pp. 117–33). New York: Routledge.

Lareau, A., and Weininger, E. (2010). Class and the transition to adulthood. In A. Lareau and D. Conley (Eds.), *Social class: How does it work?* (pp. 118–51). New York: Russell Sage Foundation.

Lawrence, T. (2009). *Private spaces in public places: Class in a suburban, public high school.* (Unpublished doctoral dissertation). SUNY at Buffalo, Buffalo, NY.

Lee, J., and Weis, L. (2012, June). *High school pathways to postsecondary education destinations: Integrated multilevel analyses of NELS, ELS and NCES-Barron's Datasets.* Final report to Association of Institutional Research.

Lee, S. (2005). *Up against whiteness: Race, school, and immigrant youth.* New York: Teachers College Press.

Leong, Nancy. (2013, June). Racial capitalism. *Harvard Law Review, 126,* 2151–2226.

Leslie, L. L., Slaughter, S., Taylor, B. J., and Zhang, L. (2012). How do revenue variations affect expenditures within U.S. research universities? *Research in Higher Education, 53*(6), 614–49.

Li, G. (2005). *Culturally contested pedagogy: Battles of literacy and schooling between mainstream teachers and Asian immigrant parents.* Albany: SUNY Press.

Lipman, P. (2011). *The new political economy of urban education: Neoliberalism, race, and the right to the city.* Routledge: New York.

Lizza, R. (2011, April 27). Leading from Behind. *New Yorker.* Retrieved from http://www.newyorker.com/online/blogs/newsdesk/2011/04/leading-from -behind-obama-clinton.html.

Losing Ground. (2002). Washington, DC: The National Center for Public Policy.

Lucas, S. (2001). Effectively maintained inequality: Education transitions, track mobility, and social background effects. *American Journal of Sociology, 106,* 1642–90.

MacLeod, J. (1995). *Ain't no makin' it: Aspirations and attainment in a low-income neighborhood* (2nd ed.). Boulder: Westview Press.

McCarthy, C., Rodriguez, A. Meecham, S., David, S. Wilson-Brown, C. Godina, H., Supryia, K. E., and Buendia, E. (2005). Race, suburban resentment, and the representation of the inner city in contempory film and television (pp. 117–32). In L. Weis and M. Fine (Eds.), *Beyond silenced voices: Class, race and gender in United States schools* (Rev. ed.). Albany: SUNY Press.

McDonough, P. (1997). *Choosing colleges: How social class and schools structure opportunity.* Albany: SUNY Press

McDonough, P. A., Antonia, A. L., Walpole, M., and Perez, L. X. (1998). College rankings: Democratized college knowledge for whom? *Research in Higher Education, 39*(5), 513–37.

McPherson, M. S., and Schapiro, M. O. (1998). *The student aid game: Meeting need and rewarding talent in American higher education.* Princeton: Princeton University Press.

———. (2002). Changing patterns of institutional aid: Impact on access and education policy. In D. Heller (Ed.), *Conditions of access: Higher education for lower income students* (pp. 73–94). Westport: American Council on Education and Praeger Series on Education.

Mickelson, R. A., and Velasco, A. E. (2006). Bring it on! Diverse responses to "acting white" among academically able black adolescents. In E. M. Horvat and C. O'Connor (Eds.), *Beyond acting white: Reframing the debate on black student achievement* (pp. 27–56). New York: Rowman and Littlefield.

Mortenson, T. (2003, March). Pell grant students in undergraduate enrollments by institution type and control, 1992–93 to 2000–2001. *Postsecondary Education Opportunity, 141.*

———. (2006). Access to what? *Postsecondary Education Opportunity, 164.*

Mullen, A. (2010). *Degrees of inequality: Culture, class, and gender in American higher education.* Baltimore: Johns Hopkins University Press.

Muller, C., Riegle-Crumb, C., Schiller, K. S., Wilkinson, L., and Frank, K. A. (2010). Race and academic achievement in racially diverse high schools: Opportunity and stratification. *Teachers College Record, 112*(4), 1038–63.

Nolan, K., and Anyon, J. (2004). Learning to do time: Willis's model of cultural reproduction in an era of postindustrialism, globalization, and mass incarceration. In N. Dolby and G. Dimitriadis (Eds.), *Learning to labor in new times* (pp. 133–50). New York: Routledge Falmer.

Oakes, J. (1985). *Keeping track: How schools structure inequality.* New Haven: Yale University Press.

Ogbu, J. (2008). *Minority status, oppositional culture, and schooling.* New York: Routledge.

Ogbu, J., and Simons, H. D. (1998). Voluntary and involuntary minorities: A cultural ecological theory of school performance with some implications for education. *Anthropology and Education Quarterly, 29,* 155–88.

Ong, A. (1999). Cultural citizenship as subject making: Immigrants negotiate racial and cultural boundaries in the United States. In R. Torres, L. Miron, and J. Inda (Eds.), *Race, identity, and citizenship: A reader.* Malden: Blackwell.

Orfield, G., and Lee, C. (2005). Segregation 50 years after *Brown*: A metropolitan change. In L. Weis and M. Fine (Eds.), *Beyond silenced voices: Class, race, and gender in United States schools* (Rev. ed., pp. 3–20). Albany: SUNY Press.

Perna, L. W. (2000). Differences in the decision to attend college among African Americans, Hispanics, and Whites. *The Journal of Higher Education, 71,* 117–41.

Perna, L. W., Rowan-Kenyon, H., Thomas, S. L., Bell, A., Anderson, R., and Li, C. (2008). The role of college counseling in shaping college opportunity: Variations across high schools. *Review of Higher Education 31*(2): 131–60.

Peshkin, A. (2001). *Permissible advantage? The moral consequences of elite schooling.* Mahwa, NJ: Lawrence Erlbaum.

Piketty, T., and Saez, E. (2003). Income inequality in the United States, 1913–1998. *The Quarterly Journal of Economics, 118*(1), 1–39.

———. (2006). The evolution of top incomes: A historical and international perspective. *American Economic Review,* 96, 200–205.

———. (2012). Top incomes and the great recession: Recent evolutions and policy implications. Paper presented at the 13th Jacques Polak Annual Research Conference. Hosted by the International Monetary Fund, Washington, DC, November 8–9.

Proweller, A. 1998. *Constructing female identities: Meaning making in an upper middle class youth culture.* Albany: SUNY Press.

Raftery, A. E., and Hout, M. (1993). Maximally maintained inequality: Expansion, reform, and higher education in Irish education, 1921–75. *Sociology of Education, 66,* 22–39.

Reardon, S. (2011). The widening academic achievement gap between the rich and the poor: New evidence and possible explanations. In G. J. Duncan and R. J. Murnane (Eds.), *Whither opportunity? Rising inequality, schools, and children's life chances* (pp. 91–116). New York: Russell Sage Foundation

Reay, D., Crozier, G., and James, D. (2011). *White middle class identities and urban schooling.* Basingstoke: Palgrave.

Reich, R. (2001). *The future of success.* New York: Alfred A. Knopf.

———. (2008). *Supercapitalism: The transformation of business, democracy, and everyday life.* New York: Vintage.

Reichert, M. (2000). Disturbances of difference: Lessons from a boy's school. In L. Weis and M. Fine (Eds.), *Construction sites: Excavating class, race and gender among urban youth* (pp. 259–73). New York: Teachers College Press.

Riegle-Crumb, C., and Grodsky, E. (2010). Racial-ethnic differences at the intersection of math course-taking and achievement. *Sociology of Education, 83*(3), 248–70.

Rimer, S., and Arenson, K. (2004, June 24). Top colleges take more blacks, but which ones? *New York Times.* Retrieved from http://www.nytimes.com/2004/06/24/us/top-colleges-take-more-blacks-but-which-ones.html?pagewanted=all&src=pm.

Rist, R. (1970). Student social class and teacher expectations: The self-fulfilling prophecy in ghetto education. *Harvard Educational Review, 40*, 411–51.

Robbins, A. (2006). *The overachievers: The secret lives of driven kids.* New York: Hyperion.

Roksa, J. (2012). Race, class, and bachelor's degree completion in American higher education: Examining the role of life course transitions. In L. Weis and N. Dolby (Eds.), *Social class and education: Global perspectives* (pp. 51–70). New York: Routledge.

Roksa, J., and Potter, D. (2011). Parenting and academic achievement: Intergenerational transmission of educational advantage. *Sociology of Education, 84*(4), 299–321.

Rosenbaum, J. E. (1978). The structure of opportunity in schools. *Social Forces, 57*, 236–56.

Rumberger, R. W., and Thomas, S. L. (1993). The economic returns to college major, quality and performance: A multilevel analysis of recent graduates. *Economics of Education Review, 12*, 1–19.

Sacks, P. (2007). *Tearing down the gates: Confronting the class divide in American education.* Berkeley: University of California Press.

Saez, E. (2013). Striking it richer: The evolution of top incomes in the United States (updated with 2012 preliminary estimates). An updated version of "Striking it richer: The evolution of top incomes in the United States," *Pathways Magazine*, Stanford Center for the Study of Poverty and Inequality, Winter 2008, 6–7.

Schneider, B. (2009). College choice and adolescent development: Psychological and social implications of Early Admissions (Discussion paper). Arlington, VA: National Association for College Admission Counseling.

Schneider, B., and Stevenson, D. (1999). *The ambitious generation: America's teenagers, motivated but directionless.* New Haven: Yale University Press.

Shavit, Y., Arum, R., and Gamoran A. (2007). *Stratification in higher education: A comparative study.* Stanford: Stanford University Press.

Sherman, A., and Aron-Dine, A. (2007). *New CBO show income inequality continues to widen.* Washington, DC: Center on Budget and Policy Priorities.

Skeggs, B. (2004). *Class, self, culture.* London: Routledge.

Sklair, L. (2001) *The transnational capitalist class.* Oxford: Blackwell.

Slaughter, S., and Rhoades, G. (2004). *Academic capitalism and the new economy: Markets, state, and higher education.* Baltimore: Johns Hopkins University Press.

Soares, J. A. (2007). *The power of privilege: Yale and America's elite colleges.* Stanford: Stanford University Press.

Solórzano, D. (1998). Critical race theory, racial and gender microaggressions, and the experiences of Chicana and Chicano Scholars. *International Journal of Qualitative Studies in Education, 11,* 121–36.

Solórzano, D., Ceja, M., and Yosso, T. (2000) Critical race theory, racial microaggressions and campus racial climate: The experiences of African-American college students. *Journal of Negro Education, 69*(1/2), 60–73.

Souza, E. H. (2004). *The launching pad: Middle class families and the transition to college.* (Unpublished doctoral dissertation). University of Massachusetts, Amherst, MA.

Spring, J. (2004). *American Education* (11th ed.). New York: McGraw Hill.

St. John, E. P. (2003). *Refinancing the college dream: Access, equal opportunity, and justice for taxpayers.* Baltimore: Johns Hopkins University Press.

St. John, E. P., Musoba, G. D., and Simmons, A. B. (2003). Keeping the promise: The impact of Indiana's Twenty-first Century Scholars program. *The Review of Higher Education 27*(1), 103–23.

Steinberg, J. (2002). *The gatekeepers: Inside the admissions process of a premier college.* New York: Penguin Books.

Stephan, J. L., Rosenbaum, J. E., and Person, A. E. (2009). Stratification in college entry and completion. *Social Science Research, 38*(3), 572–93.

Stevens, M. (2007). *Creating a class.* Cambridge, MA: Harvard University Press.

Tatum, B. D. (1997). *"Why are all the black kids sitting together in the cafeteria?" and other conversations about race.* New York: Basic Books.

Thomas, S. (2000). Deferred costs and economic returns to college quality, major and academic performance: An analysis of recent graduates in Baccalaureate and beyond. *Research in Higher Education, 41*(3), 281–313.

Thomas, S. L., and Bell, A. (2008). Education and class: Uneven patterns of opportunity and access. In L. Weis (Ed.), *The way class works: Readings on school, family and the economy* (pp. 273–87). New York: Routledge.

Thomas, S. L., and Zhang, L. (2005). Changing rates of return to college quality and academic major in the United States: Who gets good jobs in America? *Research in Higher Education, 46*(4), 437–59.

Thompson, M., and Schultz, K. (2003). The psychological experience of students of color. *Independent School Magazine, 62,* 42–49.

Tierney, W. (1997). The parameters of affirmative action: Equity and excellence in the academy. *Review of Educational Research, 67,* 165–96.

Tuan, M. (1998). *Forever foreigners or honorary whites? The Asian ethnic experience today.* New Brunswick: Rutgers University Press.

Valenzuela, A. (1999). *Subtractive schooling: U.S.-Mexican youth and the politics of caring.* Albany: SUNY Press.

Varenne, H., and McDermott, R. (1998) *Successful failure: The school America builds*. Boulder: Westview Press.

Weber, M. (1902/2003). *The protestant ethic and the spirit of capitalism*. Mineola: Dover.

Wacquant, L. (1993). From ruling class to field of power: An interview with Pierre Bourdieu on *La Noblesse d'Etat. Theory, Culture and Society, 10*, 19–44. London: Sage.

Walkerdine, V., Lucey, H., and Melody, J. (2001). *Growing up girl: Psycho-social explorations of gender and class*. London: Palgrave.

Weis, L. (1985). *Between two worlds: Black students at an urban community college*. Boston: Routledge, Kegan and Paul.

———. (1990). *Working class without work: High school students in a de-industrializing economy*. New York: Routledge.

———. (2004). *Class reunion: The remaking of the American white working class*. New York: Routledge.

———. (2008). Introduction. In L. Weis (Ed.), *The way class works: Readings on school, family, and the economy* (pp. 1–9). New York: Routledge.

Weis, L. and Dolby, N. (2012). *Social class and education: Global perspectives*. New York: Routledge.

Weis, L., and Fine, M. (1993). *Beyond silenced voices: Class, race, and gender in the United States*. Albany: SUNY Press.

———. (2000). *Speed bumps: A student-friendly guide to qualitative research*. New York: Teachers College Press.

——— (2012). Critical bifocality and circuits of privilege: Expanding critical ethnographic theory and design. *Harvard Educational Review, 82*(2), 173–201.

———. (2013). A methodological response from the field to Douglas Foley: Critical bifocality and class cultural productions. *Anthropology & Education Quarterly, 44*(3), 222–33.

Williams, T. (2011). Black students' perceptions of their access to precollege counseling practices. (Unpublished doctoral dissertation). St. John Fisher College, Rochester, NY.

Willis, P. (1977). *Learning to labour: How working class kids get working class jobs*. Westmead, England: Saxon House Press.

———. (2004) Twenty-five years on: Old books, new times. In N. Dolby, G. Dimitriadis, and P. Willis (Eds.), *Learning to labour—in new times* (pp. 167–96). New York: RoutledgeFalmer.

Yonezawa, S., and Wells, A. S. (2005). Reform as redefining the spaces of schools: An examination of detracking by choice. In L. Weis and M. Fine (Eds.), *Beyond silenced voices: Class, race, and gender in United States schools* (Rev. ed., pp. 47–61). Albany: SUNY Press.

Zernike, K. (2011, May 13). Fast-tracking to kindergarten? *New York Times*. Retrieved from http://www.nytimes.com/2011/05/15/fashion/with-kumon-fast-tracking-to-kindergarten.html?pagewanted=all.

Zweigenhaft, R. L., and Domhoff, G. W. (1991). *Blacks in the white establishment?*
A study of race and class in America. New Haven: Yale University Press.
———. (2003). *Blacks in the white elite: Will the progress continue?* New Haven:
Yale University Press.

Index

ABC (A Better Chance), 111–12, 146, 154
access to college: "access to what" question and, 18; AP (Advanced Placement) program and, 135; decreasing, at selective public colleges, 15; diversification of entering classes and, 17–18, 197–98, 247n16; expansion of, by class, 11; high school counselors' role in, 28; increasing competitiveness and, 111, 211–12; inequality in type of institution attended and, 13–14; location in educational opportunity structure and, 12–13; reorganization of opportunity structure and, 18; for women, 11
ACT (test), 90
admissions process: acceptance letters and, 250n29; applications and, 95–97, 247n18; athletic recruits and, 248n21; Black students' independence in, 112, 198; breakdowns during, 90; class solidarity and, 257nn23–24; class warfare under the surface of, 3–4; costs of, 133–35, 253n11; Early Action and Early Decision and, 94, 95, 97, 102, 131, 249–50n26; effectively maintained inequality and, 250–51n30; field of study and, 248n23, 250n28; as focal point for class positioning, 45–46; live cuts and, 250n29; marketplace of admissions and, 11–18; new upper middle class and, 3; parent and student class work and, 3; parents' organization of, 114; personal statement and, 95, 113, 121; postsecondary linking process and, 4; quantitative data in, 10; as shadow curriculum, 92; stu-

dent ownership of, 85, 89, 134–38, 141; tasks involved in, 114; three phenomena affecting outcomes of, 6–7. *See also* access to college; college matriculation patterns; college visits; parental micromanagement
Advanced Placement (AP) program. *See* AP (Advanced Placement) program
affirmative action: commodification of nonwhiteness and, 200; intended beneficiaries of, 254n3; opposition to, 112; racial capitalism and, 200; as reverse discrimination, 148
Altbach, P. G., 13
American Educational Research Association, 223, 237n14
Andre-Bechely, L., 50
Angela and Simmons family, 119–20, 183
Anna and Nalin family, 110, 150, 174, 183
Antonio, A., 29, 203, 259n32
anxiety: age of, 10; changing means of transferring class status and, 197; culture of, 193–94; increasing among privileged parents, 88; about positioning for the future, 10–11; ranking systems and, 2
AP (Advanced Placement) program: access to, 48, 58, 241n8; access to college and, 135; accumulated advantages and, 135; at Cannondale High School, 31, 32–33, 65; choice of college and, 70; course placement history and, 65; dominant college culture within, 65; expectations in, 74; grading in, 72–73; at Matthews Academy, 36; parental pressure on school and, 241n8; positioning work and, 19;

WITHDRAWAL